THE
CHICKEN PARTS
COOKBOOK

THE
CHICKEN PARTS
COOKBOOK

**225 Fast, Easy and Delicious Recipes
for Every Part of the Bird**

BY CHARLES L. PIERCE

CROWN TRADE PAPERBACKS
NEW YORK

Published by Crown Trade Paperbacks, 201 East 50th Street, New York, New York 10022. Member of the Crown Publishing Group.

Random House, Inc. New York, Toronto, London, Sydney, Auckland

http://www.randomhouse.com/

CROWN TRADE PAPERBACKS and colophon are trademarks of Crown Publishers, Inc.

Printed in the United States of America

Design by Susan DeStaebler

Library of Congress Cataloging-in-Publication Data
Pierce, Charles
    The chicken parts cookbook : 225 fast, easy and delicious recipes for every
part of the bird / by Charles Pierce.
    Includes index.
    1. Cookery (Chicken)   I. Title.
TX750.5.C45P54   1997
641.6'65—dc20   96-26001
                                                 CIP

ISBN 0-517-88789-4

10   9   8   7   6   5   4   3   2   1

First Edition

Acknowledgments

I would like to thank my editor, Katie Workman, who had the original idea for this book. She guided me through to the end with expertise, insight, and terrific good humor. Thanks to Roy Finamore, who introduced me to Katie. Thanks also go to Erica Youngren, Katie's assistant at Clarkson N. Potter, Inc., for all of her help. I would like to acknowledge my friend and partner, Wes Albinger, for his contribution to this project. His extraordinary ability to consume chicken parts at almost every meal for a year and a half is matched only by his skills as an ace editorial consultant. A special word of gratitude goes to my agent, Judith Weber, who always seems to believe in me. Thanks to Jody Weatherstone, whose contribution is greatly appreciated. And a special word of thanks to Victoria Spencer. Also, thanks to Bessie Berry at the USDA and to all those who manage the poultry hotline. Thanks go also to Dot and Nancy Tringali at the National Broiler Council and to Brad Stone in the press office at the Food and Drug Administration.

Contents

Introduction

We Americans eat a lot of chicken. Our average per person consumption, according to the National Broiler Council, is more than 75 pounds per year and rising. Chicken is healthy, easy to prepare, and economical—no wonder it is becoming our country's favorite source of protein.

Most of the chicken we buy is already cut up into parts. Packages of breasts, thighs, whole legs, drumsticks, wings, and livers abundantly line the shelves of poultry sections in grocery stores throughout the country. You see a few whole birds off to the side, but consumers seem to find cut-up pieces the simplest to purchase and easiest to prepare. *The Chicken Parts Cookbook* is full of wonderful recipes to help make the bird even more versatile and enjoyable.

The recipes are categorized by part. For each part, there are two sections, "Quick and Easy" followed by "Simply Sophisticated." "Quick and Easy" recipes are just that. The ingredients are basic, consisting of items that are either on hand or easy to obtain in any large grocery store. Cooking times are kept to a minimum, 30 minutes or less except in rare instances when the recipe calls for a few extra minutes. When a "Quick and Easy" recipe exceeds the 30-minute limit, it usually entails very simple ingredients and not much hands-on time. The second section, "Simply Sophisticated," contains recipes that either call for somewhat more exotic ingredients or use techniques that require a bit more attention to detail, although they are by no means complicated. These recipes generally take more time to prepare and warrant advance planning. I have noted in many cases where steps can be done ahead to make these special dishes easier and more convenient. The results are well worth the extra effort.

Many of the recipes for parts can be used interchangeably as long as times are respected and understood. Stewed Chicken Wings with Tuscan White Beans, for example, could be made with drumsticks and be just as good. Grilled Chicken Breasts with Salsa Cruda could be Grilled Thighs with Salsa Cruda if the cooking time is adjusted. Length of time varies from part to part and from technique to technique. A boneless breast cooked in a moderate oven takes 20 to 30 minutes to be done, but when sautéed, the same breast can be done in less than 10 minutes. Grilled thighs take 30 minutes to cook, whereas baked thighs take 45 minutes to 1 hour (direct heat vs. indirect heat). All of the recipes in this book were developed for a specific part and a particular technique. However, chicken is remarkably versatile and once you have tried a few recipes for each part, you will see how easily ingredients and techniques can be applied to all parts.

Substituting Parts

Often the part called for in a recipe can be changed. The symbols found at the end of each recipe indicate which part might be acceptable for substitution. A few guidelines are in order:

- White meat parts take less time to cook than dark meat ones.
- Boned parts cook more quickly than those with the bone left in.
- Parts prepared over direct heat, such as frying or broiling, cook more quickly than those prepared in indirect heat, such as baked in the oven.
- Use common sense when substituting parts in these recipes. A small, skinless, boneless chicken breast will cook easily in less than 10 minutes. A large thigh with the bone in will take considerably longer.
- If the original recipe calls for boneless, skinless chicken breasts, and you wish to substitute thighs, it is best to use boneless thighs. Alternatively, if you're looking to substitute a part in a recipe that calls for a bone-in part, use parts that have the bones in. You may use boneless parts, instead of bone in, and vice versa, but remember to adjust the cooking time accordingly.
- Follow the time chart on the facing page for best results. A meat thermometer helps ensure accuracy. Remember that white meat should be cooked to an internal temperature of 160°F. (165°F. with bone in) and dark meat to 175° to 180°F.

When you purchase chicken parts, there are several considerations. First, look for supermarket specials. The price of parts can fluctuate widely, and bargains are almost always available to the careful shopper. Next, check the "Sell by" date on the package label. This indicates the last day the product should be sold, although it will maintain its quality if properly refrigerated and cooked within two days. (Always keep chicken parts well wrapped in the coldest spot in the refrigerator.) For longer storage, freeze in heavy-duty foil or freezer bags. Home-frozen chicken parts should be used within two months. Lastly, when purchasing supermarket chicken, look closely before buying. If there are discolored spots, if the chicken seems to be sitting in a pool of watery blood, or if the flesh looks limp or flaccid, just say no! Look for healthy specimens with plump meat and taut, firm skin.

Cooking Times and Part Substitution Chart

	Breasts	Thighs	Drumsticks	Whole Legs	Wings
Sautéed or pan-fried	Boned: 7–12 minutes	Boned: 15–20 minutes	25–30 minutes	25–30 minutes	12–15 minutes
	Bone in: 15–18 minutes	Bone in: 25–30 minutes			
Broiled or grilled	Boned: 7–12 minutes	Boned: 30 minutes	30–40 minutes	30–45 minutes	25–30 minutes
	Bone in: 15–18 minutes	Bone in: 25–30 minutes			
Baked, stewed, or poached	Boned: 12–15 minutes	Boned: 25–35 minutes	30–45 minutes	35–50 minutes	30–40 minutes
	Bone in: 35–50 minutes	Bone in: 35–50 minutes			
Fried	Boned: 7–12 minutes	Boned: 12–15 minutes	20–25 minutes	25–35 minutes	12–15 minutes
	Bone in: 15–18 minutes	Bone in: 15–20 minutes			

The color of raw chicken varies in different sections of the country. Skin color ranges from white to deep yellow, depending on the chicken's diet. Color does not necessarily indicate a difference in flavor, tenderness, or fat content.

Available in many fine food stores and through many butchers, free-range chickens are birds that were allowed to roam freely rather than being kept in cramped quarters. Kosher chickens are slaughtered under the auspices of a rabbi and are salted during processing. Both of these kinds of chickens tend to have superior flavor and texture. For the discerning palate, they are worth the premium prices they command.

As with any perishable meats, there are some safety factors that should be considered when handling chicken parts. First, refrigerate raw chicken promptly. Never leave it out on a countertop at room temperature for more than two hours. Freeze uncooked chicken if it is not to be used within two days. Thaw frozen chicken parts in the refrigerator (not on the countertop) or in cold water. It takes three to nine hours to thaw cut-up parts. To thaw in cold water, place the chicken in its original wrap or watertight plastic bag in cold water and change the water often. Frozen parts can also be thawed in the microwave: Use the Defrost or Medium-Low setting and microwave for two minutes, then let stand for two minutes. Turn the parts often to ensure even heat distribution and repeat as needed, working in two-minute intervals. Take care to not cook the defrosting chicken in the microwave (hence the suggestion of constant turning). Do not refreeze cooked or uncooked chicken that has been previously frozen. Lastly, remember that fresh poultry now comes with food safety instructions right on the package. Look for this information and follow it to ensure the chicken you buy maintains peak quality.

There has been much talk recently of salmonella, a bacterial contamination that causes food poisoning. The salmonella bug is easily destroyed by heat, which means that hot, soapy water will take care of many risks. Always wash your hands, knives, and cutting boards thoroughly after handling raw chicken. Do not cut up raw poultry and then use the same knife or cutting board to prepare other foods until the utensils and board have been washed.

Do not use the liquid from marinades (in which raw poultry has been sitting) as a sauce or for pouring over just-cooked parts. When grilling outside or cooking inside, do not place cooked chicken on the same plate used to transport raw chicken to the grill or the stove. Remember that it takes heat to kill the bacteria. Be careful with leftovers and when holding cooked chicken for serving. Cooked chicken should be kept either hot (between 140° and 165°F.) or refrigerated at 40°F. or less.

Cook chicken parts correctly. Breasts should reach an internal temperature of 160°F. (165°F. with bone in); thighs, legs, and drumsticks should reach 175° to 180°F. A good-quality quick-reading meat thermometer is the best way to guarantee safe results without compromising flavor or texture because of overcooking.

A word about my recipe philosophy is in order here. Remember that a recipe is just a guideline. A list of ingredients followed by a set of instructions should be clear, simple, and easy for any reader to execute. The ideal recipe should be as easy for a beginner as for an experienced cook. However, the fun part of preparing food comes from the ability to use one's own inspiration, to be able to adapt to the availability of ingredients, and to substitute and experiment within the confines of the charted course. Yes, this is easier if you are used to cooking, but even a kitchen amateur can use common sense to provide creations of his or her own. A recipe should help you achieve the best final result and allow you to add your own flair along the way. My recipes attempt to do just that: offer ideas and guidelines that let you make the best use of your favorite chicken parts.

Tips and Techniques

About Fat

The total fat content in a 3-ounce edible portion of chicken is less than half that of beef and only about a third of that in pork. Most of the fat that chicken does contain is unsaturated—the good, cholesterol-lowering kind that is easier to convert to energy. It isn't necessary to remove the skin from chicken before cooking it. Although most chicken fat is in the skin, studies have shown that chicken does not absorb fat from the skin during cooking. Leaving the skin on during cooking helps to maintain the natural moisture of chicken. The key to reducing fat is to remove the skin before *eating*. This will eliminate almost half of the fat that chicken contains. A 3-ounce roasted breast with skin has 140 calories and 3 grams of fat. The same chicken breast without the skin has 116 calories and 1.5 grams of fat.

Peeling, Seeding, and Chopping Tomatoes

Bring to a boil a pot of water large enough to hold the number of tomatoes you want to peel. Cut the core out of each tomato with a small paring knife and discard. Make a small incision in the shape of a cross on the opposite side from the core of each tomato, then plunge them into the boiling water. Leave for 10 to 20 seconds (or less if the tomatoes are very ripe) and remove with a slotted spoon. The skin should be curled at the cut edges, indicating that they are ready to peel. Let cool slightly and peel, starting at the curls of the cross. Cut the tomatoes in half crosswise and gently squeeze out the insides to remove the seeds. Slice the halves, then chop as needed.

Roasting Peppers

Line an oven broiler with heavy-duty foil and brush the foil lightly with oil. Place red, green, or yellow peppers on their sides on the foil and position the broiling pan about 5 inches from the source of heat. Broil the peppers under direct heat until charred all over. Turn often to ensure even charring. When the peppers have completely blackened and blistered, remove to a paper or plastic bag and close tightly. Allow the skins to loosen in the steam, sealed in the bag, for about 30 minutes. Then remove the peppers from the bag and peel off the skins. Peeling can be done under cold running water if desired, although this will wash away some of the flavor along with the skin. (Some cooks like to hold the peppers over a bowl to capture the juices that are extruded during the peeling process. The juices make flavorful additions to salad dressings and sauces.) When the peel is removed, cut the peppers in half lengthwise to remove all seeds and membranes. Keep the roasted peppers covered in olive oil in a tightly sealed container if not to be used immediately.

Making Homemade Bread Crumbs

Remove the crusts from any white bread and discard. (I find that premium sandwich breads like those made by Pepperidge Farm or Arnold work very well.) Cut bread into large cubes and drop into the food processor with the blade in motion. Grind until powdery, pulsing several times to evenly distribute the crumbs. Place in an air-tight container if not to be used right away. Fresh crumbs should be used within two days. Leftover bread crumbs freeze very well. This is an excellent way to make good use of stale French or Italian breads, too.

Citrus Zest

The zest of citrus fruit contains an aromatic oil that adds instant flavor to many dishes. Wash oranges, lemons, or grapefruits in plenty of cold water to remove any chemical residues. Dry well before grating. Use the jagged-edged, round-hole part of a regular grater to scrape off fine zest. A special citrus grater, sold in many kitchen equipment stores, is a convenient and efficient gadget that allows you to make long strips of zest. Simply scrape the zester against the surface of the fruit to remove thin, julienne ribbons. A sharp vegetable peeler works well for making julienne strips, too. Peel away wide strips from the fruit with the peeler, cut away the bitter white pith, and with a very sharp knife make paper-thin, lengthwise slices. The strips can be used as an attractive garnish or can be finely chopped to give flavor to dishes as they cook.

Deglazing Pans

A simple, flavorful sauce can be made from pan juices when sautéing. To deglaze a pan, begin by pouring off any fat used in the browning process. Return the skillet to the top of the stove and, over high heat, pour in ¼ to ½ cup flavored vinegar, a fortified wine such as brandy, port or Madeira; cider; cream; or any flavorful liquid that complements the seasonings used in the recipe. Reduce the heat slightly and pour in enough stock or water to make 1 cup liquid total. Cook, stirring constantly to pick up any browned bits on the bottom of the skillet, until the flavors are concentrated, about 5 minutes. Season with salt and pepper to taste and pour into a sauceboat. The resulting concentrated juice is essentially gravy without flour. Just a spoonful will pep up pan-fried and sautéed chicken parts.

Blanching and Refreshing Green Vegetables

Green vegetables can be quickly boiled, then immediately drained and held under cold running water or plunged into a bowl of ice water. The "refreshed" vegetables can then be drained again and held in the refrigerator for up to 24 hours. Reheat gently in a small amount of butter or olive oil, or use in a stir-fry (or as is for crudités). This is a valuable trick of the trade that guarantees appealing taste and texture.

Grinding Nuts

When grinding nuts in the food processor or blender, add a small amount (less than 1 teaspoon) of flour to prevent the oiliness of the nuts from turning the mixture into a greasy puree; and use the pulse button to pulverize.

Peeling Fruits

Peaches, plums, apricots, and similar soft-skinned fruits can be easily peeled. Bring a pot of water to a boil and immerse the whole fruit for 10 to 20 seconds, depending on ripeness. Drain and transfer to a bowl of ice water. Use a small paring knife to gently peel away the skin from the flesh.

Cooking *en Papillote*

En papillote is a French term for cooking in a paper package. It is one of the best ways to seal in juices and preserve flavor. Chicken is an excellent choice for this cooking method, especially delicate breasts and pounded-thin, boned thighs. The chicken is enveloped in paper or aluminum foil that has been brushed lightly with butter or oil. Seasonings and ingredients that require about the same cooking time are added and the paper or foil is crimped around the edges to form a tight seal. The package is baked in a hot oven until puffed and golden.

Parchment paper is best for this technique, but foil is more readily available and works just as well. Some acids, like wine or lemon juice, will slightly discolor foil, but do not be put off—it is completely harmless.

To prepare the wrapping for this method, first cut a large, heart-shaped piece of paper or foil that measures about 12 inches wide and 15 inches long. Fold the heart in half, then unfold. Lightly butter or oil the paper or foil and place the chicken in the center of one of the halves. Add the additional seasonings or ingredients, then fold over the edges in tight pleats to close. Place on a baking sheet and cook in a hot oven (425° to 450°F.) until puffed (and golden if using paper).

The package is served right out of the oven, in its wrapping, to be opened by the diner at the table. Let guests enjoy the burst of aroma when they pierce the center of the *papillote* with their knives, but be sure to warn everyone to be careful of the hot steam. Transfer the chicken and any other contents of the package to the plate and dispose of the paper or foil before eating.

Using Phyllo Dough

These thin leaves of pastry are found in the frozen foods department of most grocery stores. Package instructions are very easy to follow, but some general tips are in order. Thaw the package of leaves completely if frozen before using. Remove only as many leaves as you need from the package and keep the rest rolled tightly in plastic wrap. Prepare fillings before working with the pastry. The leaves dry out after just a few seconds of exposure to air, so it is important to keep them covered with plastic wrap and a damp towel. Unused phyllo sheets can be refrigerated for up to one week or refrozen for up to two months. Remember to lightly brush the leaves with butter when layering. Bake according to recipe instructions, but make sure the pastry is thoroughly done. It is the crisp texture of this versatile pastry that gives a special quality. Undercooked phyllo is soggy and unappealing.

Making Crepes

Once you get the hang of it, making crepes is a cinch. It takes a little patience and, as is often the case with cooking, you finally learn how to best accomplish the task at hand when the batter is almost gone. These classic thin pancakes are versatile. They can be stuffed with a wide variety of fillings, they make great do-ahead dishes, and best of all, they freeze beautifully. Keep refrigerated for up to three days or frozen for up to two months. Make a double recipe and freeze what you don't use. Stack individual crepes between sheets of wax paper and wrap tightly in plastic wrap to store. A nonstick pan helps the cooking process immensely, as do fingers that are good at handling hot objects. I like to have the batter in a glass measuring cup when frying, as it has a great spout for pouring.

1 cup all-purpose flour

¼ teaspoon salt

3 large eggs

1 cup milk

2 tablespoons unsalted butter, melted and cooled

Additional butter for frying

1. In a medium bowl, combine the flour and the salt. Push the flour to the sides of the bowl to make a well in the center. Break the eggs into the well and add ½ cup of the milk. Mix the liquid with a whisk and gradually draw in the flour to make a smooth paste. Slowly mix in the remaining milk, stirring constantly to form a thin batter. (Strain through a fine-mesh sieve if the batter is lumpy.) Set aside at room temperature for 30 minutes. Stir in the melted butter just before frying.

2. Have the batter, a small skillet (preferably nonstick), plenty of softened butter, a plate, a flexible spatula, and several sheets of wax paper ready. Lightly butter the skillet and set over medium-high heat. When very hot, pour in enough of the batter to coat the bottom, 1 to 3 tablespoons depending on the size of the skillet. Quickly turn the pan in all directions to spread the batter over the bottom and a bit up the sides of the skillet. Do not add too much batter or the crepe will be too thick.

3. Fry the crepe until set in the center and lightly browned on the bottom, 2 to 3 minutes depending on the size of the pan. Loosen it with a spatula and turn the crepe over using two hands. Cook a minute or two longer on this side, until lightly browned. Transfer to a plate and cover with wax paper. Continue until all the batter is used, stacking the crepes between sheets of wax paper. Wipe the pan out frequently with a clean dish towel and add teaspoonfuls of additional butter only when the crepes start to stick.

Makes about twelve 7- to 8-inch crepes

Soaking Beans

Always soak dried beans in water before using. This shortens the cooking time and helps prevent splitting. (Lentils and split peas are small and tender enough to need little or no soaking.) Rinse the beans under cold running water and look carefully for any stones or loose debris that might be difficult to see. For best results, soak the beans in enough cold water to cover by two inches for 12 to 24 hours, changing the water a few times if possible. Use a large bowl, as the beans will double in bulk.

For faster soaking, place the beans in a large pot of cold water and bring to a boil. Boil for 2 minutes, then remove the pot from the heat. Cover and let soak for 2 hours.

Cook soaked beans as directed until soft. Do not use salt until the last few minutes of cooking; salt toughens the skins.

Breasts

■■■

Low in fat, high in flavor, and versatile, the breast is under-
standably a very popular chicken part. But it is all too easy to
make familiar, routine choices when preparing this favorite
part. With inspired ingredient combinations and a refreshing
variety of techniques, the following recipes help you take full
advantage of wonderful flavor and incredible versatility.

Breast Tips

- Boneless, skinless breasts are very convenient, but you will save a lot of money if
  you skin and bone the breasts yourself (see the box on page 12).
- Boneless breasts are almost always better if they are pounded flat. This makes for
  uniform cooking and more tender flesh. There is a mallet made just for flattening
  thin pieces of chicken and veal, but the bottom of a small skillet or a rolling pin
  will work just fine. Simply slip the trimmed breast between two sheets of parchment paper, wax paper, or plastic wrap and gently pound until completely flat.
  Parchment paper is best, as it is quite sturdy, but wax paper or plastic wrap is perfectly acceptable.
- Overcooked breasts are dry and unappealing. Cooking times in recipes are always
  approximate, depending on the size of the pan used, the degree of heat, and so
  on. Learn to use fingers for feeling the texture of perfectly cooked breasts. When
  in doubt, it is better to undercook than to go too far. Remember that most of the
  time the breast will continue to cook for a minute or two after it has been
  removed from the heat, and you can always return the chicken to the heat in
  order to cook for another minute.

- Because they are relatively quick cooking, breasts work especially well when wrapped in paper or foil, known in culinary terms as *en papillote*. Several recipes are included in this book that make the most of this simple cooking method. Use a good-quality parchment paper for best results. Foil will do, but the presentation of a breast served in the delicately browned paper in which it has cooked will always be more impressive.

- Breasts are either sold in one large piece, joined along the breastbone, or in singles, split along the breastbone. Boneless, skinless breasts are known as *supremes*.

- All of the recipes in this book, unless otherwise noted, are for *split breast halves,* which weigh 4 to 6 ounces each. One half-breast seems to be a perfect serving size, but if appetites are hearty, you might want to use more.

- All breasts should be plump, full, and firm, not old and mushy. The flesh should be creamy pink without dark spots or streaks of discoloration.

- Although difficult to discern with packaged breasts, the cartilage that constitutes the breastbone should be flexible, indicating that the breast comes from a young, tender bird.

- Look for taut and smooth skin on breasts. While the color of the skin is not important (this varies considerably), texture is a good indication of quality.

- There should be no "off" odors. The smell of the breast should be clean and fresh.

Boning a Whole Breast

1. Place the breast skin side down on a large work surface. Snap the breastbone with a sharp push of the wrist and remove the skin if desired.
2. Remove the wishbone with the help of a sharp paring knife, and cut the flesh along the breastbone. With the knife held as closely to the bone as possible, cut down the length of the breast, dislodging the flesh as you go.
3. Trim away and discard any of the rib cage from the sides.
4. Use the tip of the knife to remove the tough tendon that runs along the center of each half.
5. Replace the inner fillet of the breast if it becomes detached. (I like to remove the fillet when a recipe calls for flattening the breast. I freeze the fillets until I have quite a few, then use them for deep-fried "fingers.")
6. Trim the boned breasts of any excess fat or fibrous tissue.

Breasts

Quick and Easy

Chicken in Cognac Sauce

Use the good stuff for this recipe. The cooking brandy that has been hiding in the back of the pantry will not give the smooth, rounded effect of a good Cognac. Be careful when deglazing the pan. Keep the skillet away from any flame and pour slowly, keeping your face and hair away from the pan.

6 chicken breast halves, boned

Salt and freshly ground black pepper

2 tablespoons unsalted butter

2 tablespoons vegetable oil

½ cup Cognac

1 cup heavy cream

1. Pound the chicken lightly between 2 sheets of parchment paper until about ½ inch thick. Season with salt and pepper. Melt the butter with the oil in a large skillet over medium-high heat. Add the chicken and cook until well browned and cooked through, 3 to 5 minutes on each side. Remove to a plate or platter and cover with foil to keep warm.

2. Pour off all the fat from the skillet. Away from any flame, carefully pour in the Cognac and return the skillet to the heat. (The Cognac is very flammable.) Whisk or stir to pick up any cooking bits in the bottom of the skillet. Increase the heat to high, and boil, stirring or whisking occasionally, until thickened and syrupy, and reduced to about 2 tablespoons. Stir in the cream, bring back to a boil, and reduce by half, or until thickened. Season the sauce to taste with salt and pepper. Spoon a small amount of the sauce over each piece of chicken and serve at once.

 **Serves 6**

Chicken Breasts Forestière

Wild mushrooms can be substituted for the white button mushrooms if desired. Shiitakes, oyster mushrooms, chanterelles, cremini, or trumpets will lend an exotic, earthy flavor to the dish. Serve with hot buttered noodles and a simple green vegetable as accompaniments.

4 chicken breast halves, boned

¹⁄₂ teaspoon salt

¹⁄₄ teaspoon freshly ground black pepper

1 pound white button mushrooms, cleaned

2 teaspoons lemon juice

2 tablespoons unsalted butter

2 tablespoons vegetable oil

1 large onion, chopped

2 tablespoons chopped fresh sage, or 1 teaspoon dried

¹⁄₂ cup dry white wine or chicken stock

2 tablespoons chopped fresh parsley

1. Season the chicken with the salt and pepper. Cut the mushrooms into quarters (or halves, if small). Sprinkle the mushrooms with the lemon juice to prevent discoloration and set aside.

2. Melt the butter with the oil in a sauté pan large enough to hold the breasts in one flat layer. Add the chicken and cook over medium-high heat, turning once, until browned, about 3 minutes per side. Remove to a plate and cover loosely with foil.

3. Pour off all but 1 tablespoon of the fat from the pan. Add the onion and cook until slightly softened, about 2 minutes. Add the mushrooms and the sage. Cook, stirring constantly, until the mushrooms are lightly browned, about 3 minutes. Pour in the wine or stock and stir well to pick up any cooking bits in the bottom of the pan. Return the chicken to the pan, cover, reduce the heat to medium, and cook until cooked through, 7 to 10 minutes.

4. Stir in half of the parsley. Cut each of the breasts diagonally into 3 or 4 wide pieces. Place on a warmed serving platter and using a slotted spoon, transfer the mushrooms to the platter, surrounding the chicken. Cover with foil to keep warm.

5. Bring the juices in the pan to a boil over high heat. Boil until reduced by half. Pour the juices over the chicken. Sprinkle with the remaining parsley and serve at once.

 **Serves 6**

Hungarian Chicken Breasts with Paprika, Onions, and Sour Cream

As with many spices lurking in the back of our spice shelves, paprika looses its flavor in as little as a few weeks after being opened. For best results, invest in a new can from time to time. Keeping fresh staples on hand helps to make something special out of the ordinary. Low-fat sour cream works well in this recipe, but remember not to boil the sauce or it will curdle. Serve with cooked wide egg noodles or hot fluffy rice.

6 boneless, skinless chicken breast halves

2 tablespoons unsalted butter

2 tablespoons vegetable oil

1 large onion, finely chopped

1 medium tomato, peeled, seeded, and chopped

2 tablespoons imported sweet Hungarian paprika

1 cup chicken stock

1 cup sour cream

Salt and freshly ground black pepper

1. Pound the breasts between 2 sheets of parchment paper until uniformly thin, about ¼ inch. Melt the butter with the oil in a large nonstick skillet. Add the chicken and cook over medium-high heat until browned and cooked through, 3 to 4 minutes per side. Remove to a plate or platter and cover with foil to keep warm.

2. Pour off all but 1 tablespoon of the fat from the skillet. Add the onion and cook, stirring often, until softened, about 3 minutes. Add the tomato and paprika and stir to combine. Slowly add the stock, blending to form a paste. Increase the heat to high and bring to a boil, stirring constantly.

3. Remove the skillet from the heat and stir in the sour cream. Return the chicken to the skillet, along with any juices that have accumulated. Warm thoroughly over very low heat. Do not boil or the sauce will separate. Season to taste with salt and pepper. Pass extra sauce on the side.

 Serves 6

Grilled Chicken with Salsa Cruda

Don't even think of trying this recipe unless tomatoes are ripe and red, red, red! (Use bottled salsa when tomatoes are not in season.) Add a teaspoon of finely minced jalapeño pepper for a spicier version of the salsa. The smoky flavor of grilled breasts marries well with "raw" (cruda) salsa. You can make the salsa a day in advance, but do not add the cilantro until just before serving, for a truly fresh taste.

6 boneless, skinless chicken breast halves

Juice of 1 lemon

4 medium Italian plum tomatoes

¼ cup balsamic vinegar

½ medium cucumber

2 tablespoons finely chopped red onion

½ cup finely chopped fresh cilantro leaves

2 tablespoons olive oil

Salt and freshly ground black pepper

1. Pound the chicken breasts between 2 sheets of parchment paper to a thickness of about ½ inch. Place on a large platter or on 2 plates and pour over the lemon juice. Marinate, turning occasionally, for 15 to 20 minutes at room temperature, or 2 to 3 hours refrigerated.

2. Prepare a charcoal grill and burn the coals down to a gray ash. Alternatively, oil a stove-top grill and preheat well before cooking the chicken.

3. Quarter the tomatoes and use a small paring knife to remove the core, seeds, and pulp. Cut the stripped quarters into tiny dice. Place in a medium bowl and stir in the vinegar.

4. Peel the cucumber and halve lengthwise. Use a small spoon to remove the seeds. Cut the cucumber into tiny dice and add to the bowl of tomatoes. Stir in the red onion, cilantro, and olive oil. Season to taste with salt and pepper (makes about 2 cups salsa).

5. Remove the chicken from the juice and pat dry with paper towels. Season well with salt and pepper on both sides. Grill until firm and completely cooked, 3 to 5 minutes on each side. Serve on a large platter with the salsa on the side.

 Serves 6

Chicken Breasts Normandy

*The green pastures of Normandy produce some of the finest chickens, some of the finest apples, and **the** best cream in the world. They all come together in this traditional recipe. At the end of the cooking, each serving gets only a small amount of sauce, which is enough to give the chicken a rich flavor. Serve with rice or tiny boiled potatoes and follow with a simple green salad.*

6 chicken breast halves, boned

Salt and freshly ground black pepper

6 small cooking apples, preferably Golden Delicious

1 tablespoon lemon juice

2 teaspoons sugar

2 tablespoons unsalted butter

2 tablespoons vegetable oil

½ cup Calvados or similar apple brandy

½ cup heavy cream

1. Season the chicken with salt and pepper. Peel and core the apples and cut into quarters. Place the quartered apples in a large bowl and sprinkle with the lemon juice and sugar.

2. Melt the butter with the oil in a sauté pan large enough to hold the breasts in one flat layer. Add the chicken and cook over medium-high heat until well browned and cooked through, 5 to 7 minutes per side. Remove the breasts from the pan, place on a serving platter, cover loosely with foil, and keep warm in a slow oven with the door slightly ajar.

3. Pour off all but 1 tablespoon of the fat from the skillet. Add the apples and cook, carefully turning often, until golden brown all over, about 3 minutes. Pour in the Calvados, reduce the heat to medium, cover, and cook until the apples are tender, 7 to 10 minutes. Remove the apples with a slotted spoon, surround the chicken with the apples, and keep warm in a low oven while preparing the sauce.

4. Increase the heat to high and boil the remaining liquid in the skillet until reduced to 1 tablespoon. Add the cream, bring back to a boil, and cook, stirring, until thick enough to heavily coat the back of a spoon. Season to taste with salt and pepper and spoon the sauce over the chicken while very hot. Serve at once.

 **Serves 6**

Grilled Chicken Breasts with Orange and Avocado Relish

Try using a mixture of red, yellow, orange, and green peppers instead of just red. A few pitted black olives could be chopped and added, too.

6 boneless, skinless chicken breast halves

3 navel oranges

½ red bell pepper, cored, seeded, and diced

4 scallions (green onions), white parts only, thinly sliced

½ jalapeño pepper, minced

1 large avocado

2 tablespoons olive oil

2 tablespoons finely chopped fresh cilantro leaves

Salt and freshly ground black pepper

1. Pound the chicken breasts between 2 sheets of parchment paper or plastic wrap to a thickness of about ½ inch. Juice one of the oranges. Place the chicken on a large platter or 2 plates and pour over the orange juice. Marinate, turning occasionally, for 15 to 20 minutes at room temperature, or 2 to 3 hours refrigerated.

2. Prepare a charcoal grill and burn coals down to a gray ash. Alternatively, oil a stove-top grill and preheat well before cooking the chicken.

3. Remove the rind and bitter white pith from the remaining 2 oranges. Cut down between the membranes to remove whole sections of the flesh. Cut each section in half and place in a large bowl.

4. Add the bell pepper and three-fourths of the scallions to the oranges. Stir in the jalapeño. Halve the avocado, remove the pit, and peel. Cut the flesh into small dice and add to the bowl. Pour in the olive oil, add the cilantro, and season to taste with salt and pepper. Stir the relish carefully to blend (the soft avocado will easily turn to mush). Cover and set aside at room temperature.

5. Remove the chicken from the juice and pat dry with paper towels. Grill until firm and cooked through, 3 to 5 minutes on each side. Serve on a large platter with the reserved scallion sprinkled on top for garnish. Serve the relish on the side.

 Serves 6

Lemon and Herb Marinated Grilled Chicken Breasts

To have grilled chicken with herbs in the summer is reason enough to plant an herb garden, and nothing could be faster or easier. The clean, clear taste of lemon and herbs makes this simple but flavorful dish a sheer seasonal delight. Serve with fresh tomatoes and corn on the cob.

> 6 boneless, skinless chicken breast halves
>
> Juice of 2 lemons
>
> 2 tablespoons chopped mixed fresh herbs (such as rosemary, thyme, chervil, basil, or oregano)
>
> 2 garlic cloves, minced
>
> 2 tablespoons olive oil, plus additional for brushing
>
> Salt and freshly ground black pepper

1. Place the breasts in a large baking dish. Combine the lemon juice, herbs, garlic, and the 2 tablespoons of olive oil in a small bowl. Stir to blend, then pour over the chicken. Marinate for 30 minutes at room temperature, or 2 to 3 hours refrigerated, turning often.

2. Prepare a charcoal grill and burn the coals down to a gray ash. (Alternatively, line a broiling pan with oiled aluminum foil.)

3. Remove the breasts from the marinade and pat dry with paper towels. Season on both sides with salt and pepper. Grill or broil 4 to 6 inches from the source of heat until firm and cooked through, 3 to 5 minutes on each side. Brush occassionally with additional olive oil if desired.

 **Serves 6**

Chicken Nugget

Fresh vs. Frozen: *Fresh* chickens refer to birds that have been stored and shipped under standard refrigeration, which is about 35° F. *Deep-chilled* chickens are quick-cooled at the processing plant to an internal temperature of about 30° F., then shipped to market at that temperature. Technically, the bird does not freeze but comes close to it. *Frozen* chickens have been frozen solid at the processing plant and are sold that way. Fresh chicken costs more per pound than frozen.

Steamed Chinese Chicken

Vary the vegetables according to what is in season and what strikes your fancy. Choose vegetables that will take about the same amount of time to steam as the chicken. Broccoli, zucchini, yellow squash, cleaned spinach, tiny scallions, blanched and shredded cabbage, or small haricot verts are good choices. If you use a vegetable that will take longer than 5 to 7 minutes to steam, boil it for a couple of minutes before steaming, as I've done for the carrots in this recipe.

- **4 boneless, skinless chicken breast halves**
- **2 tablespoons soy sauce**
- **1 piece fresh ginger, 1 inch long, peeled and minced**
- **3 to 4 stalks lemongrass, peeled and minced**
- **8 ounces fresh carrots, peeled**
- **1 head broccoli, trimmed into small florets**
- **Salt and freshly ground black pepper**

1. Cut the chicken into 1-inch-wide fingers that measure about 3 inches long. In a small bowl, combine the soy sauce, ginger, and lemongrass. Add the chicken and turn to coat. Cover and marinate, refrigerated, for at least 4 hours and preferably overnight.

2. Bring a large pot of salted water to a boil. Cut the carrots into 1-inch pieces and plunge into the boiling water. Boil for 2 minutes, drain, and rinse under cold running water.

3. Place 2 stackable bamboo steamer layers in a wok half filled with water. Arrange the marinated chicken fingers flat in one of the steamers and season with pepper. Place the carrots and broccoli in a separate steamer and season to taste with salt and pepper. Bring the water to a boil, cover the steamers, and cook until the chicken is firm to the touch and the vegetables are tender, 6 to 8 minutes. Alternatively, set a colander inside a large pot and pour in about 1 inch of water, making sure the water does not reach the colander. Proceed as for above, arranging the vegetables in the center and the chicken around the sides. Watch carefully to prevent overcooking. Remove any vegetables as soon as they are crisp and tender. Cover and keep warm until the remaining food is done.

 Serves 6

Chicken Breast Stir-Fry with Broccoli and Lemon Soy Sauce

Simplicity itself! Vary the sauce with lime instead of lemon, sesame oil rather than corn oil, snow peas or sugar snap peas in addition to or instead of broccoli—a recipe is just a guide. The creativity of cooking comes in adding your own touch.

4 boneless, skinless chicken breast halves

1 head fresh broccoli

3 tablespoons corn or peanut oil

2 tablespoons soy sauce

2 tablespoons fresh lemon juice

1 garlic clove, minced

Salt and freshly ground black pepper

2 tablespoons chopped scallions (green onions), white part only

1. Cut the breasts into 1-inch cubes and set aside.

2. Bring a large pot of salted water to a boil. Trim the broccoli into small florets. Peel and dice the stems. Plunge florets and stems into the boiling water, bring back to a boil, and cook for 2 minutes. Drain and refresh under cold, running water. Drain on paper towels.

3. Combine 2 tablespoons of the oil with the soy sauce, lemon juice, and garlic in a small bowl.

4. Heat the remaining tablespoon of oil in a wok or large skillet over medium-high heat. Add the chicken and cook, stirring constantly, until there are no traces of pink, about 2 minutes. Add the broccoli and cook 2 minutes longer. Stir in the sauce and mix well. Season to taste with salt and pepper. Turn out onto a warmed serving platter, sprinkle with the chopped scallions, and serve at once.

 Serves 6

Chicken Nugget

When Henry IV was crowned king of France in 1589, he is reported to have said, "I wish every peasant may have a chicken in his pot on Sundays." Republican campaigners adopted this motto, and in 1928 urged voters to keep their party in power because it had "put a chicken in every pot."

Chicken Breast Stir-Fry with Green Beans, Almonds, and Plum Sauce

The plum sauce makes this recipe! If it is not available, try a combination of ¼ cup strained apricot preserves, 1 teaspoon prepared mustard, and a few drops of lemon juice in its place.

- **4 boneless, skinless chicken breast halves**
- **½ cup slivered almonds**
- **1 pound fresh green beans**
- **1 tablespoon Asian sesame oil**
- **¼ cup bottled plum sauce (available in the Asian products section of most grocery stores)**
- **Salt and freshly ground black pepper**
- **1 tablespoon chopped red onion**

1. Preheat the oven to 350°F. Cut the breasts into 1-inch cubes and set aside.

2. Spread the almonds on a small baking sheet and toast, stirring often, until lightly browned and fragrant, 10 to 12 minutes. (Watch carefully. Do not allow to burn.) Remove from the oven and cool.

3. Bring a large pot of salted water to a boil. Cut the beans into ½-inch pieces. Plunge the beans into the boiling water,

bring back to a boil, and cook until slightly tender, 2 to 3 minutes. Drain and refresh under cold running water. Drain on paper towels.

4. Heat the oil in a wok or large skillet over medium-high heat. Add the chicken and cook, stirring constantly, until there are no traces of pink, about 2 minutes. Stir in the green beans and almonds. Cook about 2 minutes longer or until the chicken is firm to the touch and the beans are warmed through. Stir in the plum sauce and season to taste with salt and pepper. Cook about 1 minute longer, stirring constantly. Turn out onto a warmed serving platter, sprinkle with the red onion, and serve at once.

 **Serves 6**

Chicken Nugget

Calling a woman "no spring chicken" makes little sense. In poultry farming, it is the young males (or cockerels) born in spring that are customarily sent to market in the fall as "spring chickens," indicating that they are older.

Smothered Chicken Breasts with Cabbage and Bacon

The hint of vinegar mixed with fennel seeds and smoky bacon gives a slightly sweet-and-sour effect to this dish. Use sliced bacon cut into small pieces instead of the slab bacon, if it is not available. I like to serve this on a cold winter's night with buttered noodles. A salad of hearty romaine lettuce with a mustardy vinaigrette would follow and, of course, lots of thickly sliced, crusty bread.

- **1 head firm green cabbage (about 2 pounds)**
- **8 ounces double-smoked slab bacon, rind removed**
- **6 chicken breast halves, boned**
- **Salt and freshly ground black pepper**
- **¼ cup red wine vinegar**
- **1 tablespoon fennel seeds**
- **1 tablespoon chopped fresh parsley**

1. Bring a large pot of salted water to a boil. Trim off the tough, outer leaves of the cabbage and cut it into quarters. Remove the core from each quarter and slice thinly. Plunge the sliced cabbage into the boiling water and bring back to a boil. Cook rapidly, stirring often, until tender, about 5 minutes. Drain and rinse under cold running water.

2. Cut the bacon into pieces that measure 1 inch long and ¼ inch wide. Place in a large skillet and cook, stirring often, until the bacon is lightly browned. Use a slotted spoon to transfer the bacon to a small bowl.

3. Season the chicken with salt and pepper. Brown the chicken in the hot bacon fat in the skillet until lightly browned, about 3 minutes on each side. Remove to a plate or platter and cover with foil to keep warm.

4. Pour off all the fat from the skillet. Add the vinegar, increase the heat to high, and boil, stirring to pick up any cooking bits from the bottom of the skillet, until reduced by half. Stir in the cabbage, the bacon, and the fennel seeds. Season the mixture well with salt and pepper. Return the chicken to the skillet, cover, and cook until the chicken is cooked through, about 5 minutes. Arrange the chicken on a large serving platter surrounded with the cabbage and bacon. Sprinkle with parsley just before serving.

 **Serves 6**

Sautéed Chicken Breasts with Spinach, Beets, and Pears

Frozen spinach can be used in many recipes, but for this dish, fresh leaves are essential. The spinach should be wilted, not thoroughly cooked. Canned beets can save time, but the home-cooked ones have a superior texture and flavor. Pears provide an interesting and different contrast.

Do not be alarmed if it appears that there is too much spinach for the skillet. Just keep cooking and add more leaves as the volume in the pan reduces as the spinach quickly cooks down.

2 bunches fresh spinach (about 10 ounces each)

2 firm Bartlett or Anjou pears, peeled, cut into ½-inch cubes

Juice of ½ lemon

6 chicken breast halves, boned

Salt and freshly ground black pepper

2 tablespoons unsalted butter

2 tablespoons vegetable oil

½ cup chicken stock

4 medium beets, cooked, peeled, and cut into ½-inch cubes

1. Remove the large, tough stems of the spinach and wash the leaves in several changes of cold water. Spin-dry in a salad spinner and set aside.

2. Place the pears in a small bowl and toss with the lemon juice.

3. Pound the chicken between 2 pieces of parchment paper or plastic wrap to ¼-inch thickness and season with salt and pepper. Melt the butter with the oil in a large skillet over medium-high heat. Add the chicken and cook until golden brown and cooked through, 4 to 5 minutes on each side. Remove to a large serving platter and cover with foil to keep warm. (Brown the chicken in 2 batches, adding additional butter and oil if necessary. Do not overcrowd the pan.)

4. Pour off all the fat from the skillet. Place the skillet over high heat and pour in the chicken stock, stirring to pick up any cooking bits left in the bottom. Bring to a boil and cook until the stock has reduced to 1 tablespoon. Mound the spinach in the skillet. Stir gently until the leaves are wilted and softened, about 3 minutes. Add the beets and cook 1 minute longer. Stir in the pears and any juices that have accumulated in the bottom of their bowl. Cook 1 minute longer. Season the mixture to taste with salt and pepper.

5. Use a slotted spoon to arrange the spinach, beets, and pears over the bottom of a large, warmed serving platter. Cut the chicken into thick, diagonal slices and place on top. Spoon over any pan juices left in the bottom of the skillet. Serve at once.

 **Serves 6**

Sautéed Chicken Breasts with Creamy Red Lentils and Cumin

The lentils might seem a bit soupy when ladled onto a serving platter. This is normal; red lentils are soft by nature and cook very quickly. Surround the platter with boiled white rice to soak up the juices and to complete an attractive presentation.

1 cup red lentils, rinsed

6 chicken breast halves, boned

Salt and freshly ground black pepper

2 tablespoons unsalted butter

2 tablespoons vegetable oil

2 tablespoons heavy cream

½ teaspoon ground cumin

1 tablespoon chopped fresh parsley

1. Place the lentils in a large saucepan and add enough salted cold water to cover by 2 inches. Bring to a boil over high heat, remove from the heat, cover, and set aside.

2. Pound the chicken between 2 pieces of parchment paper or plastic wrap to a thickness of about ½ inch. Season well with salt and pepper. Melt the butter with the oil over medium-high heat in a large skillet. Add the chicken and cook until golden brown and cooked through, 4 to 5 minutes on each side. Remove to a plate or platter and cover with foil to keep warm.

3. Pour off all the fat from the skillet. Drain the lentils and place them in the skillet. Add the cream. Bring to a boil over high heat. Reduce the heat to medium and simmer, stirring often, until thickened and creamy, about 5 minutes. Stir in the cumin and additional salt and pepper.

4. Cut the chicken into 1-inch-wide slices on the diagonal. Ladle enough of the creamy lentils to thickly cover the bottom of a large serving platter. Arrange the chicken on top. Sprinkle over the chopped parsley and serve any remaining lentils in a bowl on the side.

 Serves 6

Skewered Chicken Breasts with Scallops

This is a versatile recipe. You can add halved mushrooms, cherry tomatoes, squares of colorful bell peppers, thickly sliced bacon, or chunks of zucchini or yellow squash for variety. Scallops and cubed chicken breasts are similar in texture and cook in about the same amount of time. These are especially good when prepared on a charcoal grill.

1½ pounds boneless, skinless chicken breasts

1 pound sea scallops

1 piece fresh ginger, 3 inches long, peeled and grated

3 tablespoons soy sauce

1 lime

2 tablespoons olive oil

Salt and freshly ground black pepper

1. Cut the chicken into 2-inch pieces. Trim the scallops of any tough connective tissue and pat dry with paper towels. Place the chicken and the scallops in separate bowls.

2. Divide the ginger between the 2 bowls. Add half of the soy sauce to each bowl. Cut the lime in half and squeeze the juice of each half into the separate bowls. Toss the mixtures well, cover, and marinate for 10 to 15 minutes at room temperature.

3. Preheat the broiler to high and generously oil a broiling pan. (Alternatively, prepare a charcoal grill and allow to burn down to a gray ash.) Thread the chicken and the scallops, alternating, on six 10-inch-long metal skewers. Place the skewers on the broiling pan or oiled grill, brush evenly with the olive oil, and season well with salt and pepper. Broil or grill about 4 inches from the source of heat until golden brown, 4 to 6 minutes. Carefully turn and broil the other side for 4 to 6 minutes, or until firm to the touch and well browned.

 Serves 6

Sautéed Chicken Breasts with Lime and Ginger

Alain Senderens was one of the pioneers of the nouvelle cuisine craze that swept Paris in the late seventies while I was a student at La Varenne, a cooking school located just around the corner from his then-famous restaurant, L'Archestrate. (His current restaurant is called Lucas Carton). Monsieur Senderens was a frequent guest demonstrator for our visiting chef program, which took place every Tuesday afternoon. This recipe was inspired by one of his dishes.

I like to slice the flesh of the lime to use for a garnish. It is important to remove all of the bitter white pith before cutting the peeled lime into very thin slices. (A super-sharp knife is helpful!) Overlap a few of the nicest slices over the top of the chicken before serving—just as Alain Senderens would do!

1 large lime or 2 small

1 piece fresh ginger, 2 inches long, peeled and very finely chopped or grated

¼ cup water

1 tablespoon sugar

6 boneless chicken breast halves

Salt and freshly ground black pepper

2 tablespoons unsalted butter

2 tablespoons vegetable oil

¼ cup dry white wine

1 cup heavy cream

1. Bring a small saucepan of water to a boil. With a vegetable peeler, remove the zest from the lime, avoiding the bitter white pith. Cut the zest into long, thin, julienne strips. Plunge the strips into the boiling water and cook rapidly for 1½ minutes. Drain and rinse under cold running water.

2. Combine the lime zest, ginger, water, and sugar in the same saucepan. Bring

this mixture to a boil, reduce the heat to medium, and simmer until the water has evaporated and the lime zest and ginger are softened, about 5 minutes. Remove from the heat and set aside.

3. Pound the chicken between 2 sheets of parchment paper or plastic wrap until about ¼ inch thick. Season with salt and pepper. Melt the butter with the oil in a very large skillet over medium-high heat. Add the chicken and cook until nicely browned and cooked through, 4 to 5 minutes on each side. Remove the chicken to a plate or platter and cover with foil to keep warm. Pour off all the fat and return the skillet to the heat.

4. Pour in the wine and whisk over high heat, scraping up any cooking bits in the bottom of the skillet. Increase the heat to high and boil until the amount of liquid has reduced to about 1 tablespoon. Pour in the cream, bring back to a boil, and cook, stirring or whisking often, until reduced by half. Pour this mixture into the saucepan that contains the lime and ginger. Season the sauce with salt and pepper.

5. Spoon a small amount of sauce over each of the breasts and serve any remaining sauce on the side.

 Serves 6

Chicken Breasts with Caramelized Onions and Glazed Carrots

Watch the onions carefully while cooking over high heat, as they burn quickly. The onions should have a golden amber color, not a dark burned color which means they have become bitter.

6 boneless, skinless chicken breast halves

Salt and freshly ground black pepper

8 to 10 medium carrots (about 1 pound)

6 small yellow onions (about 1 pound), halved and thinly sliced

1 cup cold water

3 tablespoons unsalted butter

2 tablespoons sugar

2 tablespoons vegetable oil

1. Season the chicken well with salt and pepper on both sides.

2. Cut the carrots into 1-inch pieces and place in a medium saucepan. Add enough salted cold water to cover by 2 inches. Bring to a boil, reduce the heat to medium, and cook until tender, 7 to 10 minutes. Drain well.

3. Place the onions in a large skillet. Pour in the cold water and add 1 table-spoon of the butter and 1 tablespoon of the sugar. Bring to a boil over high heat. Cook, stirring often, until all the water has evaporated and the onions are softened, about 10 to 12 minutes. Reduce the heat slightly and stir constantly until the onions turn a mellow, chestnut color, about 3 to 5 minutes. Do not burn. Remove to a plate or small bowl as soon as they are properly caramelized. Set aside, covered.

4. Wipe out the skillet and melt the remaining 2 tablespoons of butter with the vegetable oil over medium-high heat. Add the chicken and cook until well browned and cooked through, 4 to 5 minutes per side. (Do in 2 batches if necessary. Do not crowd the skillet.) Remove the chicken to a plate or platter and cover with foil to keep warm.

5. Pour off all but 1 tablespoon of the fat from the skillet. Add the carrots and the remaining tablespoon of sugar. Toss and stir over medium-high heat until the carrots are warmed through and glazed, about 5 minutes. Return the caramelized onions to the skillet and stir to warm through. Season to taste with salt and pepper. Arrange the chicken on warmed individual plates or a large serving platter. Scatter the onions over the top and surround with the carrots. Serve at once.

 Serves 6

Chicken Breast Stir-Fry with Shrimp and Snow Peas

Chicken and shrimp are quick-cooking, complementary ingredients that make an easy, last-minute meal. Add some thin strips of red pepper or diced blanched carrots for color, if desired. Serve with rice or Chinese noodles.

4 boneless, skinless chicken breast halves

1½ pounds medium shrimp, peeled and deveined

Salt and freshly ground black pepper

2 tablespoons olive oil

1 garlic clove, thinly sliced

1 pound snow peas, ends trimmed and tough strings removed

¼ cup sherry wine vinegar or rice wine vinegar

1. Cut each of the breasts crosswise into 1-inch-wide strips. Halve each shrimp. Season the chicken and shrimp with salt and pepper.

2. Combine the oil and garlic in a wok. Cook over medium-high heat, stirring often, until the garlic is lightly browned on the edges, 2 to 3 minutes. Remove the cooked garlic with a slotted spoon and discard.

3. Add the chicken strips to the wok and stir constantly until there are no traces of pink, 3 to 5 minutes. Add the shrimp and stir until pink and slightly firm to the touch, 3 to 5 minutes. Add the snow peas and cook until tender but still crunchy, about 2 minutes. Pour in the vinegar, increase the heat to high, and stir well for 1 minute longer. Season with salt and pepper and serve at once.

 Serves 6

Chicken Nugget

The Shaker Manifesto of September, 1882, tells of a Connecticut farmer who mixed cayenne with his chicken feed to increase his hens' egg laying.

Grilled Chicken Breasts with Bacon, Kale, and Balsamic Vinegar

Nutritionists keep telling us to eat more leafy green vegetables, and it's a pleasure, especially if you throw in a little bacon to make them taste even better! Slab bacon can be found in the meat section of some large grocery stores or from your butcher. If it is unavailable, cut sliced bacon into 1-inch pieces. Pureed sweet potatoes make a good accompaniment.

6 boneless, skinless chicken breast halves

Salt and freshly ground black pepper

½ pound slab bacon, rind removed

1 cup chicken stock

1½ pounds kale, washed, rinsed, and stemmed

¼ cup balsamic vinegar

1. Pound the breasts lightly between 2 sheets of parchment paper or plastic wrap until about ½ inch thick. Season on both sides with salt and pepper. Set aside.

2. Cut the bacon into pieces that measure 1 inch long and ¼ inch wide. Place in a large soup pot or kettle and cook over medium-high heat, stirring often, until lightly browned, 7 to 10 minutes. Use a slotted spoon to remove the cooked bacon to a small bowl. Pour off the fat from the pot and return to the heat. Pour in the chicken stock and stir, scraping up any cooking bits left in the bottom. Increase the heat to high and boil until reduced by half.

3. Add the kale to the pot, season with salt and pepper, and stir until wilted. Reduce the heat to low, cover, and cook, stirring once or twice, until tender, about 10 minutes.

4. Meanwhile, prepare the chicken. Preheat the broiler. Line a broiling pan with foil and lightly oil the foil. Place the chicken on the foil and broil about 4 inches from the heat until firm to the touch and lightly browned, 4 to 5 minutes per side.

5. Drain off any excess liquid from the kale. Stir in the cooked bacon and the vinegar. Using a large spoon, arrange the kale over the bottom of a warmed serving platter. Place the chicken on top. Serve at once with additional vinegar on the side if desired.

 **Serves 6**

Honey-Roasted Chicken Breasts with Figs

An extra-large, well-seasoned cast-iron skillet is best for this recipe. The skillet must be very hot to properly "roast" the breasts and to honey-glaze the figs. The final presentation is very attractive. Serve with thin French green beans, known as haricots verts, tossed in a little butter with a squeeze of lemon juice.

6 chicken breast halves, boned

Salt and freshly ground black pepper

2 tablespoons unsalted butter

2 tablespoons honey

6 fresh figs (about 2 ounces each)

1. Preheat the oven to 450° F. Season the chicken breasts with salt and pepper. Place the butter and honey in a heavy ovenproof skillet large enough to hold the chicken in one flat layer. Put the skillet in the oven until the butter has melted and the skillet is very hot, 5 to 7 minutes.

2. Arrange the chicken skin side down in the hot skillet. Roast in the oven until browned on one side, about 5 minutes. Turn the pieces and roast on the other side until brown and cooked through, about 5 minutes longer. With tongs, remove to a plate or platter and cover loosely with foil to keep warm.

3. Cut each of the figs into quarters. Carefully place them in the hot skillet and spoon over the pan juices to baste. Return the skillet to the oven and cook until the figs are softened, about 3 minutes. Remove the skillet from the oven, baste the figs again with the pan juices, and cover to keep warm while slicing the chicken.

4. Cut the breasts diagonally into thick slices and decoratively arrange on individual warmed serving plates. Garnish each plate with 4 fig quarters and spoon over any pan juices. Serve at once.

 Serves 6

Sautéed Chicken Breasts with Red and Yellow Peppers

This is a summer favorite when colorful bell peppers are plentiful and reasonably priced. You can used roasted peppers if desired (see page 5). If you do, cut their cooking time in half.

Serve with hot corn fritters and grilled or broiled tomatoes.

- **1 red pepper, halved, cored, and seeded**
- **1 yellow pepper, halved, cored, and seeded**
- **6 boneless, skinless chicken breast halves**
- **Salt and freshly ground black pepper**
- **2 tablespoons olive oil**
- **1 garlic clove, minced**
- **½ cup dry white wine, chicken stock, or water**
- **2 tablespoons finely chopped fresh parsley**

1. Slice the peppers into very thin strips.

2. Season the chicken with salt and pepper. Place the oil in a heavy sauté pan large enough to hold the chicken in one flat layer. Heat over medium-high heat. Add the chicken and cook until golden brown and cooked through, 4 to 5 minutes per side. Remove to a warmed serving platter and cover with foil to keep warm.

3. Add the peppers to the pan and increase the heat to high. Cook, stirring constantly, until softened, about 5 minutes. Add the garlic and cook 1 minute longer. Pour in the wine, stock, or water and stir well. Cook, stirring constantly, until most of the liquid has evaporated and the peppers are very soft, about 5 minutes. Stir in the parsley and season to taste with salt and pepper. Spoon over the sautéed chicken and serve at once.

 **Serves 6**

Quick-Cooked Chicken Breasts with Soy and Ginger

Try using light sesame oil in place of the vegetable oil if you happen to have some on hand. Be careful, however, as it burns easily. Cook at a slightly lower temperature and if it starts to smoke, discard the oil and start again.

- **6 boneless, skinless chicken breast halves**

- **¼ cup soy sauce**

- **1 piece fresh ginger, 3 inches long, peeled and grated**

- **2 tablespoons lemon juice**

- **2 tablespoons vegetable oil, or as needed**

- **Salt and freshly ground black pepper**

1. Cut each breast into pieces that measure about 1 inch wide and 3 to 4 inches long. Combine the soy sauce, ginger, and lemon juice in a large bowl. Add the chicken and toss to coat. Cover and set aside at room temperature to marinate for 15 minutes or up to 3 hours, refrigerated.

2. Heat the oil over medium-high heat in a large sauté pan or wok. Add the chicken strips and cook, turning frequently, until lightly browned and firm to the touch, 5 to 7 minutes. Do in 2 batches if necessary; do not crowd the pan or the chicken will not properly brown. Add a small amount of additional oil if needed to prevent the chicken from sticking to the pan.

3. Arrange the chicken on a large serving platter and sprinkle with salt and pepper to taste. Serve with additional soy sauce on the side if desired.

 Serves 6

Chicken Nugget

The state bird of Rhode Island, a chicken known as the Rhode Island Red, was developed by William Tripp of Little Compton, Rhode Island, in 1902. He crossed a Malay Hen with a Brown Leghorn.

Sautéed Chicken Breasts with Tomatoes and Fennel

Use three or four ribs of celery (peeled and thinly sliced) if fennel is not available, for a milder tasting dish. Serve with crisp oven-roasted potatoes.

6 boneless, skinless chicken breast halves

1 large fennel bulb

Salt and freshly ground black pepper

2 tablespoons olive oil

2 medium onions, thinly sliced

2 garlic cloves, minced

7 or 8 Italian plum tomatoes (about 1¼ pounds), peeled, seeded, and chopped

1. Pound the breasts between pieces of parchment paper to a thickness of about ½ inch. Cover with plastic and refrigerate until ready to cook.

2. Remove the fronds from the fennel bulb and reserve for garnish. Cut the bulb into quarters, remove the tough inner core, and thinly slice the fennel.

3. Heat the oil in a large, nonstick skillet over medium-high heat. Season the chicken on both sides with salt and pepper. Add to the skillet and cook until well browned, 3 to 5 minutes on each side. Remove to a plate or platter, cover with foil, and keep warm.

4. Add the onions and fennel to the skillet and cook, stirring, until slightly softened, about 3 minutes. Add the garlic and cook 1 minute longer. Add the tomatoes, season to taste with salt and pepper, and cook, stirring often, until the fennel is tender and the liquid has thickened, 5 to 7 minutes.

5. Return the chicken to the skillet and cover. Cook about 2 minutes just to warm through. Arrange the fennel and tomato mixture over the bottom of a large, warmed platter and top with the chicken. Garnish with the fronds of the fennel and serve at once.

 **Serves 6**

Sautéed Chicken Breasts with Leeks and Tomatoes

I was lucky enough to house-sit a large château in France once upon a time. The caretaker there grew the best leeks I've ever had. He knew that I loved them and would often bring them in, with damp, fresh earth still clinging to them. I prepared them day after day and never got tired of them. I often cooked the following recipe using rabbit, which the caretaker's wife raised. I've adapted the recipe for chicken breasts—a bit tamer, but more suitable for American tastes.

6 chicken breast halves, boned

Salt and freshly ground black pepper

3 medium leeks (about 1¼ pounds before trimming)

8 to 10 small Italian or plum tomatoes (about 1½ pounds)

2 tablespoons unsalted butter

2 tablespoons vegetable oil

1/2 cup dry white wine, chicken stock, or water

1. Season the chicken breasts with salt and pepper. Trim the leeks of all but 1 inch of the green part and clean well. Cut into ½-inch-thick slices. Peel, seed, and chop the tomatoes.

2. Melt the butter with the oil in a large skillet over medium-high heat. Add the breasts skin side down and cook until browned and cooked through, turning once 4 to 5 minutes per side. Remove to an ovenproof plate and cover loosely with foil. Keep warm on the back of the stove or in a very low oven.

3. Pour off all but 2 teaspoons of fat from the skillet. Add the leeks and cook, stirring often, until slightly softened, about 3 minutes. Stir in the tomatoes and cook about 3 minutes longer. Add the wine, chicken stock, or water and stir well. Cover and simmer until the leeks are very soft, 5 to 7 minutes. Transfer the mixture to a food processor and puree until smooth. Clean out the skillet and return the puree to it. Bring to a simmer over medium heat.

4. Cut the breasts diagonally into large, thick slices and arrange on warmed plates or a serving platter. Season the tomato and leek puree to taste with salt and pepper. Spoon some of the puree around the chicken and serve at once.

 **Serves 6**

Sautéed Chicken Breasts with Lemon Noodles

This sort of very simple recipe is often the best! For a festive touch, serve with sautéed fava beans and wild mushrooms.

6 boneless, skinless chicken breast halves

Salt and freshly ground black pepper

1 package (16 ounces) broad egg noodles

2 tablespoons unsalted butter

2 tablespoons vegetable oil

½ cup chicken stock

1 cup heavy cream

2 tablespoons fresh lemon juice

2 tablespoons chopped fresh parsley

1. Preheat the oven to 250° F. Season the chicken with salt and pepper.

2. Prepare the noodles according to package directions. Meanwhile, melt the butter with the oil in a large skillet. Sauté the chicken over high heat until lightly browned and cooked through, 4 to 5 minutes on each side. Transfer the breasts to a large ovenproof serving platter, cover loosely with foil, and place in the oven with the door slightly ajar to keep warm while preparing the sauce.

3. Pour off all the fat from the skillet. Add the chicken stock and whisk over medium-high heat to pick up any cooking bits from the bottom of the skillet. Increase the heat to high and boil until the liquid has reduced by half. Pour in the cream, bring back to a boil, and cook until reduced and thickened, 5 to 7 minutes.

4. Drain the noodles and add to the skillet. Remove from the heat and stir in the lemon juice. Season to taste with salt and pepper.

5. Pour the noodles around the chicken breasts on the warm platter. Sprinkle with the parsley and serve at once.

 Serves 6

Chicken Nugget

Queen Henrietta Maria, the wife of Charles I, had concentrated chicken stock made from a whole hen and boiled down to less than a pint for her morning cup of *bouillion de santé*.

Chicken Breasts Parmesan

Purchase a chunk of good-quality Parmesan and grate it yourself. The flavor of the real thing makes all the difference in the world. You can add an extra tablespoon or so of cheese to the sauce if you prefer an intense flavor. Serve with tiny boiled potatoes and fresh spinach.

- ¼ cup all-purpose flour
- ½ teaspoon salt
- Freshly ground black pepper
- 6 boneless, skinless chicken breast halves
- 3 tablespoons unsalted butter
- 2 tablespoons vegetable oil
- 1 small onion, finely chopped
- ½ cup dry white wine
- 1 cup chicken stock
- ⅓ cup plus 1 tablespoon grated Parmesan cheese
- Additional salt and freshly ground black pepper
- 1 tablespoon chopped fresh parsley

1. Combine the flour, salt, and pepper in a large bowl and mix well. Add the chicken in batches and turn several times to coat evenly. Set the breasts aside and reserve the flour.

2. Melt 2 tablespoons of the butter with the oil in a heavy nonstick skillet over medium-high heat. Add the breasts and cook until lightly browned, 3 to 4 minutes per side. Remove to a plate or platter and cover with foil to keep warm.

3. Pour off all but 1 tablespoon of the fat. Add the onion and cook over medium heat, stirring often, until softened, 2 to 3 minutes. Stir in the remaining tablespoon of butter until melted. Sprinkle over the reserved flour and stir to blend. Add the wine and chicken stock. Increase the heat to high and stir until the liquid comes to a boil. Stir for 1 to 2 minutes or until the sauce is thickened and smooth. Return the chicken to the skillet, reduce the heat to medium, cover, and simmer until the chicken is firm to the touch, about 5 minutes. Remove the breasts to a warmed platter.

4. Stir the ⅓ cup cheese into the sauce and season with salt and pepper. Spoon a small amount of sauce over the breasts and serve the remaining sauce on the side. Sprinkle the chicken with the tablespoon of grated Parmesan and the parsley just before serving.

 Serves 6

Sautéed Chicken Breasts with Quick Red Pepper Sauce

This is a great dish to do in summer. Peppers are at their best then, and the locally grown kind have more flavor than the imported ones available the rest of the year. You can add some chopped fresh herbs to the sauce, if desired.

6 boneless, skinless chicken breast halves

Salt and freshly ground black pepper

4 red bell peppers (about 1½ pounds)

2 tablespoons unsalted butter

2 tablespoons vegetable oil

½ cup water

½ cup heavy cream

1. Pound the breasts between 2 pieces of parchment paper to a thickness of ½ inch. Season with salt and pepper.

2. Halve the peppers lengthwise and remove the stems, cores, and seeds. Cut ½ of one of the peppers into long, thin julienne strips. Set aside for garnish. Cut the remaining peppers crosswise into ¼-inch-thick slices.

3. Melt the butter with the oil in a large, heavy skillet over medium-high heat. Add the chicken breasts and cook about 4 minutes on each side or until lightly browned and cooked through. Remove the breasts to a plate or platter and cover with foil and place in a low oven to keep warm.

4. Pour off the fat from the pan and add the water. Increase the heat to high and stir to pick up any bits left from cooking in the bottom of the pan. Add the peppers and stir well. Reduce the heat to medium-high, cover, and cook until the peppers are slightly softened, about 10 minutes. Drain well and transfer to a food processor. Puree until smooth. Return the puree to the skillet and stir in the cream. Season the sauce with salt and pepper.

5. Arrange the chicken breasts overlapping on a serving platter. Ladle a small amount of the sauce over each breast. Garnish with the reserved julienne strips of pepper and serve the remaining sauce on the side.

 **Serves 6**

Chicken Breasts with Fresh Tomato Pan Sauce

This is a summer dish meant to be prepared with tomatoes and basil fresh from the garden or farmstand. Serve with angel hair pasta (cappellini) and with an arugula salad. Add a pinch of sugar to the sauce if the tomatoes are acidic.

- **6 boneless, skinless chicken breast halves**

- **Salt and freshly ground black pepper**

- **2 tablespoons olive oil**

- **1 medium onion, finely chopped**

- **1 garlic clove, minced**

- **4 cups diced plum tomatoes (10 to 12 small tomatoes)**

- **2 tablespoons chopped fresh parsley**

- **1 cup loosely packed shredded basil leaves**

- **Several small basil leaves, for garnish**

1. Season the breasts with salt and pepper. Heat the oil in a large nonstick skillet over medium-high heat. Add the chicken and cook until well browned and cooked through, 4 to 5 minutes on each side. Remove to a plate or platter and cover with foil to keep warm.

2. Pour off all but 1 tablespoon of the oil. Add the onion and cook, stirring often, until softened, about 3 minutes. Add the garlic and cook 1 minute longer. Stir in the tomatoes, reduce the heat to medium, and cover. Cook, stirring often, until the tomatoes are softened and have formed a chunky sauce, 12 to 15 minutes. Add the parsley and basil and season to taste with salt and pepper.

3. Slice each breast on a bias into 4 or 5 strips. Place on a warmed serving platter and spoon over enough of the sauce to cover. Garnish with basil leaves and serve at once with any remaining sauce on the side.

 Serves 6

Chicken Breast Curry

The use of vanilla in a savory dish might seem strange. However, the sweetness of the vanilla balances the natural tartness of the yogurt as well as the spiciness of the curry. Serve with plenty of white rice to soak up the sauce!

6 boneless, skinless chicken breast halves

Salt and freshly ground black pepper

2 tablespoons olive oil

1 small onion, finely chopped

⅓ cup raisins

2 tablespoons curry powder (see Note)

2 cups low-fat vanilla yogurt

⅓ cup toasted, slivered almonds

1. Season the chicken with salt and pepper. Heat the oil in a large skillet over medium-high heat. Add the chicken and cook until well browned, 3 to 4 minutes per side. Remove to a plate or platter and cover with foil to keep warm.

2. Add the onion to the skillet. Cook, stirring often, until softened, about 3 minutes. Stir in the raisins and the curry powder. Cook about 2 minutes longer, stirring constantly. Reduce the heat to low and slowly stir in the yogurt to blend. Return the chicken and any accumulated juices to the skillet. Cover and cook over very low heat until warmed through, 5 to 7 minutes. Do not boil or the yogurt will separate.

3. Remove the chicken from the sauce and cut on a bias into wide strips. Transfer to a large, warmed platter and spoon over a small amount of the sauce. Sprinkle over the almonds and serve at once with the remaining sauce on the side.

 **Serves 6**

NOTE: *Curry powder will have a more mellow, rounded taste if cooked for a minute or two before adding liquid to make a sauce. Be careful, however. Too much cooking will give a burned, bitter taste to this most famous blend of spices.*

Chicken Breast Caesar Salad

The chicken can be prepared ahead of time and refrigerated until you are ready to assemble the salad, or it can be tossed in while still warm. Either way is delicious!

½ cup lemon juice

2 garlic cloves, minced

½ cup olive oil

½ teaspoon salt

½ teaspoon freshly ground black pepper

½ teaspoon sugar

½ cup mayonnaise

6 boneless, skinless chicken breast halves

2 heads romaine lettuce, cut into 1-inch pieces

½ cup grated Parmesan cheese

6 anchovy fillets, packed in oil, drained and patted dry

Croutons, store-bought or home-made, for garnish (see Note)

1. Whisk together the lemon juice, garlic, olive oil, salt, and pepper in a small bowl. Pour half of this into another bowl and whisk in the sugar and mayonnaise. Cover and refrigerate this dressing until needed.

2. Pour the remaining lemon juice and oil mixture into a nonreactive bowl or baking dish. Add the chicken breasts, turn to coat, cover, and marinate for 20 to 25 minutes.

3. Preheat a stove-top grill or broiler. Remove the chicken from the marinade and grill or broil until browned and cooked through, 4 to 5 minutes per side. Transfer to a plate and let cool slightly.

4. Combine the lettuce, cheese, and anchovies in a large salad bowl. Pour over the reserved refrigerated dressing and toss to coat. Cut the chicken into small pieces and add to the salad. Garnish with croutons and additional freshly ground black pepper.

 **Serves 6**

NOTE: *Packaged croutons come in a wide variety of types and flavors, many of which are very good. However, you may want to make your own from stale bread, a simple and inexpensive process.*

Preheat the oven to 350°F. In a large bowl, toss 3 cups of stale bread cubes, cut into 1-inch pieces, with 2 to 3 teaspoons minced garlic, 1 teaspoon dried parsley, 1 teaspoon dried oregano, and ¼ cup olive oil. Spread the bread cubes on a baking sheet and bake for 12 to 15 minutes, shaking the pan occasionally, until golden. Cool on paper towels.

You can place the croutons (while still warm) in a paper bag with ¼ cup grated Parmesan cheese and shake, if desired.

Sautéed Chicken with Arugula and Toasted Almonds

Tossed with cooked pasta, this chicken sauté makes a colorful and unusual main dish. Arugula is a bitter green with a nutty flavor that is enhanced by the toasted almonds. If not available, spinach, chard, or blanched kale could be used in its place.

6 boneless, skinless chicken breasts

Salt and freshly ground black pepper

2 tablespoons olive oil

¼ cup sherry wine vinegar

½ cup chicken stock

½ pound arugula, torn into large pieces

½ cup whole blanched almonds, toasted

1. Cut the chicken into 3 × 1-inch slices and season them with salt and pepper. In a large, nonstick skillet, heat the oil over medium-high heat and add the chicken pieces. Cook until well browned, tossing occasionally, about 4 minutes. Do in 2 batches if necessary; do not crowd the pan or the chicken will not properly brown. Transfer the chicken to a plate or platter and cover with foil to keep warm.

2. Carefully pour the vinegar into the skillet. Increase the heat to high and boil, stirring to pick up any bits on the bottom of the pan, until the vinegar has reduced to 2 tablespoons. Return the chicken pieces to the pan. Pour in the chicken stock and bring to a boil. Boil until the liquid is thickened and slightly syrupy, 3 to 4 minutes.

3. Remove from the heat and add the arugula. Stir until the arugula is wilted and well mixed with the chicken. Season to taste with salt and pepper and scatter over the almonds. Serve at once.

 **Serves 6**

Chicken Nugget

The finest chickens in France come from Bresse, a small village just south of Dijon. The *poulet de Bresse* is known the world over for its tender flesh and fine flavor. Fed a special diet and allowed to roam free, these birds are labeled with metal rings that attest to their authenticity.

Chicken Breasts with Sautéed Spinach and Orange

Serve with wild rice mixed with dried cranberries for a low-fat main dish that is full of contrasting flavors and texture.

- **1 large seedless orange**
- **6 boneless, skinless chicken breast halves**
- **Salt and freshly ground black pepper**
- **3 tablespoons olive oil**
- **1 red bell pepper, halved, cored, and seeded**
- **2 pounds cleaned spinach, stems removed (1½ pounds without stems)**

1. Preheat the oven to 300° F. Lightly oil a large ovenproof serving platter and place it in the oven.

2. Grate the zest from the orange and set aside. Remove the bitter white pith from the orange and cut down between the membranes to remove whole sections. Keep the sections covered until ready to serve.

3. Season the chicken breasts with salt and pepper. Heat 2 tablespoons of the oil in a large nonstick skillet and add the breasts. Cook over medium-high heat until well browned and cooked through, 4 to 5 minutes per side. Do in 2 batches if necessary; do not crowd the pan or the chicken will not brown properly. Transfer to the warmed platter and cover with foil to keep warm.

4. Cut the pepper into long, thin strips. Heat the remaining tablespoon of oil in a wok or large skillet. Add the pepper strips and cook over medium-high heat, stirring constantly, until slightly softened, 1 to 2 minutes. Add the spinach and cover. (It may seem like too much spinach but it will reduce greatly.) Cook, stirring often, until just wilted, 2 to 3 minutes. Uncover and cook about 2 minutes more or until the spinach is tender but not mushy. Stir in the grated orange zest, season to taste with salt and pepper, and remove from the heat.

5. Transfer the chicken from the platter to a large cutting surface. Pour any accumulated juices from the platter into the spinach. Cut each breast on a bias into 4 or 5 thick slices. Mound some spinach in the center of warmed individual serving plates and fan the chicken slices on top. Garnish with the orange sections and serve warm.

 **Serves 6**

Five-Ingredient Chinese Ginger Chicken Breasts

In a real rush? Skip the two- to three-hour marinade and proceed. The distinctive flavor will not be quite as intense, but it will be a welcome last-minute dish. Add a pinch of chopped fresh lemongrass for an even more exotic flavor.

- **6 boneless, skinless chicken breast halves**
- **6 tablespoons soy sauce**
- **1 piece fresh ginger, 3 inches long, peeled and grated**
- **1 teaspoon Asian sesame oil**
- **¼ cup minced scallions (green onions)**

1. Cut the chicken into 1-inch-wide strips and place in a large bowl. Add the soy sauce, ginger, and sesame oil. Cover, refrigerate, and marinate for 2 to 3 hours.

2. Preheat the oven to 350° F. Fold 6 large sheets of parchment paper in half. Use scissors to cut out a heart shape large enough to hold a mound of the chicken strips with a 2-inch border to spare. Brush each heart lightly with butter or vegetable oil.

3. Divide the chicken evenly among the hearts, placing the strips in the center of one side. Sprinkle each with scallions. Starting at the curve of the heart, fold the other side over the strips and crimp the edges closed by making small pleats to seal.

4. Place the packages on 2 large baking sheets. Bake until puffed and brown, 15 to 20 minutes. Serve the *papillotes* on individual plates and let each guest cut or break open the package at the table.

 **Serves 6**

Chicken Breast Satay with Peanut Sauce

Serve plain white rice mixed with golden raisins and chopped peanuts. Mound the rice in the center of a large platter and place the skewered chicken on top. Pass the sauce separately in a decorative bowl.

Coconut milk is widely available in the specialty foods departments of many large grocery stores. Use whole milk, if not available; the coconut milk adds an extra dimension, but it is not essential to the texture of the sauce.

6 boneless, skinless chicken breast halves

2 tablespoons vegetable oil, preferably peanut oil

Salt and freshly ground black pepper

1 medium onion, finely chopped

1 garlic clove, minced

1 teaspoon curry powder

1 tablespoon brown sugar

¼ cup creamy peanut butter

¾ cup unsweetened coconut milk

1. Soak approximately 30 wooden skewers in warm water for at least 30 minutes.

2. Place each chicken breast between 2 sheets of wax paper, and use a wooden mallet or the handle of a large knife to flatten each breast to ¼-inch thickness. Cut each breast into 1½-inch-wide strips. Thread each breast strip flat on a skewer. Brush lightly with half of the oil. Season with salt and pepper. Place on an oiled broiling pan and set aside while preparing the sauce.

3. Heat the remaining tablespoon of oil in a medium saucepan over medium-high heat. Add the onion and cook, stirring often, until softened, about 2 minutes. Stir in the garlic, curry powder, and brown sugar. Cook 1 minute longer. Whisk in the peanut butter and coconut milk. Reduce the heat to medium low and simmer, stirring often, until thickened and smooth, 5 to 7 minutes. Season to taste with salt and pepper.

4. Preheat the broiler and set the pan about 6 inches from the heat source. Broil the chicken until opaque and firm to the touch, 3 to 4 minutes. Carefully turn and cook 3 to 4 minutes longer on the other side. Serve at once with the sauce on the side.

 Serves 6

Broiled Chicken Breasts with Lemon and Roasted Garlic

Garlic becomes mellow when cooked. Here we've pan-"roasted" the cloves in a skillet over direct heat. You can do this in a hot oven, too, but it takes twice as long. Making the paste can be done very efficiently with a mortar and pestle. Proceed in the same manner described below—crush the garlic with the salt, then work in the lemon juice to form a paste.

6 boneless, skinless chicken breast halves

Salt and freshly ground black pepper

4 large garlic cloves, unpeeled

About 1/2 teaspoon salt

1/2 teaspoon chopped fresh thyme, or 1/4 teaspoon dried

3 tablespoons lemon juice

1. Preheat the broiler or prepare a charcoal fire and allow the coals to burn down to a gray ash. Oil a broiling pan or grill and set aside. Season the chicken breasts with salt and pepper.

2. Place the garlic cloves in a small, heavy sauté pan. "Roast" over medium-high heat, stirring the garlic or shaking the pan often, until the cloves are golden brown on the outside and slightly tender on the inside, about 20 minutes. Let cool slightly, then peel. Place the garlic in a small bowl and add a large pinch of salt and the thyme. Use a fork to crush the garlic with the salt and thyme against the side of the bowl. Add the lemon juice slowly, working constantly with the fork until the mixture forms a thick paste.

3. Rub each chicken breast with an equal amount of the garlic mixture. Broil or grill 6 inches from the heat source until the chicken is opaque and cooked through, about 5 minutes on each side.

 **Serves 6**

Sautéed Chicken Breasts with Balsamic Vinegar and Capers

Balsamic vinegar is dark, rich, and perfect for deglazing a pan to make a simple sauce for chicken breasts. However, you can substitute any good-quality vinegar with excellent results.

6 boneless, skinless chicken breast halves

3 tablespoons unsalted butter, softened

2 tablespoons vegetable oil

¼ cup balsamic vinegar

½ cup chicken stock

2 tablespoons imported capers, coarsely chopped

Salt and freshly ground black pepper

1. Preheat the oven to 250° F. Pound the chicken breasts between 2 sheets of parchment paper until about ½ inch thick. Melt 2 tablespoons butter with the oil in a large nonstick skillet over medium-high heat. Add the chicken and cook until browned and cooked through, 4 to 5 minutes on each side. Remove to a large ovenproof plate or platter and keep warm in the oven, covered. Do in 2 or 3 batches if necessary; do not crowd the pan or the breasts will not properly brown. Add additional butter and oil as needed.

2. Pour off all the fat from the skillet. Return the skillet to the heat and add the vinegar. Stir, picking up any bits left from browning the chicken, and increase the heat to high. Boil until reduced by half. Pour in the chicken stock and bring back to a boil. Boil rapidly, stirring often, until the liquid has reduced again by half or until thickened and slightly syrupy. Add the capers, reduce the heat to medium low, and warm through, about 1 minute. Remove the skillet from the heat and swirl in the remaining tablespoon of softened butter. Season the sauce with salt and pepper. Pour the sauce over the chicken and serve at once.

 **Serves 6**

Chicken Nugget

A full colonel in the U.S. army is known as a "chicken" colonel, probably because of his eagle insignia.

Chicken Breasts with Cranberries

Cranberries are not just for Thanksgiving! They are plentiful for many months of the year now, so here is a recipe to make good use of an American favorite. I like to serve this with a puree of root vegetables, such as turnips, parsnips, or rutabagas.

Crème de Cassis is a black currant liqueur widely available in wine stores. It is used to make a popular apéritif called a Kir (white wine or Champagne flavored with just a drop of Cassis). But you can substitute a fortified wine like Port or Madeira, if desired.

2 cups cranberries

2 tablespoons sugar

2 tablespoons crème de Cassis

½ cup chicken stock or water

2 tablespoons unsalted butter

2 tablespoons vegetable oil

6 chicken breast halves, boned

Salt and freshly ground black pepper

2 tablespoons red wine vinegar

1. Combine the cranberries, sugar, crème de Cassis, and stock or water in a small saucepan. Simmer over low heat, stirring often, until the cranberries have given off liquid and are slightly tender, about 5 minutes. Remove from the heat and set aside, covered.

2. Melt the butter with the oil in a large sauté pan over medium-high heat. Season the chicken breasts with salt and pepper. Add the chicken and cook until browned and cooked through, 4 to 5 minutes per side. Remove to a plate or platter and cover loosely with foil to keep warm.

3. Pour off the fat from the sauté pan. Return the pan to the heat and carefully add the vinegar. Use a whisk to stir and pick up any bits left in the pan from browning. Cook over medium-high heat, whisking often, until reduced by half. The reduced juices should be slightly thickened and syrupy. Add the cranberry mixture, reduce the heat to low, and gently stir until warmed through, 3 to 5 minutes. Season to taste with salt and pepper. Cover and keep warm.

4. Cut the chicken breasts into large slices on a diagonal. Arrange on a warmed platter or warmed individual serving plates. Spoon over a small amount of the cranberries and sauce. Serve at once with any additional sauce passed on the side.

 **Serves 6**

Chicken Breasts in Mustard Sauce

It is amazing what can be done with ingredients you already have in your kitchen. A little mustard, some cream, and voilà, an ordinary chicken part becomes a gourmet delight. Don't be alarmed by the cup of cream called for here. One cup of cream, reduced and divided six ways, is not a lot. A small spoonful of rich sauce is all that is needed to really dress up a chicken breast.

6 chicken breast halves, boned

Salt and freshly ground black pepper

2 tablespoons unsalted butter

2 tablespoons vegetable oil

½ cup chicken stock

1 cup heavy cream

2 tablespoons Dijon mustard

1. Season the chicken with salt and pepper. Melt the butter with the oil in a large skillet over medium-high heat. Add the chicken and cook until well browned and cooked through, 4 to 5 minutes on each side. Remove to a plate or platter and cover with foil to keep warm.

2. Pour off all the fat from the skillet and return the skillet to the heat. Pour in the chicken stock and increase the heat to high. Boil, whisking to pick up any cooking bits in the bottom of the skillet, until thickened, syrupy, and reduced to about 2 tablespoons. Stir in the cream, bring back to a boil, and reduce again by half, or until thickened. Remove from the heat and stir in the mustard. Season to taste with salt and pepper. Spoon a small amount over each breast and serve at once.

 Serves 6

Chicken Nugget

"Chicken has often been considered a luxury. In 817 the Council of Aachen ruled that chicken was a dish too sumptuous for fast days and forbade monks to eat it except during four days at Easter and four more at Christmas. The chicken had its fast-day status restored temporarily in the thirteenth century when St. Thomas Aquinas held that it was of aquatic origin and thus edible on the same terms as fish; the Church later decided that St. Thomas had underestimated the chicken and ruled it definitely too good for fasting."

—Waverly Root, in *Food*

Chicken Breasts in Parsley Sauce

This is a low-fat recipe that makes good use of one of nature's most abundant herbs. Fresh parsley has a clean and fresh taste, and should not be reserved just for garnishing. Be sure to remove the tough stems for this recipe. The tender leaves make the best sauce.

- 6 boneless, skinless chicken breast halves
- Salt and freshly ground black pepper
- 1 tablespoon olive oil
- 2 celery stalks, finely chopped
- 1 medium onion, finely chopped
- 4 cups lightly packed fresh parsley leaves (about 4 ounces)
- ½ cup dry white wine
- ½ cup plain low-fat yogurt

1. Preheat the oven to 300°F. Pound the chicken between 2 sheets of parchment paper to about ½-inch thickness. Season with salt and pepper. Heat the oil over medium-high heat in a large nonstick skillet. Add the chicken and cook until lightly browned and cooked through, about 4 minutes on each side. Remove to an ovenproof plate or platter and transfer to the oven while preparing the sauce.

2. Add the celery and the onion to the skillet. Cook over medium heat, stirring constantly, until softened, about 3 minutes. Add the parsley and cook, stirring, until wilted, about 2 minutes. Pour in the wine, increase the heat to high, and boil until most of the liquid has evaporated. Transfer the contents of the skillet to a food processor and process until smooth, scraping down the sides of the work bowl as necessary. Return the parsley mixture to the skillet and add the yogurt. Add any juices that have accumulated around the chicken breasts. Stir over very low heat until thick and blended. Do not boil. Season to taste with salt and pepper.

3. Place the chicken breasts on warmed individual serving plates. Spoon a small amount of the sauce on top and serve the rest on the side.

 **Serves 6**

Chicken Nugget

"And we meet, with champagne and a chicken, at last."
—Lady Mary Wortley Montagu, "The Lover," a poem, 1748

Southern Fried Chicken Breasts

Fried chicken has a special place in my heart. I grew up in Georgia, and our big meal of the day was always at noon. Fried chicken was a real treat, usually served with turnip greens, sweet potatoes, and cornbread. I always looked forward to these lunches. The aroma of the chicken in the noonday heat was downright intoxicating.

Southern cooks know the exact amount of time it takes to fry breasts to that crunchy-on-the-outside, melt-in-the-mouth tender inside. This recipe calls for soaking the breasts in buttermilk, a trick I picked up in Georgia. The buttermilk not only lends a tangy flavor, but also seems to tenderize the sweet flesh.

6 large chicken breast halves

1 quart buttermilk

Vegetable oil, for deep-frying

1 cup all-purpose flour

½ tablespoon mild paprika

Salt and freshly ground black pepper

1. Trim the breasts and place in a deep bowl. Pour over the buttermilk and soak, turning occasionally, for 30 minutes at room temperature or up to 6 hours in the refrigerator. Drain, discard the buttermilk, and pat chicken dry.

2. Fill a deep-fat fryer or Dutch oven with several inches of vegetable oil. Heat to 350°F. or until a small piece of bread sizzles when thrown into the hot oil. Combine the flour, paprika, and a pinch each of salt and pepper in a large paper bag. Place the breasts in the bag a few at a time and shake well until all of the pieces are well coated. Remove 1 at a time, shake off excess flour, and submerge in the hot oil. Reduce the heat to medium, partially cover to avoid messy splattering (see Note), and cook, turning occasionally, until golden brown and crisp, 25 to 30 minutes. Cook in batches if necessary so that the pieces do no touch; crowding the pan will prevent the chicken from becoming crisp and evenly browned.

3. Drain on paper towels and sprinkle with additional salt, if desired. Serve hot or at room temperature.

 Serves 6

NOTE: *A device called a splatter screen is handy when deep-frying. It is a screen on a round frame with a long handle that is used in place of a lid. The cook can see what is happening but avoid messy and painful grease splatters.*

Chicken Breasts *en Papillote* with Fennel and Orange

Fennel and orange make a nice contrast in texture and flavor. If you're lucky enough to have a bottle of pastis (the strong aniseed-flavored drink so popular in the south of France), add a teaspoon or so to each of the packages. This will really bring out the taste of the fennel. People love to open the pretty paper packages at the table. Serve the breasts with parsleyed rice or quick-cooking couscous.

- **1 large fennel bulb (about 1½ pounds)**
- **1 tablespoon olive oil, plus additional for brushing**
- **2 small navel oranges**
- **6 boneless, skinless chicken breast halves**
- **6 tablespoons orange juice**
- **Salt and freshly ground black pepper**

1. Preheat the oven to 375°F. Quarter the fennel, remove the tough core, and slice thinly. Heat the oil over medium-high heat in a medium saucepan. Add the fennel and cook, stirring often, until tender, about 10 minutes.

2. Meanwhile, finely grate the oranges, being careful to avoid the bitter white pith underneath the brightly colored skin. Using a serrated knife, remove the pith and remaining peel of the oranges. Cut between the membranes and separate the flesh into sections.

3. Fold 6 large sheets of parchment paper in half and cut into large heart shapes. Be sure to make each side of the hearts at least 2 inches larger all around than the chicken breasts. Brush the insides of the hearts lightly with olive oil. Arrange the breasts in the center of one side of each heart. Scatter equal amounts of the fennel over each breast, top with a few orange sections, and spoon over a tablespoon of orange juice. Add a pinch of grated orange zest and season with salt and pepper. Fold the other side of the heart over the chicken and, starting at the curve of the heart, crimp the edges together to form a tight seal. Place the packages on 2 large baking sheets. Cook for about 20 minutes or until puffed and browned. Break or cut open the packages at the table. (Be careful when opening the packages, from which steam will escape quickly, possibly harming unsuspecting guests.)

 **Serves 6**

Breasts

Simply Sophisticated

Apricot-Glazed Chicken Breasts

In this stunningly simple dish, the dried apricots give plain chicken breasts a wonderful flavor and beautiful color. Add golden raisins that have been plumped in Grand Marnier, if desired. Serve with buttered noodles or spätzle for a memorable meal.

24 dried pitted apricots (about 4 ounces)

½ cup sugar

½ cup water

6 large chicken breast halves

Salt and freshly ground black pepper

2 tablespoons unsalted butter, cut into small pieces

1. Preheat the oven to 400°F. In a small saucepan, combine the apricots, sugar, and water. Stir over medium heat until the sugar is dissolved. Increase the heat to medium high and cook, uncovered, until the apricots are softened, about 20 minutes. Transfer the contents of the saucepan to a food processor and puree until smooth.

2. Season the chicken with salt and pepper. Place in a large greased roasting pan and dot with the butter. Spoon over the apricot mixture and place the pan in the oven. Cook, turning the chicken and basting every 10 to 15 minutes, until glazed and lightly browned, about 1 hour.

 Serves 6

Chicken Breasts Grenadine

Grenadine is a sweet syrup made from pomegranate seeds. It is used for making many exotic cocktails and can, therefore, often be found in liquor stores.

6 large chicken breast halves

Salt and freshly ground black pepper

2 tablespoons unsalted butter, softened

½ cup grenadine syrup

2 medium navel oranges

1 pomegranate (about ¾ pound)

1. Preheat the oven to 400°F. Season the chicken with salt and pepper. Spread the butter over the bottom of a large baking dish or roasting pan, add the chicken, and drizzle over the grenadine. Bake, uncovered, turning often until the chicken is glazed and cooked through, about 45 minutes.

2. Meanwhile, remove the peel of the oranges, avoiding the bitter white pith. Cut the peel into long, thin julienne strips. Remove any remaining white pith from the orange. Cut down between the membrane to remove whole sections of the flesh. Place the sections in a bowl and set aside.

3. Fill a small saucepan with water and bring to a boil. Add the julienne strips of orange peel and bring back to a boil. Boil for 1 minute, then rinse under cold running water. Repeat this procedure once more, then drain and remove the strips to dry on paper towels.

4. Break open the pomegranate and carefully remove the small red seeds of the fruit. Set them aside for garnish.

5. Transfer the chicken to a serving platter and cover with foil to keep warm. Gently transfer the orange sections and the julienne strips to the baking dish. Use a spoon to carefully turn the sections in the pan juices for color. Arrange the sections on top of the chicken and scatter the strips decoratively around the platter. Sprinkle over the pomegranate seeds and spoon over any cooking juices left in the baking dish. Serve at once.

 **Serves 6**

Chicken Nugget

The ancient Romans thought the chicken sacred and employed roosters for fortune-telling.

Chilled Poached Chicken Breasts with Green Peppercorn Sauce

This is a lovely luncheon or brunch buffet dish. The sauce can be made in advance, the chicken can be poached well ahead of time, and all can be assembled just before serving.

On those dog days of summer, when heating up the kitchen is the last thing you want to do, try poaching the chicken in the microwave instead of the oven. Follow manufacturers instructions for best results. Low-fat sour cream works perfectly well for the sauce.

½ cup sour cream

¼ cup mayonnaise

1 tablespoon Dijon mustard

1 heaping teaspoon grated lemon zest

1½ teaspoons lemon juice

½ teaspoon sugar

2 tablespoons green peppercorns, drained

2 cups dry white wine

2 cups chicken stock

10 whole black peppercorns

2 sprigs fresh thyme

6 boneless, skinless chicken breast halves

12 cups loosely packed mixed salad greens, such as watercress, red lettuce, and arugula

Salt and freshly ground black pepper

1. To make the sauce, combine the sour cream, mayonnaise, mustard, lemon zest, lemon juice, sugar, and green peppercorns in a small bowl. Cover and refrigerate until ready to serve.

2. Preheat the oven to 350°F. Combine the wine, stock, black peppercorns, and thyme in a nonreactive baking dish large enough to hold the chicken in one flat layer. Place the breasts in this poaching liquid and cover with foil. Place in the oven and bake for about 30 minutes or until the chicken is firm to the touch and cooked through.

3. Remove the chicken from the poaching liquid and cool to room temperature. Cover and refrigerate until chilled, at least 1 hour. (The chicken can be poached up to 2 days in advance.)

4. Divide the salad greens among 6 individual serving plates. Cut each breast into ½-inch slices and fan them out over the greens. Taste the sauce and season with salt and pepper. Spoon the sauce over the top and garnish with additional freshly ground pepper.

 Serves 6

Chicken and Leek Cabbage Bundles

Stuffed cabbage is comfort food at its best. Serve these bundles with rice. Chopped, cooked bacon can be added to the stuffing just before filling the leaves.

1 medium head green cabbage (1½ to 2 pounds)

3 medium leeks, white part only, thinly sliced

3 large carrots, peeled and cut into ½-inch cubes

3 slices white sandwich bread, crusts removed

Salt and freshly ground black pepper

4 boneless, skinless chicken breast halves, cut into 1-inch cubes

1 recipe Tomato Sauce (page 226)

1. Bring a large stockpot of salted water to a boil. Use a small knife to cut away the tough core at the base of the cabbage and immerse the head in the boiling water. Use 2 large spoons to peel off the outer layers as they cook and soften. Transfer about 12 of the largest leaves to a colander and refresh under cold running water. (Leave the remaining cabbage in the kettle.) Cut out the thick rib at the base of each of the 12 leaves, and pat dry with paper towels.

2. Add the leeks to the pot and boil with the remaining cabbage until tender, about 3 minutes. Drain and rinse the leeks and cabbage under cold running water. Use your hands to squeeze out excess moisture from the vegetables, then chop coarsely.

3. Bring a large saucepan of salted water to a boil. Add the carrots and cook until just tender, 5 to 7 minutes. Drain and rinse under cold running water. Lay out on paper towels to drain.

4. In the bowl of a food processor, combine the chopped cabbage and leeks with the bread and process until smooth. Season well with salt and pepper.

5. Preheat the oven to 350°F. On a large work surface, lay the blanched cabbage leaves out flat and sprinkle each with salt and pepper. Place 1 to 2 tablespoons of the cabbage and leek mixture in the center of each leaf. Add equal amounts of the chicken and carrots to each leaf. Season again with salt and pepper. Carefully fold the sides of the leaves in toward the center, then roll the leaves into bundles.

6. Place all but ½ cup of the tomato sauce in the bottom of a large baking dish. Arrange the bundles snugly in the dish, seam side down, and dab over the remaining sauce. Cover the dish lightly with foil and bake until the sauce is bub-

bling hot and the bundles are cooked through, 45 minutes to 1 hour. Serve at once.

 Serves 6

Baked Chutney Chicken Breasts with Seckle Pears

Seckle pears are a small American variety with an excellent tangy flavor. If not available, use any larger firm pear. Peel the pears and cut into 1-inch cubes. Diced cooking apples, such as Golden Delicious, could be used, too.

1 cup golden raisins

¹/₂ cup dark rum

6 chicken breast halves

Salt and freshly ground black pepper

1 small jar (8¹/₂ ounces) Major Grey's Mango Chutney

Juice of ¹/₂ lemon

8 to 10 small seckle pears (about 1¹/₄ pounds), peeled, quartered, and cored

1 tablespoon chopped fresh parsley

1. Preheat the oven to 400°F. Combine the raisins and rum in a small saucepan and bring to a boil. Remove from the heat and set aside, covered, to plump.

2. Butter a large baking dish. Season the chicken with salt and pepper. Arrange the breasts snugly in the dish and spoon over the chutney. Squeeze over the lemon juice and add the raisins with the rum. Surround with the pears. Bake, uncovered, for about 1 hour or until the pears are tender and the skin side of the chicken is browned. Turn the chicken every 10 to 15 minutes to stir and coat the breasts, ending by cooking the breasts skin side up.

3. Serve the chicken on a large, warmed platter. Surround with the pears, spoon over any pan juices, and sprinkle with the parsley.

 Serves 6

Chicken Breasts with Lentils and Sausage

Lentils and sausage are a natural combination. I prefer the tiny, green lentils imported from LePuy, a town in France. They tend to have more flavor and the texture is firmer. I've often used a reduced-fat sausage in this recipe, with excellent results.

2½ cups dried lentils (about 1 pound)

4 tablespoons olive oil

2 medium carrots, peeled and coarsely chopped

1 medium onion, coarsely chopped

1 celery stalk, coarsely chopped

Several sprigs fresh thyme

2 garlic cloves, peeled and crushed

1 bay leaf

1 pound sweet Italian sausage, cut into 3-inch lengths

½ cup dry white wine

6 boneless, skinless chicken breast halves

Salt and freshly ground black pepper

1 tablespoon white wine vinegar

1 tablespoon chopped fresh parsley, for garnish

1. Rinse the lentils under cold running water and drain well.

2. Heat 2 tablespoons of the oil in a large, deep skillet over medium-high heat. Add the carrots, onion, and celery. Cook, stirring often, until slightly softened, 3 to 5 minutes. Add the thyme, garlic, and bay leaf. Stir in the drained lentils and enough cold water to cover. Increase the heat to high and bring to a boil. Reduce the heat to medium and simmer, uncovered, until tender, 30 to 40 minutes. Add more water if necessary to prevent scorching. Season with salt to taste during the last 10 minutes of cooking time. Discard the thyme stems, garlic, and bay leaf.

3. Meanwhile, place the remaining 2 tablespoons olive oil in a large nonstick skillet. Add the sausages and cook, turning often, until lightly browned on all sides. Remove to a plate and cover to keep warm. Pour off all but 1 or 2 tablespoons of fat from the skillet. Over high heat, add the wine and boil, scraping up any bits from browning, until the liquid is mostly evaporated.

4. Season the chicken with salt and pepper. Add to the skillet and cook, turning often, until browned on both sides, about 5 minutes.

5. Return the sausages to the skillet. With a slotted spoon, cover the chicken and sausages with the cooked lentils. Cover the skillet, reduce the heat to medium low, and cook until very hot and the chicken and sausage are cooked through, 10 to 12 minutes. Stir in the vinegar just before serving and garnish with parsley.

 Serves 6

Baked Chicken Breasts with Prunes and Lemon

Simple and tasty, this dish is meant to be served on a cold day with hot buttered noodles or mashed potatoes. Watch the baking dish carefully during cooking. If the liquid starts to evaporate, add a little water to prevent scorching.

1 medium lemon

12 ounces large, pitted prunes (about 2 cups, loosely packed)

2 cups boiling water

6 chicken breast halves

Salt and freshly ground black pepper

1. Use a vegetable peeler to cut wide lengthwise strips from the lemon, avoiding the bitter white pith. Cut the strips into long, thin, julienne pieces. Squeeze the juice from the lemon; you should have 3 to 4 tablespoons of juice. In a bowl, combine the prunes, the julienned lemon strips, and the lemon juice. Pour over the boiling water, cover, and let stand for 10 minutes.

2. Preheat the oven to 350°F. Butter a large baking dish and season the chicken with salt and pepper. Drain the prunes, reserving ¼ cup of the soaking liquid. Place the breasts skin side down in one flat layer on the bottom of the baking dish. Surround with the drained prunes and lemon strips. Pour over the ¼ cup reserved soaking liquid. Cover the dish with foil and bake for 15 minutes. Remove the foil, turn the chicken over, and return the dish to the oven. Bake, turning often, for 45 minutes to 1 hour or until the chicken is lightly browned and cooked through and the prunes are plump.

3. Arrange the breasts on a large, warmed serving platter. Surround with the prunes. Pour over any juices that have accumulated in the bottom of the pan and serve at once.

 **Serves 6**

Crepes with Chicken Breast, Leeks, and Mushrooms

This is one of those dishes some folks call a labor of love. It takes time and patience to prepare, but the praise you earn will soothe any qualms about the effort. Serve with just a green salad and a good dessert. The crepes can be done well in advance and the sauce can be made a day or two ahead. Take the sauce out of the refrigerator and let it come to room temperature before filling the crepes.

3 large boneless, skinless chicken breast halves

3 cups chicken stock, preferably homemade

3 medium leeks, white part only, cleaned and trimmed

4 tablespoons (½ stick) unsalted butter

10 medium mushrooms (about ½ pound), halved

Salt and freshly ground black pepper

3 tablespoons all-purpose flour

12 crepes 7 inches in diameter (see page 8)

½ cup freshly grated Parmesan cheese

1. Place the chicken breasts in a medium skillet and pour in the chicken stock. Bring to a boil over high heat, reduce the heat to medium, and cook until firm to the touch and cooked through, turning once or twice, about 15 minutes. Remove, cool slightly, and cut the breasts into 1-inch cubes. Set aside, covered. Reserve the cooking liquid.

2. Halve the leeks lengthwise and cut into ¼-inch-thick slices. Melt 1 tablespoon of the butter in a medium saucepan over medium-high heat. Add the leeks and cook, stirring often, until softened, about 7 minutes. Do not brown. Add the mushrooms and cook about 2 minutes longer. Season with salt and pepper. Remove from the heat, cover, and set aside.

3. Melt the remaining 3 tablespoons butter in a large saucepan over medium-high heat. Stir in the flour and cook, stirring often, until lemon-colored and bubbling, about 3 minutes. Pour in the reserved liquid that the breasts were cooked in and increase the heat to high. Stir constantly until boiling. Reduce the heat to medium low and cook, stirring often, until smooth and thickened and reduced to 1 cup. Season to taste with salt and pepper. Place two-thirds of the sauce in a large bowl. Add the cooked chicken, leeks, and mushrooms. Stir well to blend. Season with salt and pepper. Reserve the remaining third cup of sauce and set aside.

4. Preheat the oven to 375° F. On a large work surface, lay the crepes flat. Fill each crepe with about ¼ cup of the chicken and leek mixture. Gently roll into a loose cylinder and place in a large, buttered baking dish, seam side down. Pour over the remaining third of the sauce and sprinkle over the cheese. Bake for about 20 minutes or until the sauce is bubbling hot. Serve at once.

 Serves 6

Baked Chicken Niçoise Stuffed with Black Olives and Capers

Serve with oven-roasted red potatoes tossed with fresh thyme.

6 chicken breast halves

24 pitted black olives, preferably oil-cured, finely chopped

2 tablespoons capers, finely chopped

2 tablespoons chopped fresh parsley

1 tablespoon lemon juice

1 garlic clove, minced

2 to 3 tablespoons olive oil

Freshly ground black pepper

1. Preheat the oven to 350° F. Lightly oil a large covered baking dish that will hold the chicken in a flat layer. To prepare the chicken for the filling, carefully lift the skin of each breast and insert a finger to loosen the skin from the flesh.

2. To make the filling, combine the olives, capers, 1 tablespoon of the parsley, the lemon juice, and garlic in a large bowl. With a fork, blend in enough olive oil to make a spreadable paste. Season with black pepper. (The olives should make the mixture salty enough.)

3. Fill the loosened space under the skin of the breasts with 1 to 2 teaspoonfuls of the olive mixture. Use your fingers to spread the filling evenly and uniformly, being careful not to tear the skin.

4. Arrange the prepared breasts snugly together in the baking dish. Drizzle over a small amount of additional olive oil and squeeze over a little more lemon juice, if desired. Cover the dish and bake, basting occasionally, for about 45 minutes or until the flesh is quite firm to the touch and the chicken is cooked through. Serve on a warmed platter and sprinkle with the remaining tablespoon of chopped parsley.

 **Serves 6**

Chicken Strudel with Cabbage and Bacon

The filling for this hearty winter dish can be prepared a day or two in advance if desired. Serve with tomato sauce and lots of hot, fluffy rice.

4 boneless, skinless chicken breast halves

Salt and freshly ground black pepper

3 medium carrots (about ½ pound), peeled and cut into ¼-inch slices

1 head green cabbage (about 2½ pounds)

5 slices bacon, cut into ½-inch pieces

1 medium onion, finely chopped

8 sheets phyllo dough

Melted unsalted butter, for brushing

1. Cut the chicken into 1½-inch pieces, season with salt and pepper, and set aside. Bring a large pot of salted water to a boil. Add the carrots, bring back to a boil, and cook rapidly for 2 minutes to blanch. Drain and rinse under cold running water.

2. Halve the cabbage lengthwise and remove the tough inner core. Use a large knife to shred the leaves into ¼-inch-thick slices.

3. Cook the bacon in a large saucepan over medium-high heat, stirring often, until lightly browned and the fat has been rendered. Use a slotted spoon to remove the cooked bacon to a bowl. Add the chunks of chicken to the pan and cook, stirring often, over medium-high heat until lightly brown and cooked through, about 3 minutes. Remove the chicken to a bowl with a slotted spoon.

4. Add the onion to the pan and cook, stirring often, until softened, about 2 minutes. Add the cabbage and cook, stirring often, until tender, about 10 minutes. Pour the cabbage mixture into a colander to drain off excess liquid, then transfer to a bowl. Stir in the carrots, bacon, and chicken. Combine well and season to taste with salt and pepper. Set aside to cool.

5. Preheat the oven to 350° F. Cover a large work surface with several sheets of parchment paper. Working quickly according to package directions, place the first sheet of phyllo dough flat on the paper. Brush with melted butter. Place a second sheet of dough on top and brush again with melted butter. Repeat this process until all of the sheets of dough have been used.

6. Spoon the cooled chicken and cabbage mixture lengthwise over the bottom third of the phyllo layers. Carefully lift the end with the filling and roll into

a tight cylinder and fold in the sides. Gently transfer to an oiled baking sheet and twist the ends inward to form a slight crescent. Brush the top of the strudel with butter and bake for 35 to 40 minutes or until the filling is bubbling hot and the top is browned. Cut into thick slices with a serrated knife and serve at once.

Serves 6

Grilled Chicken with Tropical Salsa

This is an excellent low-fat recipe. Tomatillos are found in many Latin American markets. They have a fresh, clean taste that works well in a spicy salsa. If they are not available and if green tomatoes are not to be found, firm red tomatoes can be used with good results.

6 boneless, skinless chicken breast halves

Juice of 1 lemon

½ cup golden raisins

½ red bell pepper, cored, seeded, and diced very small

½ medium red onion, very thinly sliced

2 small tomatillos, paperlike skins removed, or 1 medium green tomato, cored and diced very small

1 small mango, peeled and diced very small

1 cup ¼-inch dice fresh or canned pineapple

2 tablespoons sherry wine vinegar

2 tablespoons olive oil

Salt and freshly ground black pepper

1. Pound the breasts between 2 sheets of parchment paper to a thickness of about ½ inch.

2. Prepare a charcoal grill and let the coals burn down to a gray ash. Alternatively, oil a stove-top grill and preheat well before cooking the chicken.

3. Combine the lemon juice and raisins in a small heatproof bowl. Pour over just enough boiling water to cover. Set aside for 10 minutes.

4. Combine the red pepper, red onion, tomatillos or green tomato, mango, and pineapple in a large bowl. Drain the raisins, discard the soaking liquid, and add the raisins to the bowl. Just before serving, stir in the vinegar and oil. Season with salt and pepper (makes about 2½ cups salsa).

5. Grill the breasts until firm and completely cooked, 4 to 5 minutes on each side. Serve on a large platter with the salsa on the side.

 **Serves 6**

Chicken Breast and Spinach Roulades with Yogurt Sauce

The sauce can be made a day or two in advance. Be sure to reheat gently to prevent the sauce from separating. This recipe makes a very attractive plate presentation. Mound cooked rice into small (1/2-cup) buttered ramekins. Keep warm in a hot water bath on top of the stove. Unmold the rice onto the plate with the roulades and sauce just before serving.

6 boneless, skinless chicken breast halves

Salt and freshly ground black pepper to taste

1 1/2 pounds fresh spinach, or 2 packages (10 ounces each) frozen spinach

1/2 cup dried bread crumbs

2 tablespoons lemon juice

1 large egg, beaten

1 cup white wine or chicken stock

2 tablespoons olive oil

1 medium onion, finely chopped

1 garlic clove, minced

1 cup plain yogurt

2 tablespoons chopped fresh parsley

1. Place the chicken breasts between sheets of parchment paper and pound to a uniform thickness of about 1/4 inch. Season with salt and pepper.

2. Remove the large stems from the fresh spinach and wash well in several changes of cold water. Place the spinach in a large nonreactive pan and sprinkle with salt. (Do not add additional water. There should be enough moisture from washing to prevent scorching.) Cook, stirring often, over medium heat until wilted and tender, 5 to 7 minutes. Drain well and rinse under cold, running water. Drain again and use hands to gently squeeze excess moisture from the cooked spinach. Transfer to a work surface and coarsely chop. Or follow package directions for preparing frozen spinach. Squeeze and remove excess moisture as for fresh spinach.

3. Preheat the oven to 375°F. Combine the spinach, bread crumbs, lemon juice, egg, and salt and pepper in a large bowl. Use a fork to blend into a smooth filling. Lay the pounded chicken breasts flat on a work surface. Place 1 heaping tablespoon of the filling in the center of each breast. Roll into a tight cylinder, like a jelly roll, and secure with toothpicks.

(Reserve any leftover filling for another use or bake separately in a buttered small ramekin and serve with the chicken.) Place the roulades in a baking dish large enough to hold all of them in one flat layer. Bring the wine or stock to a boil in a small saucepan and pour into the bottom of the dish. Cover with foil and bake until the chicken is opaque, firm to the touch, and filling is set, 35 to 40 minutes.

4. Meanwhile, prepare the sauce. Heat the olive oil in a small skillet over medium-high heat. Add the onion and cook, stirring often, until softened, about 3 minutes. Add the garlic and cook 1 minute longer. Transfer the contents of the skillet to a food processor and add the yogurt. Process until smooth. Wipe out the skillet that the onion was cooked in and pour in the sauce. Stir in half of the parsley and season to taste with salt and pepper. Keep the sauce warm over very low heat, stirring occasionally, until ready to serve. Do not allow the sauce to boil or it will separate.

5. Remove the roulades from the baking dish. Use a very sharp, serrated knife to carefully cut the cylinders into ¼-inch-thick rondelles. Arrange the rondelles on heated individual serving plates. Spoon a small amount of the sauce over each plate and serve the rest on the side. Garnish with sprinkles of the remaining parsley.

 Serves 6

Chicken Nugget

A chicken brick is not an item of masonry, but rather the name given to an unglazed clay casserole often used to cook a bird. The dish is soaked in water, the bird placed inside, and both put in a cold oven set to a hot temperature. The *brick* refers to the brick-oven effect of hot steam from the wet clay, which helps tenderize the meat.

Wine-Baked Chicken Breasts with Carrots, Leeks, and Mushrooms

I do the same recipe with a piece of hearty cod with excellent results. Julienning vegetables, or cutting them into matchstick-size pieces, is something I'm particularly good at, but it takes some practice, time, and patience. I use a tool called a mandoline that is popular with chefs in France. This manual slicer makes clean, uniform julienne strips with little effort. There have been some excellent knockoffs of the classic mandoline in the last few years, most made of durable plastic. (The real version is made of stainless steel and therefore rather expensive.) Most food processors have a blade for making julienne strips, but I find that they work too fast and are difficult to control. You can also use a sharp knife. Carrots and celery are the easiest vegetables to julienne. Leeks are the most difficult. Save all the scraps from julienned vegetables to use in making stock.

6 large boneless, skinless chicken breast halves

Salt and freshly ground black pepper

2 medium carrots, peeled and cut into thin julienne strips

1 medium leek, cut into thin julienne strips

3 tablespoons unsalted butter, softened

5 or 6 medium mushrooms, trimmed of stems and cut into matchstick-size pieces

½ cup dry white wine

1. Season the chicken with salt and pepper.

2. Bring a large saucepan of salted water to a boil. Add the carrots and the leek. Bring back to a boil and cook rapidly over high heat until slightly tender, about 1 minute. Pour into a strainer and rinse well under cold running water. Drain well and transfer to a plate lined with paper towels; pat dry.

3. Preheat the oven to 400° F. Using 2 tablespoons of the butter, coat a glass baking dish large enough to hold the chicken in one flat layer. Place the chicken on top and cover with the carrots, leek, and mushrooms. Season with salt and pepper. Pour over the wine. Bake for 20 to 25 minutes or until the chicken is firm to the touch and the vegetables are tender.

4. Use a spatula to hold the contents of the baking dish in place while you pour the cooking juices into a small saucepan. Cover the baking dish with foil to keep the chicken warm. You should have slightly over ½ cup liquid. Boil over high heat until the juices are syrupy and

reduced by half, about 3 minutes. Remove from the heat and gently stir in the remaining tablespoon of butter. Season to taste with salt and pepper.

5. Remove the chicken to a work surface and slice each breast diagonally into 4 equal pieces. Transfer to a warmed platter and distribute the vegetables over the chicken. Spoon over the sauce and serve at once.

 Serves 6

Sautéed Chicken Breasts with Fava Beans and Pecorino Cheese

The soft texture and subtle earthy flavor of tender, young fava beans are enhanced by sharp pecorino cheese. This unexpected flavor contrast was inspired by a recent spring visit to a wonderful restaurant in Florence, named Cibreo. There, chef Fabio renders his version of hearty Tuscan cuisine based on daily forays to local markets. Serve this dish with orzo cooked in chicken stock and a salad of tender mixed greens.

6 chicken breast halves

Salt and freshly ground black pepper

2 tablespoons unsalted butter

2 tablespoons vegetable oil

¼ cup dry white wine

3 cups cooked fresh or dried fava beans

¼ pound pecorino cheese, cut into small cubes (about 1 cup)

2 tablespoons olive oil

1. Season the chicken with salt and pepper. Melt the butter with the oil in a large, heavy skillet over medium-high heat. Cook the chicken until well browned and cooked through, about 5 minutes on each side. Remove the chicken to a plate or platter and cover with foil to keep warm.

2. Pour off all the fat from the skillet and return skillet to the heat. Pour in the wine and, whisking constantly to pick up any bits left on the bottom from cooking the chicken, boil until reduced by half. Add the fava beans and stir over medium-high heat until most of the liquid is absorbed and the beans are heated through, 2 to 3 minutes. Remove from the heat, stir in the cheese and the olive oil, and season to taste with salt and pepper. Spoon the fava bean mixture around the browned chicken and serve at once.

 **Serves 6**

Grilled Chicken Breasts with Orzo, Spinach, and Red Peppers

Frozen spinach will do nicely here, but the flavor of the real thing is better. This is an especially satisfying chicken dish, and a great last-minute single-dish dinner for cooks on the run!

6 boneless, skinless chicken breast halves

Juice of 1 lemon

1 package (1 pound) orzo

1 large red bell pepper, cored, seeded, and diced into small cubes

1 bunch fresh spinach (about ¾ pound), or 1 package (10 ounces) frozen

2 tablespoons olive oil

Salt and freshly ground black pepper

1. Place the breasts in a large bowl or baking dish and squeeze over the lemon juice. Cover with plastic wrap and marinate for 20 to 30 minutes, turning often. Prepare a stove-top or charcoal grill to cook the chicken.

2. Bring a large pot of salted water to a boil and prepare the orzo according to package directions.

3. Meanwhile, bring a small pot of salted water to a boil. Add the pepper to the water and bring back to a boil. Boil for 1 minute, drain, and refresh under cold running water. Drain on paper towels.

4. Remove the large, tough stems from the fresh spinach. Wash the leaves in several changes of cold water. Place the damp leaves in a large nonreactive pot and set over medium-high heat. Season with salt and cook, stirring constantly, until the leaves have wilted, 3 to 5 minutes. Remove from the heat and cover. When cool enough to handle, squeeze out the excess moisture and coarsely chop. Or, cook the frozen spinach per package directions, cool, squeeze out the excess moisture, and chop.

5. Grill the chicken over high heat, turning once, until cooked through, with no trace of pink in the center, 10 to 12 minutes in all. Remove from the grill, cover with foil, and keep warm.

6. Drain the orzo well and return it to the pot it cooked in. Add the olive oil, red pepper cubes, and spinach. Stir well and season to taste with salt and pepper. Spoon this mixture into the bottom of a large, warmed serving bowl. Cut the chicken into wide pieces and arrange attractively on top.

 **Serves 6**

Chicken Roulades with Olive and Anchovy Stuffing

Use a small (3¼-ounce) can of drained tuna in place of the anchovies if these tiny fish are not popular in your home. New potatoes tossed with a pinch of chopped fresh dill makes a nice accompaniment for these roulades.

- **6 boneless, skinless chicken breast halves**
- **4 ounces anchovy fillets, soaked in warm water for 10 minutes**
- **12 black olives, preferably oil-cured, pitted**
- **1 tablespoon grated lemon zest**
- **½ cup coarsely chopped fresh flat parsley**
- **4 large slices white sandwich bread, crusts removed**
- **Salt and freshly ground black pepper**
- **6 thin slices good boiled ham**
- **2 tablespoons olive oil**
- **1 cup all-purpose flour, for dredging**
- **½ cup dry white wine**

1. Pound the breasts between 2 pieces of parchment paper to a uniform thickness of about ½ inch thick.

2. Drain the anchovies and squeeze out excess moisture. Combine the anchovies, olives, lemon zest, and parsley in the bowl of a food processor. Place the bread in a large bowl of cold water and soak for 1 minute. Squeeze out the excess moisture with your hands and add to the food processor. Process the mixture until smooth. Season to taste with salt and pepper.

3. Lay the chicken breasts flat on a large work surface and season with salt and pepper. Spread each with an equal amount of the stuffing. Top with a layer of the ham. Roll the chicken into a tight cylinder, like a jelly roll, and secure with toothpicks.

4. Heat the oil in a large skillet over medium-high heat. Place the flour in a large bowl. Dredge each roulade in the flour and shake off the excess. Cook the roulades in the hot oil, turning often, until lightly browned on all sides, about 5 minutes. Lower the heat, pour in the wine, cover, and cook until firm to the touch, about 12 minutes. Transfer the roulades to a warmed serving dish. Boil the pan juices for a minute or two to thicken, stirring the bottom of the skillet to pick up any bits left from cooking. Pour the juices over the chicken and serve at once, reminding guests to remove the toothpicks before eating.

 **Serves 6**

Chicken Breasts *en Papillote* with Spinach and Tomato

The hardest part of this recipe is cleaning the spinach! Be sure to wash and rinse the leaves several times to remove sand or grit. This is a good recipe for those who are watching their weight and fat intake. The fat content is low and the flavor is exceptional.

6 boneless, skinless chicken breast halves

5 plum tomatoes (about 12 ounces)

1 bunch (¾ pound) fresh spinach

Salt and freshly ground black pepper

2 to 3 tablespoons olive oil

1. Preheat the oven to 400° F. Pound the chicken between 2 sheets of parchment paper until about ½ inch thick. Tear off 6 large pieces of parchment paper that each measure 16 to 18 inches long. Fold each in half and cut out large heart shapes 2 inches larger all around than the chicken breast halves.

2. Bring a large pot of water to a boil. Cut a cross in the bottom of each tomato and cut out the core from the opposite end. Plunge the tomatoes into the boiling water and leave for 20 to 30 seconds.

Drain well and slip off the skins while holding the tomatoes under cold running water. Cut the peeled tomatoes in half crosswise, squeeze out the seeds, and chop finely.

3. Remove the tough stems from the spinach and wash the leaves in several changes of cold water. Spin-dry in a salad spinner or shake off excess moisture with your hands.

4. Place each chicken breast in the center of one side of each paper heart. Season with salt and pepper then spread on a large spoonful of the chopped tomatoes. Mound the spinach leaves over the chicken and tomatoes, piling them high. Dribble on a small amount of olive oil and sprinkle on salt. Fold over the other side of the heart, and starting at the curved end, crimp the edges tightly to close. (The spinach will make this operation difficult, but keep working until all of the leaves are inside the package. They will wilt down to more than half their original bulk as the packages cook. Do not be concerned if some of the leaves are folded into the crimped edges.)

5. Place the *papillotes* on 2 large baking sheets. Brush the tops with a small amount of olive oil and immediately place in the oven. Cook for 12 to 15 minutes or until the paper is golden brown and puffed. Serve at once, in the paper

or not, on individual plates. (Be careful when opening the packages. Hot steam will escape quickly and could be harmful to unsuspecting guests.)

 Serves 6

Sautéed Chicken Breasts with Saffron Noodles

Serve a bright green vegetable, such as fresh peas, tiny green beans, or sugar snap peas, with these creamy, exotic noodles and chicken.

6 boneless, skinless chicken breast halves

Salt and freshly ground black pepper

1 large pinch imported saffron threads

1 cup heavy cream

½ pound broad egg noodles

2 tablespoons unsalted butter

2 tablespoons vegetable oil

½ cup dry white wine

1 tablespoon chopped fresh parsley

1. Pound the breasts between 2 sheets of parchment paper until about ½ inch thick. Season with salt and pepper.

2. Combine the saffron and cream in a small saucepan. Warm over medium heat just until tiny bubbles appear around the edges of the pan. Remove from the heat, stir well, cover, and set aside for the flavors to infuse.

3. Cook the noodles according to package directions, usually 8 to 10 minutes. Drain well and set aside, covered.

4. Meanwhile, melt the butter with the oil in a large skillet. Add the chicken and cook until browned and cooked through, 4 to 5 minutes per side. Remove to a plate or platter and cover with foil to keep warm.

5. Pour off the fat from the skillet. Return the skillet to medium-high heat and pour in the wine. Increase the heat to high and bring to a boil. Boil, stirring to pick up any cooking bits in the bottom of the skillet, until reduced by half. Pour in the saffron cream and boil to reduce again by half.

6. Add the cooked noodles to the sauce and stir until warmed through and coated with the sauce. Season to taste with salt and pepper. Arrange the sauced noodles over the bottom of a warmed serving bowl or deep platter. Arrange the browned chicken on top. Sprinkle with parsley and serve at once.

 **Serves 6**

Chicken Breast Roulades with Mushroom Filling

Bread, soaked in milk and squeezed dry, binds the filling for these roulades. Stir 1 egg yolk into the filling for a firmer texture. Be sure to slice the cooked roulades carefully with a very sharp knife, as they shred easily. Serve with a light tomato sauce or thin yogurt-based herb sauce.

- **6 boneless, skinless chicken breast halves**
- **4 large slices white sandwich bread, crusts removed**
- **1 cup milk**
- **2 tablespoons olive oil**
- **3 large shallots minced**
- **16 to 18 medium mushrooms (12 ounces), trimmed and coarsely chopped**
- **¼ cup (loosely packed) coarsely chopped fresh parsley leaves**
- **1 tablespoon lemon juice**
- **Salt and freshly ground black pepper**

1. Pound the chicken between 2 sheets of parchment paper to an even thickness of about ¼ inch. Set aside.

2. Tear the bread into large pieces and combine with the milk in a small bowl. Let stand about 1 minute for the liquid to absorb, then squeeze dry with your hands.

3. Heat the oil in a medium skillet over medium-high heat. Add the shallots and cook, stirring often, until slightly softened, about 2 minutes. Add the mushrooms and cook 2 minutes longer. Add the parsley and lemon juice. Reduce the heat to medium low, cover, and cook until the mushrooms are tender and have given up their liquid, 3 to 5 minutes. Transfer to the bowl of a food processor and add the bread. Process until the mixture is smooth. Season with salt and pepper.

4. Bring a large skillet of water to a boil. Spread a thin layer of the filling over the flattened chicken breasts. Place each of the breasts on separate pieces of parchment paper several inches larger than the chicken. Roll the chicken into a long, thin cylinder, like a jelly roll, and secure by twisting the ends tightly closed. Reduce the heat to medium low and carefully place the roulades in the simmering water. Cover and poach for 12 minutes. Remove from the heat and, holding the hot chicken with a paper towel, using a very sharp, thin blade knife, cut the cylinder into ¼-inch-thick rondelles. Remove the paper before serving.

 **Serves 6**

Sautéed Chicken Breasts with Asparagus and Shiitake Mushrooms

Serve with glazed carrots, tiny onions, and rice or pasta for a perfect spring dinner.

6 boneless, skinless chicken breast halves

1½ pounds asparagus

2 tablespoons unsalted butter

2 tablespoons vegetable oil

Salt and freshly ground black pepper

2 large shallots, minced

8 ounces shiitake mushrooms, stems trimmed and heads thickly sliced

¼ cup dry white wine

1 cup heavy cream

1. Flatten the chicken between 2 pieces of parchment paper to a thickness of about ¼ inch.

2. Bring a large pot of salted water to a boil. Trim the asparagus of the tough lower part of the stem and use a vegetable peeler to peel the green skin up to the tips. Plunge the spears into the boiling water and bring back to a boil.

Boil rapidly until slightly tender, about 2 minutes. Drain and refresh under cold running water. Drain on paper towels.

3. Melt the butter with the oil in a large skillet over medium-high heat. Season the chicken with salt and pepper. Cook until lightly browned and cooked through, 4 to 5 minutes on each side. Remove to a plate or platter and cover with foil to keep warm.

4. Pour off all but 1 tablespoon of the fat. Add the shallots and cook, stirring constantly, until barely softened, about 1 minute. Add the mushrooms and cook, stirring constantly, 2 minutes longer. Pour in the wine, increase the heat to high, and cook until all of the liquid has evaporated, about 2 minutes. Add the cream and boil rapidly until slightly reduced and thickened, about 5 minutes. Add the asparagus, lower the heat to medium, and warm through. Season to taste with salt and pepper.

5. Arrange the chicken on warmed individual serving plates or a large platter. Spoon over a small amount of the asparagus and cream mixture. Serve at once with rice or pasta.

 Serves 6

Homemade Chicken Potpie

There must be as many chicken potpie recipes in the world as there are chickens! This one uses frozen puff pastry, which makes an elegant presentation and gives a fine-flavored buttery crust. The pie can be prepared in stages, assembled, refrigerated, and baked at the last minute.

- **1 package (12 to 14 ounces) frozen puff pastry, thawed**

- **4 boneless, skinless chicken breast halves**

- **2 cups chicken stock**

- **4 tablespoons (½ stick) unsalted butter**

- **2 tablespoons vegetable oil**

- **10 ounces white button mushrooms, halved or quartered**

- **Salt and freshly ground black pepper**

- **3 large carrots, cut into ½-inch cubes**

- **3 small white potatoes, peeled and cut into ½-inch cubes**

- **1 package (10 ounces) frozen green peas, thawed**

- **3 tablespoons all-purpose flour**

- **1 cup heavy cream**

- **1 large egg**

1. Lightly butter a 6- to 8- cup ovenproof baking dish or casserole. Roll out the dough to a ¼-inch thickness, making sure that it extends 1 inch longer than the circumference of the dish or casserole circumference. Place on a baking sheet and refrigerate until ready to assemble the dish.

2. Place the chicken breasts in a large skillet. Pour over the chicken stock and bring to a simmer over medium-high heat. Reduce the heat to medium, cover and poach gently until opaque and firm to the touch, about 10 minutes. Remove from the stock and set aside to cool. Reserve the cooking liquid.

3. Melt 2 tablespoons of the butter in a large saucepan. Add the oil and melt together over medium-high heat. Add the mushrooms and sauté until they begin to give off their liquid and are lightly browned, about 5 minutes. Season to taste with salt and pepper. Drain on paper towels.

4. Bring a small saucepan of salted water to a boil over high heat. Add the carrots and bring back to a boil. Cook rapidly until slightly tender, about 3 minutes. Drain and rinse under cold running water. Wipe out the pan and add the potatoes. Pour in enough cold water to

cover, add a pinch of salt, and bring to a boil. Cook until tender, about 5 minutes. Drain well.

5. Melt the remaining 2 tablespoons butter in a medium saucepan over medium-high heat. Stir in the flour and blend well. Cook, stirring constantly, until bubbling and lemon-colored, 2 to 3 minutes. Do not brown. Pour in the reserved chicken cooking liquid, increase the heat to high, and, whisking constantly, bring to a boil. When thickened and boiling, reduce the heat to medium and pour in the cream. Season to taste with salt and pepper. Cook, stirring often, until creamy and blended, about 5 to 7 minutes.

6. Cut the chicken breasts into 1-inch cubes. Combine the chicken, mushrooms, carrots, potatoes, and peas in a large bowl. Pour over the sauce and stir to blend. Set aside to completely cool. (The recipe can be covered and kept refrigerated up to a day in advance at this point.)

7. Preheat the oven to 375°F. Spread the chicken mixture over the bottom of the baking dish or casserole. Place the rolled-out dough on top, tucking in the edges to form a thick border. Use the tip of a very sharp knife to make decorative slits in the top of the dough to allow steam to escape. Beat the egg with a teaspoonful of cold water to form a wash. Brush the entire surface of the dough with the wash. Bake in the middle of the oven for 35 to 40 minutes or until the crust is golden brown. Serve at once.

 Serves 6

Chicken Nugget

"The greatest of all chicken dishes, of course, is . . . the chicken pot pie, an English invention. . . . Like the mazurkas of Chopin, it leaves room for the self expression of the artist."

—H. L. Mencken, in the *Baltimore Evening Sun* (1910)

Chicken Breast Roulades with Broccoli Filling

A rolled, filled chicken cylinder cooks well wrapped in parchment paper. Do not be alarmed at the first reading of this recipe. The paper is strong enough to stand up to the heat of simmering water. Slicing the still-hot poached chicken requires a little patience and a very sharp knife. The cooked roulade will shred easily if not properly handled.

6 boneless, skinless chicken breast halves

1 head broccoli

2 slices white sandwich bread, crusts removed

1 large egg yolk

1 tablespoon lemon juice

Salt and freshly ground black pepper

1 recipe Tomato Sauce (page 226)

1. Pound the breasts between 2 sheets of parchment paper to a thickness of about ¼ inch.

2. Bring a large saucepan of salted water to a boil and line a colander with a piece of cheesecloth, allowing ends to over-hang. Trim the broccoli into large florets. Peel and thickly slice the stems. Plunge the broccoli into the boiling water, bring back to a boil, and cook rapidly until just tender, 2 to 3 minutes. Drain and rinse under cold running water. Place the cooked broccoli in the colander, bring up the overhanging ends, and gently squeeze out as much moisture as possible. Transfer to a food processor, and add the bread, egg yolk, lemon juice, and salt and pepper. Blend until smooth (makes about 1 cup of filling).

3. Fill a large, covered skillet with 2 or 3 inches of water and bring to a boil. Tear off 6 large pieces of parchment paper from a roll and lay them flat on a work surface. Place one of the pounded breasts in the center of each parchment piece and season with salt and pepper. Spoon a thin layer of the filling over each breast and spread just to the edges with a knife. Roll lengthwise, like a jelly roll, into a tight cylinder. Crimp the ends of the roulades to firmly seal. The roulade should resemble a fat sausage. Gently transfer each roll to the skillet of boiling water. Reduce the heat to medium, cover, and cook the roulades until firm to the touch and completely cooked, 10 to 12 minutes.

4. Meanwhile, heat the tomato sauce over medium heat. Spoon ¼ cup over the bottom of 6 warmed serving plates. Remove the roulades from the skillet and, working with one at a time, carefully take away and discard the paper. Holding the cylinder with a clean

kitchen towel or paper towels, use a very sharp, thin knife to cut into ½-inch-thick slices. Arrange the slices decoratively over the tomato sauce. Serve at once.

 Serves 6

Baked Chicken Breasts with Goat Cheese and Sun-Dried Tomatoes

Serve with garlicky mashed potatoes and blanched sugar snap peas that have been tossed in a little butter.

- **6 chicken breast halves**
- **6 ounces fresh goat cheese, very well chilled**
- **6 small sun-dried tomatoes (about 2 ounces)**
- **6 whole basil leaves**
- **¼ cup olive oil**
- **Salt and freshly ground black pepper**

1. Preheat the oven to 375°F. Lift the skin of each of the breasts and loosen the skin from the fresh to form a fillable pocket. Do not tear the skin. Cut the goat cheese into 6 equal portions and slip one piece just under the skin in the center of each breast. Use your fingers

to place one of the tomatoes and one basil leaf on top of each cheese piece.

2. Pour half of the olive oil in the bottom of a baking dish large enough to hold the chicken in one flat layer. Arrange the breasts snugly in the dish and drizzle over the remaining olive oil. Season with salt and pepper. Bake for 45 minutes to 1 hour or until lightly browned and cooked through.

 Serves 6

Chicken Nugget

More than 90 percent of the nation's production of chicken comes from an area commonly referred to as "the broiler belt." This area includes all or parts of seventeen states that lie along the Gulf of Mexico and the Atlantic seaboard. The top five broiler states are Arkansas, Alabama, Georgia, North Carolina, and Mississippi.

Chicken Breast Roulades with Zucchini Filling

Zucchini, like most squash, contains a large amount of water. For a filling like this, it is important to extract as much of this water as possible. The best way to do so is to squeeze in cheesecloth, as described below. You can find zucchini almost year-round these days. However, I like to make this dish in midsummer, when small, tender, young zucchini (preferably locally grown!) are at their best.

6 boneless, skinless chicken breast halves

2 medium zucchini

1 large egg, lightly beaten

1 to 1½ cups fresh bread crumbs

Salt and freshly ground black pepper

1 recipe Tomato Sauce (page 226)

1 tablespoon chopped fresh parsley

1. Pound the breasts between 2 sheets of parchment paper to a thickness of about ¼ inch.

2. Line a colander with cheesecloth, allowing the ends to hang over the edge. Coarsely grate the zucchini and place in the colander. Bring the edges of the cheesecloth together and squeeze as much moisture as possible from the grated zucchini. Transfer to a medium mixing bowl and stir in the egg and enough of the bread crumbs to form a stiff filling. Season to taste with salt and pepper. You should have about 1 cup tightly packed zucchini filling.

3. Fill a large, covered skillet with 2 or 3 inches of water and bring to a boil. Tear off 6 large pieces of parchment paper from a roll and lay flat on a work surface. Place one of the pounded breasts in the center of each parchment piece and season with salt and pepper. Spoon a thin layer of the filling over each breast and spread just to the edges with a knife. Roll lengthwise, like a jelly roll, into a tight cylinder. Crimp the ends of the roulades to firmly seal. The roulade should resemble a fat sausage. Gently transfer each roll to the skillet of water. Reduce the heat to medium, cover, and cook the roulades until firm to the touch and completely white, 10 to 12 minutes.

4. Meanwhile, heat the tomato sauce over medium heat. Spoon ¼ cup over the bottom of 6 warmed serving plates (reserve the remaining tomato sauce for another use). Remove the roulades from the skillet and, working with one at a time, carefully take away and discard the paper. Holding the cylinder with a clean kitchen towel or paper towels, use a very

sharp, thin knife to cut into ½-inch-thick slices. Arrange the slices decoratively over the tomato sauce. Serve at once, garnished with a pinch of chopped parsley.

 Serves 6

Pineapple Baked Chicken Breasts with Dried Cranberries

Dried cranberries are relatively easy to find these days. If not available, raisins can be substituted.

6 chicken breast halves

Salt and freshly ground black pepper

2 cups canned or fresh pineapple chunks

1 cup dried cranberries

¼ cup dry white wine

2 teaspoons sugar

1 tablespoon finely chopped fresh mint leaves

1. Preheat the oven to 375° F. Season the chicken with salt and pepper. Lightly oil a baking dish large enough to hold the chicken in one flat layer, and place the breasts in the dish. Scatter over the pineapple chunks and cranberries. Pour over the wine and sprinkle the sugar evenly over the dish.

2. Bake, turning the chicken often and stirring the fruit, until the skin of the chicken is lightly browned and the cooking juices are thickened, about 1 hour. Baste frequently. Add a small amount of additional wine or water if the liquid evaporates. Serve on a warmed platter and garnish each breast with a small pinch of chopped mint.

 Serves 6

Chicken Nugget

A broiler or roasting chicken weighs 3 to 5 pounds. A boiling fowl or large hen weighs 6 to 9 pounds. A guinea fowl or guinea hen weighs 2 to 3 pounds. A capon (a neutered male chicken) weighs 5 to 11 pounds. A poussin or baby chicken weighs 8 to 16 ounces, and a Cornish game hen weighs 1 to 1½ pounds.

Thai Steamed Chicken with Coconut-Shallot Chutney

This recipe works best with a bamboo steamer. Three tiers of these steamers are inexpensive and incredibly versatile. If not available, place the rolled chicken on a metal collapsible steamer that fits inside a large saucepan. Or fill a colander with the rolled chicken breasts and place inside a casserole or Dutch oven large enough to hold the colander suspended over an inch of water. Be sure that the cover will fit tightly so that the chicken can be properly steamed.

Fresh coconut makes this dish really special. Dried shredded coconut is fine, too; just be sure that it is unsweetened. Unsweetened, shredded coconut is often available in health food stores.

1 cup shredded, unsweetened coconut

2 tablespoons vegetable oil

3 large shallots, thinly sliced

2 tablespoons golden raisins

1 piece fresh ginger, 1 inch long, peeled and grated

¼ cup lime juice

½ cup chopped fresh cilantro

2 scallions (green onions), white part only, thinly sliced

½ jalapeño pepper, seeded and minced

1 teaspoon sugar

6 boneless, skinless chicken breast halves

⅓ cup sake

1 tablespoon soy sauce

1 teaspoon Asian sesame oil

1. Preheat the oven to 400°F. Spread the coconut on a sheet pan and toast, stirring often, until crisp and golden, 12 to 15 minutes.

2. Heat the oil in a large skillet over medium-high heat. Add the shallots and cook, stirring often, until the edges are browned, about 5 minutes. Add the raisins and ginger, and cook 2 minutes longer. Stir in the lime juice, cilantro, scallions, jalapeño, and sugar. Remove from the heat and add the coconut. Cool to room temperature. (The chutney can be made up to 3 days in advance.)

3. Place the chicken breasts between 2 pieces of parchment paper or plastic wrap and pound to a uniform thickness of ¼ inch. Spread about 3 tablespoons of the chutney in the center of each breast and roll up to enclose. Secure the rolls with toothpicks. (Reserve any remaining chutney for serving.) Place seam side down in a heatproof bowl set inside a bamboo steamer basket. Combine the sake, soy sauce, and sesame oil in a small bowl. Pour this mixture over the chicken.

4. Bring 1 inch of water to a boil in a wok or in a large saucepan. Set the steamer over the water and steam, tightly covered, until the chicken is firm, 15 to 20 minutes. Remove and slice each breast into 3 crosswise pieces. Serve on individual plates or on a large platter with any remaining chutney and extra soy sauce on the side.

Serves 6

Olive and Goat Cheese–Stuffed Chicken Breasts

I used to prepare this recipe with bacon, but like everybody else these days, reducing saturated fats sometimes crosses my mind. The small amount of lean boiled ham gives some of that bacon flavor without as much fat. I like the strong flavor of oil-cured olives, but any ripe olive will work just fine.

12 pitted black olives, preferably oil-cured, finely chopped

¼ pound lean boiled ham, finely chopped

4 ounces fresh goat cheese, at room temperature

2 teaspoons lemon juice

1 tablespoon chopped fresh parsley leaves

6 chicken breast halves

Olive oil, for drizzling

Salt and freshly ground black pepper

1. Preheat the oven to 375°F. Oil a baking dish large enough to hold the breasts in one flat layer.

2. Combine the olives, ham, goat cheese, 1 teaspoon of the lemon juice, and the parsley in a small bowl. Use a fork to work the mixture into a firm paste.

3. Use your fingers to separate the skin from the flesh of the breasts, being careful to not tear the skin. Spread 1 scant tablespoon into each pocket formed by lifting the skin, using fingers to spread the mixture as uniformly as possible.

4. Place the breasts skin side up in the baking dish. Drizzle over a small amount of olive oil and the remaining teaspoon of lemon juice. Season the breasts with salt and pepper. Bake, turning often, until the chicken is lightly browned and cooked through, 45 minutes to 1 hour.

 Serves 6

Chicken Breasts Tonnato

*This is a variation on a classic Italian veal dish, **vitello tonnato**. Our version is made with chicken breasts for a less costly and just as flavorful alternative. The sauce is made with more tuna than mayonnaise to reduce the caloric content and add more flavor. Chicken Breasts Tonnato can be served in individual servings as instructed, or presented on a large platter, fancifully garnished and served buffet style. Since it is served cold, this is a great summer, do-ahead dish.*

6 boneless, skinless chicken breast halves

Salt and freshly ground black pepper

1½ cups chicken stock

2 or 3 sprigs fresh thyme

2 cans (2 ounces each) anchovies, packed in oil

2 cans (6 ounces each) tuna, packed in olive oil, preferably imported Italian

¼ cup lemon juice

¼ cup capers, plus 1 tablespoon for garnish

¼ cup mayonnaise

Thinly sliced lemon, for garnish

1. Preheat the oven to 350° F. Season the chicken breasts with salt and pepper. Arrange them on the bottom of a casserole large enough to hold them in one layer.

2. Bring the stock to a boil in a medium saucepan and pour over the chicken. (Increase the amount of stock or add water to ensure that the chicken is completely covered. The amount of liquid required depends on the size of the casserole.) Add the thyme sprigs and cover the casserole tightly with foil. Cook in the oven until the chicken is cooked through, 20 to 25 minutes. Remove the chicken from the casserole and cool to room temperature. Reserve the cooking liquid for another use. When cooled, transfer the chicken to 6 individual serving plates, cover with plastic wrap, and refrigerate for several hours or overnight.

3. To make the sauce, place the anchovies in a small bowl and cover with warm water. Let stand for 10 minutes. Drain, rinse, and lay them out on paper towels to dry. Drain the tuna, reserving the oil.

4. Combine the tuna, lemon juice, 10 to 12 of the anchovies, ¼ cup capers, and the mayonnaise in the bowl of a food processor. Process until smooth. With the motor running, add the reserved oil from the tuna and process until the sauce is thick and emulsified. You should have about 2 cups.

5. Slice each of the chilled breasts in half horizontally. Spread 1 to 2 tablespoons of the sauce thinly over the bottom half of each breast. Cover with the other breast slice and top with another layer of the sauce. Cut the remaining anchovies into long, thin strips. Garnish each breast with the anchovy strips, the remaining tablespoon of capers, and lemon slices. Serve at once or cover and refrigerate for several hours, if desired.

 Serves 6

Baked Chicken Breasts with Spinach, Goat Cheese, and Pine Nuts

To concentrate the spinach flavor, squeeze as much moisture out of the cooked spinach as possible. (Frozen spinach is already at least partially cooked.) Over the sink, gather the spinach leaves in the cupped palm of your hand and press firmly to squeeze.

Add a small amount of freshly ground nutmeg to the spinach mixture, if desired.

6 chicken breast halves

½ cup tightly packed cooked or thawed frozen spinach, squeezed dry

4 ounces fresh goat cheese

⅓ cup toasted pine nuts

1 teaspoon grated lemon zest

Salt and freshly ground black pepper

Olive oil, for drizzling

1. Preheat the oven to 375°F. Lift the skin of each of the breasts and insert a finger to form a fillable pocket without tearing the skin.

2. Combine the spinach, goat cheese, pine nuts, and lemon zest in the bowl of a food processor. Process until smooth and blended, working in several quick pulses. Scrape the sides of the bowl often to ensure even blending. Season the filling with salt and pepper (makes about 1 cup of filling).

3. Stuff about 1 tablespoon of filling under the skin of each breast. Use your fingers to force the filling into the far corners of the pockets without tearing the skin. Do not overstuff the chicken. Save any leftover filling for another use.

4. Place the breasts in a baking dish large enough to hold them in one flat layer. Drizzle over a small amount of olive oil and season with salt and pepper. Bake, basting often, until the skin is lightly browned and the chicken is cooked through, about 45 minutes.

 **Serves 6**

Almond-Coated Chicken with Honey-Thyme Sauce

When grinding almonds in the food processor, add a teaspoonful or so of flour (or sugar for sweet dishes). This absorbs some of the oil and makes a cleaner, finer grind.

4 boneless, skinless chicken breast halves

Salt and freshly ground black pepper

2 cups (8 ounces) toasted, slivered almonds

1 cup all-purpose flour

2 large eggs, lightly beaten

⅔ cup mild honey

2 tablespoons fresh thyme, or 1 teaspoon dried

3 tablespoons red wine vinegar

⅔ cup plus 2 tablespoons chicken stock

1 teaspoon cornstarch

1. Cut the chicken into 1½-inch-wide strips or "fingers." Season with salt and pepper.

2. Preheat the oven to 350°F. Place the toasted almonds in the bowl of a food processor and process until finely ground but not powdery, about 10 seconds. Empty into a baking dish for dipping. Place the flour in a separate dish and put the eggs in a bowl next to these 2 dishes. Line a large cookie sheet with foil and lightly oil. Dip the chicken first in the flour and shake off any excess. Next dip in the egg and drain off excess. Then roll the strips in the ground almonds until well coated. Place on the sheet and bake, turning once, for 20 to 25 minutes or until lightly browned.

3. Meanwhile, prepare the sauce. Combine the honey and thyme in a medium saucepan. Bring to a boil over high heat, then reduce to medium high. Cook until slightly caramelized, about 2 minutes. Stir in the vinegar and ⅔ cup stock. Simmer, stirring often, for 5 minutes. In a small bowl or cup, whisk together the cornstarch and remaining 2 tablespoons stock. Add to the sauce and continue simmering, stirring constantly, until shiny and slightly thickened, 3 to 4 minutes.

4. When the chicken is done, transfer to a warmed serving platter. Dribble a small amount of the sauce over the top and serve the rest on the side.

 Serves 6

Mediterranean Baked Chicken Breasts

Serve with saffron-flavored rice and garlicky Caesar salad.

6 chicken breast halves

Salt and freshly ground black pepper

2 tablespoons unsalted butter

2 tablespoons olive oil

2 garlic cloves, minced

1 cup thinly sliced sun-dried tomatoes

½ cup dry white wine

1 cup chicken stock

½ cup pitted black olives, thinly sliced

2 tablespoons grated Parmesan cheese

1 tablespoon chopped fresh parsley

1. Preheat the oven to 350° F. Season the chicken with salt and pepper. Heat the butter with the oil in a large, heavy skillet over medium-high heat. Add the chicken and cook until browned, about 5 minutes on each side. Remove to a plate and keep warm.

2. Pour off all but 2 tablespoons of the fat from the pan. Add the garlic and tomatoes. Cook, stirring constantly, until the tomatoes are softened, about 2 minutes. Add the wine and chicken stock and increase the heat to high. Boil until reduced by half, scraping up any bits in the bottom of the pan. Return the chicken to the pan and scatter the olives over the top. Reduce the heat to medium, cover, and cook until the chicken is tender, 15 to 20 minutes. Season with salt and pepper to taste.

3. Transfer the chicken to a large warmed platter and surround with the tomatoes and olives. Spoon any pan juices over the top. Garnish with the Parmesan cheese and parsley. Serve at once.

 **Serves 6**

Mexican Chicken Breasts with Pumpkin Seed Sauce

Dried ancho chilies are available at Latin American markets and some specialty stores and supermarkets. Epazote is an herb often used in Mexican cooking. It also can be found in many Latin American markets and in some specialty food stores. However, you may omit it from this recipe if it's not available.

6 dried ancho chilies (see Note)

1 cup boiling water

6 chicken breast halves

**Salt and freshly ground black
    pepper to taste**

2 tablespoons olive oil

1 cup hulled, raw pumpkin seeds

1 medium onion

2 garlic cloves

**1 sprig fresh epazote, or
    2 teaspoons dried**

4 medium tomatoes

1 cup chicken stock

1 tablespoon tomato paste

1 teaspoon sugar

**2 tablespoons chopped fresh
    cilantro**

1. Remove the stem, seeds, and veins from the chilies. Place the chilies in a bowl and top with boiling water. Soak for 15 to 30 minutes, drain, and reserve the liquid.

2. Season the chicken breast halves with salt and pepper.

3. Heat the oil in a large, heavy skillet over medium-high heat and stir in the pumpkin seeds. Cook, stirring often, until the seeds are fragrant and toasted, 2 to 3 minutes. Remove the seeds with a slotted spoon and set aside to cool.

4. Add the chicken to the skillet and cook until well browned, about 5 minutes on each side. Remove to a plate or platter and cover with foil to keep warm. Pour off and discard all but 1 tablespoon of the fat from the skillet.

5. Combine the pumpkin seeds, onion, garlic, epazote, and tomatoes in the bowl of a food processor. Add the chilies with their soaking liquid and puree until smooth. Empty this puree into the skillet and add the chicken stock and tomato paste. Bring to a boil, reduce heat to low, and simmer for 5 minutes. Stir in the sugar and season to taste with salt and pepper.

6. Return the chicken to the skillet and cook, covered, over medium-low heat until firm to the touch and cooked through, 20 to 25 minutes. Remove the lid and stir in the cilantro. Cook 5 min-

utes longer or until the flavors have blended. Serve at once.

 Serves 6

NOTE: *Other chilies can be substituted for the anchos, or a combination of chilies can be used.*

- Chipotle *chilies lend a smoky, earthy taste with more heat.*
- Guajillos *are mild and lend a nice red color to the sauce.*
- Pasillas *are less rich and more pungent in flavor.*

Do not be too concerned with the names of chilies; they tend to change from one area to another. Varieties of fresh chilies often have another name when dried. Ancho chilies are actually dried poblano, for example. Play around with what is available in your local marketplace. Any mild chili will do. Just remember to always remove the seeds, stem, and veins before using.

Chicken Nugget

Richard Olney calls the capon a "martyr to the cause of cooking." A castrated male chicken, prized for its thick layer of fat just under the skin, makes an excellent roasted bird. Caponizing originated in ancient Greece but became widespread in classical Rome after a law was passed forbidding the consumption of fattened hens, which were considered to be a delicacy. With a simple surgical operation, Roman poultry breeders began to produce a bird that grew to twice the size of an ordinary chicken, while retaining all the succulence of a young bird.

Simply Sophisticated

Moroccan Chicken and Eggplant Kebabs with Red Onion Confit

Low in fat and full of earthy spiciness, these kebabs are even better if cooked over a charcoal grill. Squares of red or yellow bell peppers could be threaded on the skewers for color, if desired. Serve with mounds of hot, cooked couscous tossed with toasted pine nuts. Thinly sliced cucumbers in yogurt with chopped mint makes a nice side dish, too.

2 teaspoons chili powder

1 teaspoon ground cumin

1/2 teaspoon ground cinnamon

1 teaspoon turmeric

1/4 teaspoon cayenne pepper

1/2 teaspoon freshly ground black pepper

6 boneless, skinless chicken breast halves, cut into 1-inch cubes

1 large eggplant (about 2 pounds), cut into 1-inch cubes

1 teaspoon coarse salt

2 tablespoons olive oil, plus additional for brushing

4 red onions, halved and thinly sliced

2 tablespoons red wine vinegar

1 teaspoon sugar

2 tablespoons capers, drained

1. Combine the chili powder, cumin, cinnamon, turmeric, cayenne pepper, and black pepper in a large bowl. Add the chicken and toss well to coat. Cover and refrigerate for at least 1 hour and for up to 6 hours.

2. Toss the eggplant with the salt and place in a colander set over a bowl. Let stand for 30 minutes. Pat dry with paper towels.

3. Meanwhile, prepare the confit. Heat the 2 tablespoons oil in a large, heavy skillet over very low heat. Add the red onions and cook, stirring often, until soft but not browned, about 15 minutes. Stir in the vinegar and sugar. Cover and cook 10 to 15 minutes longer or until the onions are very tender. Stir in the capers.

4. Preheat and lightly oil a stove-top grill or broiler. (Alternatively, prepare a charcoal grill and burn down the coals to a gray ash.)

5. Place alternating pieces of chicken and eggplant on each of 12 metal skewers and lightly brush each with olive oil. Grill or broil the kebabs, turning often, until the chicken is browned and cooked through and the eggplant is lightly charred, 10 to 12 minutes. Serve 2 hot kebabs per person, with the onion confit on the side.

 **Serves 6**

Chicken Breasts and Oysters with Champagne Sauce

Plump oysters marry well with the tender flesh of chicken breasts. This recipe is a simple yet rich dish that is meant for special occasions. Sometimes I add some julienned carrot strips along with the leeks. The added color is nice, if you have the time.

Serve with parsleyed rice and a bright green vegetable, such as steamed spinach.

6 boneless, skinless chicken breast halves

¼ cup all-purpose flour

½ teaspoon salt

½ teaspoon freshly ground black pepper

4 tablespoons (½ stick) unsalted butter

2 medium leeks, cut into fine julienned strips (about 3 cups)

½ cup clam juice

1½ dozen shucked oysters, with their liquor

¾ cup Champagne

1½ cups heavy cream

1. Place the chicken breasts between 2 pieces of parchment paper or plastic wrap and pound to a ½-inch thickness. Place the flour in a shallow bowl and season with the salt and pepper. Dip the chicken in the seasoned flour and shake off the excess.

2. Melt the butter in a large, heavy skillet over medium-high heat. Add the chicken and cook until well browned, 5 to 6 minutes per side. Remove the chicken to a plate or platter and cover with foil to keep warm.

3. Add the leeks to the skillet and stir over medium heat until just wilted, about 2 minutes. Place the clam juice in a measuring cup and add enough of the liquor from the oysters to measure ¾ cup. Add this to the skillet along with the Champagne. Increase the heat to high and bring to a boil. Boil until reduced by half, 5 to 7 minutes. Add the cream and bring back to a boil. Reduce again, stirring often, until the sauce is thick enough to coat the back of a spoon.

4. Return the chicken to the skillet and warm through over medium-low heat. Add the oysters and cook until the edges begin to curl, about 2 minutes. Do not overcook. Season to taste with salt and pepper, if desired.

 Serves 6

Chicken Breast Mole Enchiladas

The addition of a little cocoa powder gives this dish an interesting and unusual flavor. Chocolate is a typical ingredient in the mole dishes of Mexico. Make sure that the baking dish is large enough to hold the filled tortillas in one flat layer. They cook better this way.

6 boneless, skinless chicken breast halves, cut into 2 × ½-inch strips

3 teaspoons chili powder

Salt and freshly ground black pepper

2 tablespoons vegetable oil

1 medium onion, finely chopped

2 garlic cloves, crushed

1 cinnamon stick, 2 inches long, or ½ teaspoon ground cinnamon

1 teaspoon ground cumin

1 large can (28 ounces) crushed tomatoes

1 tablespoon unsweetened cocoa powder

6 flour tortillas, 10 inches in diameter

About 2 cups shredded Monterey Jack cheese

2 tablespoons chopped fresh cilantro

1. Toss the chicken strips with the chili powder in a large bowl. Season with salt and pepper.

2. Heat the oil in a large, heavy skillet or Dutch oven over medium-high heat. Add the chicken and cook, turning often, until lightly browned on all sides, about 5 minutes. Remove the chicken from the skillet and set aside. Pour off all but 1 tablespoon of the fat from the skillet. Add the onion, garlic, cinnamon, and cumin. Cook over medium-high heat, stirring often, until the onion is slightly softened, about 2 minutes. Add the tomatoes, reduce the heat to medium, and simmer, uncovered, until slightly thickened, about 10 minutes. Stir in the cocoa and cook 5 minutes longer.

3. Preheat the oven to 350°F. Spread ¼ cup of the sauce in the bottom of a large baking pan. Divide the chicken evenly among the 6 tortillas, placing several pieces in a strip down the center of each. Top the chicken with about 3 tablespoons of sauce and roll into a cylinder. Lay the rolled tortillas, seam side down, in the baking pan and pour over the remaining sauce. Sprinkle with the cheese.

4. Bake for 20 to 25 minutes or until the cheese is melted and the sauce is bubbly. Sprinkle with the cilantro and serve at once.

 Serves 6

Cornmeal Crusted Chicken Breasts with Black Bean Salsa

The salsa can be served right away if pressed for time. However, it develops more flavor if allowed to chill for several hours. Add the mint just before serving, if making in advance. Try using chicken tenders in place of the breasts and serving them as an appetizer!

3 cups cooked black beans

1 tablespoon olive oil

1 tablespoon white wine vinegar

Zest and juice of 1 orange

¼ cup coarsely chopped fresh mint leaves

1 medium tomato, peeled, seeded, and chopped

1 small jalapeño pepper, seeded and minced

Salt and freshly ground black pepper

6 boneless, skinless chicken breast halves

½ cup milk

¾ cup fine ground yellow cornmeal

¼ teaspoon salt

¼ teaspoon cayenne pepper

3 tablespoons unsalted butter

3 tablespoons vegetable oil

1. Toss the beans with the oil, vinegar, orange zest, orange juice, mint, tomato, and jalapeño in a large bowl. Season to taste with salt and pepper. Cover the salsa with plastic wrap and refrigerate until chilled.

2. Place the chicken between 2 sheets of parchment paper or plastic wrap and pound to an even thickness of about ¼ inch.

3. Place the milk in a large bowl for dipping. Combine the cornmeal with the salt and cayenne pepper in another bowl.

4. Melt the butter with the oil in a large, heavy skillet over medium-high heat. Dip the chicken in the milk and dredge in the cornmeal. Transfer to the skillet and cook until golden brown and cooked through, about 5 minutes on each side. Serve with the salsa on the side.

 Serves 6

Chicken Nugget

At $26 billion in annual retail sales, chicken alone accounts for 6 percent of the total U.S. expenditures for food.

Pan-Sautéed Chicken Breasts with Melted Leek Sauce

Serve with crisp, oven-roasted potatoes and follow with a seasonal green salad. The sauce can be made a day or two in advance and kept tightly covered in the refrigerator until you're ready to brown the chicken.

- **6 tablespoons (¾ stick) unsalted butter**
- **2 large leeks, white part only, thinly sliced**
- **2 garlic cloves, peeled and halved**
- **1 bouquet garni (see Note)**
- **1 teaspoon salt**
- **1½ cups chicken stock**
- **¼ cup all-purpose flour**
- **Salt and freshly ground black pepper**
- **6 boneless, skinless chicken breast halves**
- **¼ cup dry white wine**
- **2 tablespoons chopped fresh parsley**

1. Melt 4 tablespoons of the butter in a small, heavy skillet over medium-high heat. Add the leeks, garlic, bouquet garni, and salt. Reduce the heat to low and cook, stirring often, until very soft, 15 to 20 minutes. Remove the bouquet garni and transfer the mixture to a food processor. With the motor running, add the stock and puree until smooth.

2. Melt the remaining 2 tablespoons butter in a large, heavy skillet over medium-high heat. Combine the flour with a pinch each of salt and pepper in a large bowl. Dip the chicken in the flour to coat and shake off the excess. Cook the chicken in the hot butter until browned, 3 to 4 minutes per side. Remove to a plate and pour off the fat from the skillet.

3. Over high heat, add the wine to the skillet and bring to a boil. Whisk constantly to scrape up any browned bits on the bottom. Boil until all but 1 tablespoon of the liquid has evaporated, about 2 minutes. Pour in the leek sauce, reduce the heat to medium, and return the chicken to the skillet. Cover and simmer gently until the chicken is firm and cooked through, about 10 minutes.

4. Transfer the chicken to a large, warmed serving platter. Season the sauce to taste with additional salt and pepper. Spoon the sauce over the chicken, sprinkle with the chopped parsley, and serve at once.

 **Serves 6**

NOTE: *To prepare a bouquet garni, combine several parsley stems, 2 bay leaves, 8 to 10 peppercorns, and 2 sprigs fresh thyme in a large*

square of rinsed cheesecloth. Gather the ends together to form a small pouch and tie securely with kitchen string.

Grilled Chicken Breasts with Herbed Potato Ragoût

Use small, red-skinned new potatoes for the best results. A tablespoonful or so of coarsely chopped capers will add zest.

6 boneless, skinless chicken breast halves

Salt and freshly ground black pepper

4 medium Italian plum tomatoes, or 1 can (14 ounces) plum tomatoes, peeled, seeded, and chopped

10 to 12 medium, firm-fleshed potatoes (about 1½ pounds), peeled and cut into ½-inch cubes

1 to 2 cups chicken stock

2 teaspoons chopped fresh thyme, or 1 teaspoon dried

1 teaspoon chopped fresh rosemary, or ½ teaspoon dried

2 teaspoons chopped fresh parsley

1. Prepare a charcoal grill and let coals burn down to a gray ash. Alternatively, prepare a stove-top grill for cooking the chicken, generously oiling the grates of either.

2. Flatten the chicken breasts between sheets of parchment paper to a uniform thickness of about ½ inch. Season both sides with salt and pepper.

3. Combine the tomatoes and potatoes in a medium skillet. Pour in enough stock to barely cover the mixture. (The amount will vary according to the size of the skillet used.) Season with salt and pepper. Bring to a boil over high heat, reduce the heat to medium-high, and cook uncovered, stirring often, until the potatoes are tender and the liquid has boiled down to a thick sauce, 20 to 30 minutes.

4. Grill the chicken over hot coals or on stove-top grill. Grill until cooked through, 4 to 5 minutes on each side.

5. Stir the thyme, rosemary, and half of the parsley into the potato mixture. Turn out onto a large, warmed serving platter and surround with the grilled breasts. Sprinkle over the remaining parsley and serve at once.

 Serves 6

Tamarind Marinated Chicken Breasts with Apricot Sauce

Tamarind is commonly found in Asian or specialty food stores. Usually sold in dehydrated block form (as is called for in this recipe), tamarind sometimes comes as a concentrated paste. To substitute the paste in this recipe, dissolve 1 tablespoon in ¾ cup hot water and proceed as indicated.

1 piece tamarind pulp, about the size of a golf ball

1 cup boiling water

¼ cup vegetable oil

½ teaspoon salt

½ teaspoon fennel seeds

1 piece fresh ginger, 1 inch long, peeled and minced

2 tablespoons white wine vinegar

1 teaspoon black peppercorns

6 boneless, skinless chicken breast halves

4 or 5 dried apricots, cut into small dice (about ⅓ cup)

2 tablespoons apricot preserves

¼ cup plain lowfat yogurt

1. Place the tamarind in a small bowl and pour over the boiling water. Let stand for 15 to 20 minutes.

2. Combine the oil, salt, fennel seeds, ginger, vinegar, and peppercorns in a small bowl. Drain the tamarind through a fine-mesh strainer, pressing down on the pulp. Discard the stems and skin. Add this liquid to the bowl and mix the marinade well.

3. Place the chicken in a large nonreactive bowl. Pour over the marinade, cover, and refrigerate for at least 1 hour and for up to 6 hours.

4. Preheat a stove-top grill or broiler. Remove the chicken from the marinade and pat dry. Place the marinade in a small saucepan and add the apricots. Bring to a boil, lower the heat to medium low, and simmer for 5 minutes. Transfer the mixture to a food processor and puree until smooth. Return the puree to the pan and stir in the preserves and yogurt. Heat gently over very low heat. Do not boil.

5. Meanwhile, grill or broil the chicken until lightly browned and cooked through, about 5 minutes on each side. Slice each breast on a bias into 4 to 5 pieces. Serve with the sauce drizzled over the top.

 **Serves 6**

Baked Chicken Breasts with Tomatoes, Onions, and Olives

Mediterranean cuisine, with its sun-drenched appeal, is low in fat and full of strong, vivid flavors. Ingredients like those used in this recipe make ordinary chicken a baked delight. Chopped, drained anchovy fillets can be added to the casserole for a more authentic touch.

- **6 split chicken breasts**
- **Salt and freshly ground black pepper**
- **2 tablespoons olive oil**
- **2 medium onions, peeled, halved, and thinly sliced**
- **1 garlic clove, minced**
- **10 to 12 plum tomatoes, peeled, seeded, and chopped, or 1 large can (2 pounds, 3 ounces) peeled Italian plum tomatoes, seeded and chopped**
- **½ cup pitted black olives (about 4 ounces before pitting), preferably oil-cured, coarsely chopped**
- **¼ cup dry white wine**
- **2 tablespoons chopped fresh parsley**

1. Preheat the oven to 350° F. Season the chicken with salt and pepper. Heat the oil in a large, heavy skillet. Over medium-high heat, cook the chicken until lightly browned, 2 to 3 minutes per side. Transfer to a large, covered ovenproof casserole and set aside.

2. Add the onions to the skillet and cook, stirring often, until softened but not browned, about 2 minutes. Add the garlic and cook 1 minute longer. Stir in the tomatoes, olives, wine, and half of the parsley. Season to taste with salt and pepper. Simmer for 2 to 3 minutes, then pour over the chicken in the casserole. Cover tightly and bake, turning the chicken occasionally, until tender, 45 minutes to 1 hour. Arrange the breasts on a large, warmed platter. Spoon over the contents of the casserole and garnish with the remaining parsley. Serve at once.

 Serves 6

Sautéed Chicken Breasts with Asparagus and Morels

Spring is the best season for asparagus. Use firm green stalks with tight heads. Fresh morels are a delicacy—if you have a source and can find them during their very short growing season, by all means use them in place of the dried ones called for here. To complete the spring menu, serve with steamed tiny new potatoes.

6 boneless, skinless chicken breast halves

Salt and freshly ground black pepper

24 fresh asparagus spears, trimmed and cleaned

2 ounces dried morel mushrooms

2 tablespoons unsalted butter

2 tablespoons vegetable oil

$\frac{1}{2}$ cup chicken stock

1 cup heavy cream

2 tablespoons chopped fresh parsley

1. Place the chicken between 2 sheets of parchment paper or plastic wrap and pound to a thickness of $\frac{1}{2}$ inch. Season the breasts with salt and pepper. Bring a large pot of salted water to a boil. Add the asparagus and bring back to a boil. Cook rapidly for 2 minutes. Drain and rinse under cold running water.

2. Bring a large pot of water to a boil. Place the morels in a heatproof medium bowl. Pour in enough boiling water to cover by 1 inch and soak for 10 minutes. Strain and rinse under cold running water to remove any grit. Squeeze out excess moisture and coarsely chop.

3. Melt the butter with the oil in a large, heavy skillet over medium-high heat. Add the chicken and cook until browned, 4 to 5 minutes on each side. Remove to a plate or platter and cover with foil to keep warm. Pour off all but 1 tablespoon of the fat from the skillet. Add the morels and cook, stirring, until most of the liquid has evaporated, 2 to 3 minutes. Add the chicken stock, increase the heat to high, and boil, stirring or whisking to pick up any cooking bits left in the bottom of the pan, until reduced by half, 2 to 3 minutes. Add the cream and boil until the total amount of liquid has reduced by half and the sauce is thickened. Reduce the heat to medium, and gently stir in the asparagus and half of the parsley. Season to taste with salt and pepper. Cook just until warmed through, 2 to 3 minutes. Arrange the chicken on warmed individual serving plates or on a large platter. Spoon over the asparagus and morel mixture and garnish with a sprinkle of the remaining parsley.

 **Serves 6**

Thighs

∎∎∎

This rich meat from the upper portion of the leg goes well with fresh and dried fruits, fortified wines, and robust spices.

Thigh Tips

- Thighs have a thick layer of fatty skin, more so than other parts. If you want to reduce fat, leave the skin on during cooking but remove it afterward.
- You'll find that direct-heat cooking methods such as grilling, broiling, and pan-frying are favorite techniques with this particular part, which will make the skin crisp and crunchy but keep the meat moist.
- Thighs are often a very good buy, and the richness of dark meat makes for a more substantial serving. There is hardly any tough sinew or gristle, unlike drumsticks or wings.
- Cook thighs until the juices run clear. Pierce the thigh at its thickest point with a sharp knife. Press the flesh to release the liquid; if these juices are pink, cook longer, until done. The internal temperature should read 170°F. on a meat thermometer.
- For convenience, look for packages of already-boned thighs. Cut into small pieces, boneless thighs can be stir-fried, sautéed, or made into fajitas and kebabs.

Boning Thighs

1. Place the thigh skin side down on a cutting board and cut along the thin side from joint to joint.
2. Cut the meat from one joint, then use the knife to scrape against the bone, dislodging the flesh.
3. Cut the meat from the opposite joint and gently pull to remove the bone.

Thighs

Quick and Easy

Broiled Thighs with Sour Cream and Dill Sauce

Reduced-fat sour cream and mayonnaise make this dish rich in flavor, but not in fat. The sauce is also good with cold chicken or grilled fish, like salmon.

2 cups reduced-fat sour cream

1 tablespoon reduced-fat mayonnaise

1 tablespoon lemon juice

¼ cup chopped fresh dill

Salt and freshly ground black pepper

6 large or 12 small chicken thighs

1. Preheat the broiler or prepare a charcoal grill and allow the coals to burn down to a gray ash. Oil the broiling pan or grill to prevent sticking.

2. Combine the sour cream, mayonnaise, lemon juice, and dill in a large bowl. Season to taste with salt and pepper. Set aside while preparing the thighs. (The sauce can be made up to 2 days in advance. Keep covered in the refrigerator until 30 minutes before serving.)

3. Place the thighs skin side toward the heat on a broiling pan or charcoal grill. Cook about 6 inches from the source of heat, turning once, until the skin is lightly browned and the flesh nearest the bone shows no sign of pink when tested with a fork, about 30 minutes.

4. Spoon a small amount of the sauce over the thighs while still hot. Serve the remaining sauce on the side.

 **Serves 6**

Chicken and Salsa Stir-Fry

Colorful and zesty, this quick recipe is great with cornbread. Serve with a refreshing green salad tossed with a garlicky dressing.

- ¼ cup all-purpose flour
- ½ teaspoon salt
- ¼ teaspoon freshly ground black pepper
- 6 boneless, skinless chicken thighs, cut into 1-inch pieces
- 2 tablespoons olive oil
- 2 cups fresh corn kernels or thawed frozen corn
- 2 cups cooked kidney beans, or 1 can (15 ounces), drained and rinsed
- 1½ cups bottled or homemade tomato salsa
- Salt and freshly ground black pepper
- 2 tablespoons chopped fresh cilantro

1. Combine the flour with the salt and pepper in a wide, shallow bowl. Add the chicken pieces and toss well to coat. Shake off excess flour. Heat the oil in a large, heavy skillet or in a wok over medium-high heat. Add the chicken and cook, turning often, until well browned and cooked through, about 10 minutes. Remove the chicken to a warmed plate or platter and cover with foil to keep warm.

2. Add the corn to the hot skillet or wok and cook, stirring often, until toasted and golden brown, about 2 minutes. Stir in the beans and salsa. Reduce the heat to medium. Return the chicken to the skillet and cook until the corn is cooked and all the ingredients are warmed through, about 5 minutes. Season to taste with salt and pepper, transfer to a serving platter, and sprinkle with cilantro.

 Serves 6

Chicken Nugget

The Literary Chicken: **Among the dishes at the feast for Charles Bovary's wedding to Emma Rouault, described by Gustav Flaubert in his novel *Madame Bovary*, are "six dishes of hashed chicken." "Minced chicken" is served to guests for supper at the home of Jane Austen's eponymous heroine Emma. "Minced chicken with saffron" is one of the "old-fashioned dishes" the Subotchev family dine on in Turgenev's *Virgin Soil*.**

Stir-Fried Thighs with Artichokes and New Potatoes

Fresh artichokes take a lot of time and trouble to prepare. This recipe uses the handy frozen variety, but if you are so inclined, use the real thing. Simply remove the leaves, cut away the chokes, and boil in water with a couple of teaspoons of lemon juice or vinegar for 15 to 20 minutes, until tender. Drain well, cut into quarters, and use here in place of the thawed artichokes. You'll need six to eight large artichoke globes.

- **1 pound red new potatoes, scrubbed and cut into 1-inch pieces**
- **¼ cup all-purpose flour**
- **½ teaspoon salt**
- **¼ teaspoon freshly ground black pepper**
- **6 large boneless, skinless chicken thighs, cut into 1 inch pieces**
- **3 tablespoons olive oil**
- **1 teaspoon fennel seeds**
- **2 garlic cloves, thinly sliced**
- **1 package (9 ounces) frozen artichoke hearts, thawed**
- **1 tablespoon Worcestershire sauce**
- **2 tablespoons lemon juice**
- **Additional salt and freshly ground black pepper**

1. Place the potatoes in a large saucepan and pour over enough cold water to cover. Add a pinch of salt and bring to a boil over high heat. Reduce the heat to medium high, and cook until almost tender, about 10 minutes. Drain well and set aside.

2. Combine the flour, salt, and pepper in a wide, shallow bowl. Add the chicken pieces and toss or stir to coat well. Heat 2 tablespoons of the oil in a large skillet or wok over medium-high heat. Add the chicken and cook, turning often, until well browned and cooked through, about 10 minutes. Transfer to a warmed plate and cover with foil to keep warm.

3. Add the remaining tablespoon of oil to the skillet. Stir in the fennel seeds and garlic. Cook, stirring often, until the garlic is fragrant and begins to color, 1 to 2 minutes. Add the artichokes and potatoes. Cook, partially covered, until heated through, about 3 minutes. Return the chicken to the skillet, stir in the Worcestershire sauce, and cook until very hot, about 2 minutes. Sprinkle over the lemon juice and season to taste with salt and pepper. Serve at once.

 Serves 6

Curried Chicken Thigh and Eggplant Sauté

For an exotic meal inspired by Middle Eastern cuisines, sauté thighs and eggplant in curry and serve with red lentils cooked in chicken stock. Basmati rice is an excellent accompaniment.

- ¼ cup all-purpose flour
- ½ teaspoon salt
- ¼ teaspoon freshly ground black pepper
- 6 large boneless, skinless chicken thighs, cut into 1-inch pieces
- 3 tablespoons olive oil
- 2 garlic cloves, minced
- 1 medium eggplant, cut into 1-inch dice
- Additional salt and freshly ground black pepper
- ½ cup chicken stock
- ½ cup heavy cream
- 2 teaspoons curry powder
- 1 package (10 ounces) frozen peas, defrosted

1. Combine the flour, salt, and pepper in a large, shallow bowl. Add the chicken pieces and toss to coat well. Heat 2 tablespoons of the oil over medium-high heat. Shake off the excess flour from the thighs and cook, turning often, until well browned, about 8 minutes. Remove the chicken to a plate and cover with foil to keep warm.

2. Add the remaining tablespoon of oil and the garlic to the skillet. Cook, stirring often, until fragrant, about 30 seconds. Add the eggplant, sprinkle with additional salt and pepper, and cook, stirring and tossing occasionally, until softened, 7 to 10 minutes.

3. Combine the chicken stock, cream, and curry powder in a small bowl. Return the chicken to the skillet and pour in the curry and cream mixture. Bring to a simmer, cover, and cook 6 to 8 minutes. Uncover, stir well, and cook until the sauce is thickened, 3 to 4 minutes. Season to taste with salt and pepper, add the peas, and cook just to heat through.

 Serves 6

Stir-Fried Chicken with Shrimp and Peanuts

Serve this South Pacific–inspired dish with cellophane (bean thread) noodles or steamed rice and crisp-cooked snow peas.

- 1 piece fresh ginger, 1 inch long, peeled and minced
- 1 tablespoon cornstarch
- 1 tablespoon soy sauce
- 2 tablespoons dry sherry
- 2 tablespoons water
- 6 large boneless, skinless chicken thighs, cut into 1-inch pieces
- 2 tablespoons peanut oil
- 24 large shrimp, peeled and deveined
- 2 garlic cloves, minced
- 3 tablespoons bottled oyster sauce (available in the Asian food section of most large grocery stores)
- ½ cup chicken stock
- ½ cup unsalted, roasted peanuts

1. Blend together the ginger, cornstarch, soy sauce, sherry, and water in a large bowl. Add the chicken, turn to coat, and let stand for 10 minutes.

2. Heat the oil in a wok over high heat. Add the shrimp and cook, tossing and stirring constantly, until just pink and opaque, 2 to 3 minutes. Remove to a plate and set aside.

3. Add the garlic to the wok and cook until fragrant, about 30 seconds. Drain the chicken from the marinade and reserve the liquid. Add the chicken to the wok and cook, tossing frequently, until firm and cooked through, 5 to 6 minutes. Add the oyster sauce, the reserved chicken marinade and the chicken stock. Lower the heat and simmer until the sauce is thickened and glossy, 2 to 3 minutes. Add the shrimp and peanuts and cook 1 to 2 minutes longer to warm through. Serve at once.

 **Serves 6**

Chicken Nugget

Chicken is sold in parts more than ever these days. Over 57 percent leaves the processing plants as cut-up chicken, compared to about only a third ten years ago.

Quick Chicken Thigh, Cumin, and Pepper Sauté

Cumin is an earthy and aromatic spice long used in North African and Middle Eastern cuisines. The ground spice is increasingly easy to find and adds an exotic flavor to simple dishes like this quick thigh sauté.

- **6 large boneless, skinless chicken thighs, cut into strips ¼ inch wide and 1½ inches long**

- **Salt and freshly ground black pepper**

- **2 tablespoons olive oil**

- **1 medium onion, finely chopped**

- **3 tablespoons white wine vinegar**

- **1 tablespoon ground cumin**

- **1 tablespoon chopped fresh oregano, or 1 teaspoon dried**

- **3 large bell peppers, cored, seeded, and cut into strips**

- **1 cup chicken stock**

1. Season the chicken pieces with salt and pepper. Heat the oil in a large non-stick skillet over medium-high heat. Add the chicken and cook, tossing occasionally, until well browned, about 8 minutes. Remove to a plate with a slotted spoon and cover with foil to keep warm.

2. Add the onion to the skillet and cook until softened, 2 to 3 minutes. Add the vinegar, increase the heat to high, and cook, stirring to scrape up any browned bits from the skillet, until the liquid has evaporated. Stir in the cumin and the oregano. Add the peppers and cook until slightly softened, 3 to 4 minutes. Return the chicken to the skillet, add the stock, and bring to a boil. Reduce the heat to medium and simmer until the peppers are soft and the liquid is reduced and slightly thickened, 8 to 10 minutes.

 Serves 6

Chicken Nugget

The United States was seized with "hen fever" for a brief period in the mid-nineteenth century, when new breeds were brought from China and chickens became very fashionable. They were exhibited, admired, painted, and written about.

Sweet-and-Sour Chicken Kebabs

Every now and then, when you're in the mood for something different, think of chicken kebabs. They are crunchy and light, and this sweet-and-sour glaze is particularly appealing. Serve over a bed of fluffy couscous studded with toasted pine nuts and currants.

1 can (8 ounces) pineapple chunks, drained, juice reserved

1/3 cup strained apricot preserves

1 tablespoon Dijon mustard

1 tablespoon Worcestershire sauce

Pinch of red pepper flakes

6 large boneless, skinless chicken thighs, cut into 1 inch pieces

24 small dried apricots

1 large red bell pepper, cut into 1-inch pieces

1. Whisk together the pineapple juice, apricot preserves, mustard, Worcester-shire sauce, and red pepper flakes in a small bowl. Place the chicken pieces in a nonreactive bowl and pour over half the sauce. Turn to coat all of the pieces and let stand for 10 minutes.

2. Preheat the broiler and lightly oil a broiling pan. Alternatively, light a charcoal fire and allow it to burn down to a gray ash, then lightly oil the grill.

3. On each of 12 skewers, thread 1 apricot, 1 piece of chicken, 1 pineapple chunk, and one pepper slice. Repeat the sequence so that you have 2 of each component per skewer.

4. Place the skewers on the broiling pan or grill. Broil or grill, turning and basting frequently with the remaining half of the marinade, until lightly browned and cooked through, 10 to 12 minutes.

 Serves 6

Chicken Nugget

All the world loves chicken! U.S. exports rose from $296 million in 1984 to $720 million in 1988 and could reach $1 billion in the 1990s.

Pan-Fried Thighs with Apple Butter

Nothing really replaces the flavor of a good apple brandy like the Calvados called for here. If it is absolutely not to be found, the same amount of dry white wine can be used in its place. I like to make my own apple butter. I can control the sugar content as I see fit, and can flavor it with lots of vanilla instead of cinnamon or nutmeg. But there are plenty of commercial apple butters of outstanding quality to be found these days. Farmers' markets are good sources, especially in the fall. Serve these thighs with baked sweet potatoes and a simple green vegetable like broccoli or spinach.

6 large boneless chicken thighs, boned

Coarse salt and freshly ground black pepper

2 tablespoons unsalted butter

1 tablespoon vegetable oil

1 large onion, finely chopped

½ cup Calvados or apple jack

½ cup store-bought or homemade apple butter

1. Season the thighs with salt and pepper. Melt the butter with the oil in a large, heavy skillet over medium-high heat. Add the chicken skin side down and cook until well browned, 10 to 12 minutes. Turn and cook until firm to the touch and cooked through, 5 to 7 minutes longer. Pour off excess fat that is rendered from time to time. There should be just enough fat in the skillet to brown the thighs. Remove the chicken to a warm platter and cover with foil to keep warm.

2. Pour off all but about 1 tablespoon of the fat, add the onion, and cook, stirring often, until lightly browned, about 5 minutes. Pour in the Calvados, increase the heat to high, and bring to a boil. Cook, stirring to pick up any bits left in the bottom of the skillet, until reduced by half, about 3 minutes.

3. Remove the skillet from the heat and stir in the apple butter. Season to taste with salt and pepper and spoon a heaping tablespoonful of the apple butter sauce over each thigh. Spread evenly and serve at once.

 **Serves 6**

Baked Thighs with Eggplant, Tomato, and Goat Cheese

The overlapping of the eggplant is important when preparing this recipe. If the slices are too thick, the circles will not be flat enough to form a base. Small eggplants are easier to work with but are difficult to find. You might need two baking sheets to hold the assembled circles. (Count on an additional 5 to 10 minutes cooking time if using two baking sheets.) Use a very large spatula to transfer the cooked circles to serving plates; they fall apart easily while warm.

2 small eggplant or 1 large (about ¾ pound)

Coarse salt

2 tablespoons unsalted butter

2 small onions, thinly sliced

1 tablespoon chopped fresh thyme leaves, or 1 teaspoon dried

Freshly ground black pepper

2 large tomatoes, sliced ¼ inch thick

6 large boneless, skinless chicken thighs, pounded to ½ inch thick

1 small log (3½ ounces) goat cheese, cut into 6 even disks

2 tablespoons olive oil

1. Trim the ends of the eggplants and cut into ¼-inch-thick slices. Place in a large bowl and sprinkle liberally with salt. Toss to coat and leave to stand for 20 minutes.

2. Melt the butter in a small, heavy skillet over medium-high heat. Add the onions and thyme, reduce the heat to medium low, and cook, stirring often, until the onions are soft but not browned, 10 to 12 minutes. Season with salt and pepper. Set aside.

3. Preheat the oven to 375° F. and lightly oil a large baking sheet with a rim. Quickly rinse the eggplant slices under cold running water and pat dry. Arrange 4 or 5 slices of small eggplant overlapping (or only 1 or 2 slices if using 1 large eggplant) to form a circle that measures about 4 inches in diameter. Top with a slice of tomato and season with salt and pepper. Place a chicken thigh on top and spoon over about 1 tablespoon of the onion mixture. Arrange a disk of the goat cheese on top and drizzle with a small amount of the olive oil. Continue with the remaining ingredients, making 6 circles in all. Bake for 30 minutes or until the chicken is opaque and the cheese is lightly browned. To serve, use a spatula to transfer to individual, warmed plates. Lift carefully just under the circle of eggplants and move in one quick motion.

 **Serves 6**

Provençal Chicken Stir-Fry

Squash, tomatoes, and fresh herbs are pungent full-summer flavors that evoke the magic of Provence. Serve with polenta and Parmesan cheese for an authentic Mediterranean delight.

6 large boneless, skinless chicken thighs

½ cup all-purpose flour

1 teaspoon salt

½ teaspoon freshly ground black pepper

3 tablespoons olive oil

2 garlic cloves, minced

2 shallots, minced

2 teaspoons *herbes de Provence* (see Note)

2 small or 1 large yellow squash, cut into 1-inch dice

2 small or 1 large zucchini, cut into 1-inch dice

24 small cherry tomatoes

Salt and freshly ground black pepper

1. Trim the thighs of all fat and cut into 1½-inch pieces. Combine the flour, salt, and pepper in a large bowl. Add the chicken and toss to coat.

2. Heat 2 tablespoons of the oil in a large skillet over high heat. Add the chicken pieces and cook, stirring and turning constantly, until browned, about 5 minutes. Remove and set aside.

3. Add the remaining tablespoon of oil to the skillet and add the garlic and shallots. Cook, stirring often, until softened, about 2 minutes. Add the *herbes de Provence* and cook 1 minute longer. Add the squash and zucchini and cook, stirring often, until they just begin to brown, about 3 minutes. Toss in the reserved chicken, reduce the heat slightly, cover, and cook until the chicken pieces are cooked through and the squash is tender, 3 to 4 minutes.

4. Add the cherry tomatoes to the skillet and cook, covered, until the tomato skins start to wrinkle, about 1 minute. Season to taste with salt and pepper and serve at once.

 Serves 6

NOTE: ***Herbes de Provence*** *is a popular mixture of dried herbs including thyme, savory, fennel, rosemary, and sometimes marjoram. The commercial blend is sold in many specialty stores. If not available, use a homemade mixture of dried thyme and dried rosemary mixed with chopped fresh parsley.*

Chicken Thigh Saté with Prunes and Bacon

These satés can be made with smaller skewers or large toothpicks and served with drinks. Use thinly sliced bacon for best results.

24 large pitted prunes

12 bacon slices, halved crosswise

6 large boneless, skinless chicken thighs, each cut into 8 small pieces

½ cup plum sauce (available in Asian food section of most supermarkets)

¼ cup soy sauce

2 tablespoons peanut oil

1. Preheat the oven to 450° F. If using bamboo skewers, soak in water for at least 30 minutes before using.

2. Wrap each of the prunes with one of the halved bacon strips. Thread one of the wrapped prunes on a 10- or 12-inch bamboo or metal skewer, securing the seam with the skewer. Alternate 2 pieces of chicken with 1 wrapped prune. Repeat with the remaining skewers. Each skewer should have 4 wrapped prunes and 1 whole chicken thigh.

3. Place the skewers on a lightly oiled rack set over a roasting pan. Combine the plum sauce, soy sauce, and peanut oil in a small bowl. Brush the skewers with half of this mixture and bake for 10 minutes. Reduce the oven temperature to 350° F., turn the skewers, brush on the remaining sauce, and cook until the bacon is crisp and the chicken is cooked through, 12 to 15 minutes longer. Serve at once.

 **Serves 6**

Chicken Nugget

Mimi Sheraton, writing about chicken soup as penicillin in her book, *The Whole World Loves Chicken Soup:* "On the chance that your mother never told you, chicken soup is good for just about everything that ails you. Could such a widely held belief be false? Did people ever believe that the earth was flat or that the sun revolved around it?"

Chicken Thigh Succotash Stir-Fry

*Succotash comes from a Narragansett Indian word, **miskquatash,** which means "boiled corn kernels." This vegetable stew has many variations, but always includes beans and corn. My version is a quick one using frozen lima beans and corn kernels. Peeled, seeded, and chopped tomatoes could be added as well as cubes of cooked summer squash or zucchini. Serve with plain white rice or tiny boiled potatoes.*

> **6 large boneless, skinless chicken thighs**
>
> **1 package (10 ounces) frozen lima beans**
>
> **1 package (10 ounces) frozen corn kernels**
>
> **2 tablespoons olive oil**
>
> **1 small onion, finely chopped**
>
> **2 tablespoons heavy cream**
>
> **1 tablespoon chopped fresh thyme leaves, or 1 teaspoon dried**
>
> **Salt and freshly ground black pepper**
>
> **1 tablespoon chopped fresh chives**

1. Trim the thighs of all fat and cut into 1½-inch pieces. Prepare the lima beans and the corn according to package directions. Drain well and pat dry with paper towels.

2. Heat the oil in a wok or large skillet over medium-high heat. Add the chicken and cook, stirring or tossing often, until well browned, 5 to 7 minutes. Reduce the heat to medium, add the onion, and cook, stirring often, until softened, about 3 minutes. Add the lima beans, corn, and cream. Season with the thyme and salt and pepper to taste. Cover and cook 2 to 3 minutes or until heated through. Transfer to a warmed serving platter and sprinkle with the chives. Serve at once.

 **Serves 6**

Quick and Easy

Chicken Thigh Sauté with Beets, Walnuts, and Blue Cheese

Serve this unusual and exotic stir-fry over a bed of salad greens lightly tossed with a lemon dressing for a luncheon dish or a first course.

6 large boneless, skinless chicken thighs

1 cup walnut pieces

½ cup all-purpose flour

1 teaspoon salt

½ teaspoon freshly ground black pepper

¼ cup peanut oil

1 small onion, finely chopped

1 teaspoon grated lemon zest

2 tablespoons balsamic vinegar

2 cups diced cooked or canned beets

½ cup crumbled blue cheese

1. Trim the thighs of all fat and cut into 1½-inch pieces. Heat a large wok or skillet over medium-high heat and add the walnuts. Toast, tossing or stirring often, until fragrant, about 2 minutes. Remove the nuts and set aside. Wipe out the wok or skillet with a paper towel.

2. Combine the flour, salt, and pepper in a large bowl. Add the chicken pieces and toss to coat. Heat the oil in the wok or skillet over high heat, swirling to cover all sides. Add the chicken and cook, tossing often, until lightly browned, 4 to 5 minutes. Drain on paper towels and discard excess oil from the wok.

3. Add the onion to the wok and cook, stirring often, over medium-high heat until softened, about 3 minutes. Add the lemon zest and vinegar. Stir, scraping up any browned bits from the bottom, then return the chicken to the wok or skillet and cook until well browned and cooked through, 2 to 3 minutes. Add the beets and walnuts. Toss to combine, lower the heat to medium, and cook 2 minutes or until heated through.

4. Remove the wok from the heat, toss in the blue cheese, transfer to a serving platter, and serve at once.

 **Serves 6**

Quick Chicken Thigh Sauté with Cherry Tomatoes and Mozzarella

Pinch off the tiny leaves from the tops of fresh basil sprigs to use for garnish. I like to use mozzarella cheese that is made from buffalo milk, which has a better texture and flavor, for this recipe. Try using a mixture of yellow and red cherry tomatoes for a colorful variation.

6 large boneless, skinless chicken thighs

Salt and freshly ground black pepper

2 tablespoons olive oil

12 to 15 cherry tomatoes (about ¹⁄₂ pound), halved or quartered

6 ounces mozzarella cheese, diced (about 1¹⁄₂ cups loosely packed)

¹⁄₂ cup thinly shredded fresh basil

2 tablespoons balsamic vinegar

Hot cooked pasta or couscous

1. Trim the thighs of all fat and cut into 1-inch pieces. Season well with salt and pepper. Heat the oil in a large, heavy skillet over high heat. Sauté the chicken, turning often, until lightly browned, 2 to 3 minutes. Add the tomatoes, reduce the heat to medium high, cover, and cook until the tomatoes are softened and the chicken is cooked through, about 5 minutes.

2. Remove the skillet from the heat and add the cheese, basil, and vinegar. Stir well to blend, and season to taste with salt and pepper. Serve at once with pasta or hot, fluffy couscous.

 Serves 6

Chinese Fried Chicken and Green Beans

Serve with Chinese fried rice flavored with lots of fresh scallions.

1½ pounds green beans, trimmed
of stems

Oil for deep-frying

½ cup cornstarch

½ cup plus 2 tablespoons sherry

2 tablespoons white wine vinegar

6 large boneless, skinless chicken
thighs, trimmed and cut into
1-inch dice

1 tablespoon peanut oil

1 piece fresh ginger, 1 inch long,
peeled and minced

1 garlic clove, minced

½ teaspoon sugar

2 tablespoons soy sauce

1. Bring a large pot of salted water to a boil. Add the green beans and cook until tender, 3 to 5 minutes. Drain and rinse under cold, running water. Set aside on paper towels.

2. Heat 2 inches of oil in an electric fryer to 375°F. Alternatively, heat 2 inches of oil in a wok or large skillet over medium-high heat. Drop a small piece of bread in the oil after a few minutes to gauge the temperature. If the bread sizzles and floats to the surface, it is hot enough. If not, continue heating before frying the chicken.

3. In a bowl, combine the cornstarch, ½ cup of the sherry, and the vinegar. Whisk to form a batter. Dip a few pieces of the chicken in the batter at a time, transfer to the hot oil, and fry until crisp and lightly browned, 4 to 5 minutes. Remove with a slotted spoon to drain on paper towels. Continue with all of the chicken.

4. Heat the peanut oil in a separate skillet or wok. Add the ginger and garlic. Cook over medium-high heat, stirring constantly, until the garlic is slightly softened, 1 to 2 minutes. Add the green beans and toss to coat. Remove from the heat and add the remaining 2 tablespoons sherry, the sugar, and the soy sauce. Stir or toss well, transfer to a serving platter, and surround with the chicken pieces. Serve at once.

 Serves 6

Rosemary and Lemon Baked Chicken Thighs

Use the freshest rosemary possible for this recipe. The tender tips of the plant are easier to chop and blend better with the lemon than do the larger, more brittle leaves. Serve with oven-roasted potatoes and sautéed zucchini.

3 small lemons

3 sprigs fresh rosemary

6 large chicken thighs

¼ cup all-purpose flour

½ teaspoon salt

½ teaspoon freshly ground black pepper

2 tablespoons olive oil

Lemon slices, for garnish

1. Using a vegetable peeler, remove the zest from the lemons in long strips. Avoid the bitter white pith underneath the colored skin. Reserve the peeled lemons for their juice. Remove the leaves from the rosemary and place them on a cutting surface. Finely chop the lemon zest with the rosemary to form a fragrant mixture.

2. Use fingers to gently loosen the skin from the chicken thigh to form a pocket. Insert a generous pinch of the lemon-rosemary mixture between the flesh and the skin. (Use about half of the lemon-rosemary mixture in all. Set the remaining mixture aside.)

3. Combine the flour with the salt and pepper on a plate. Dip the chicken in the flour and shake off the excess.

4. Preheat the oven to 400° F. Heat the oil in a cast-iron or other ovenproof skillet over medium-high heat. Place the chicken in the skillet skin side down and cook, turning often, until golden brown, 6 to 8 minutes. Remove from the heat, sprinkle with the remaining lemon-rosemary mixture, and squeeze over the juice from the peeled lemons. Place the skillet in the oven and cook, turning once, until well browned and there are no traces of pink near the bone, about 20 minutes. Serve at once, garnished with thin slices of fresh lemon, if desired.

 **Serves 6**

Chicken Thigh Hash

This delicious hash is sure to please just about everyone! It is great for brunch or for a light dinner. There are several simple preparation steps to this recipe, but they can be done simultaneously to save time.

Poached eggs and a good salad are perfect accompaniments. This is a good recipe for using up leftover chicken. Use about 2½ cups of diced, cold chicken in place of the thighs.

6 large boneless, skinless chicken thighs

2 cups chicken stock

Salt

9 to 12 medium red potatoes (about 1½ pounds), scrubbed and cut into ½-inch dice

1 tablespoon olive oil

1 large onion, finely chopped

1 green bell pepper, finely chopped

½ cup heavy cream

1 tablespoon chopped fresh thyme, or 1 teaspoon dried

Freshly ground black pepper

6 poached large eggs (optional; see Note)

1. Place the chicken in a large skillet and pour over the stock. Add enough cold water to cover and season with a pinch of salt. Bring to a simmer over medium-high heat, then cook until opaque, about 5 minutes. Remove from the heat and let stand, covered, until there are no traces of pink, about 20 minutes. Cut into ½-inch dice. Reserve the stock for another use.

2. Meanwhile, place the potatoes in medium saucepan and add enough cold water to cover. Season with salt and bring to a boil over high heat. Reduce the heat to medium and cook, uncovered, until tender, about 15 minutes. Drain well and spread on paper towels to dry.

3. Heat the oil in a large, heavy skillet over medium-high heat. Add the onion and bell pepper. Cook, stirring often, until softened, about 5 minutes. Remove with a slotted spoon. Wipe the skillet clean.

4. Combine the chicken, potatoes, and onion mixture in a large bowl. Stir in the cream, add the thyme, and season to taste with salt and pepper. Lightly oil the skillet that the onion and pepper were cooked in and place over medium-high heat. Add about one-third of the hash mixture and press down with a spatula. Cook, turning often with the spatula, until lightly browned, 5 to 7 minutes. Season with salt and pepper. The hash is done when there are some nicely crisp sections as well as some soft, tender sec-

tions. Transfer to a warmed plate, keep warm in a low oven, and continue with the remaining hash. Mound the hash on a large platter and top with poached eggs, if desired.

 Serves 6

NOTE: *To poach eggs, fill a medium saucepan with about 2 inches of cold water. Add 1 tablespoon of white vinegar and bring to a boil. Break an egg into a saucer and gently slide it into the water. Reduce the heat to medium high and simmer for 3 to 5 minutes. Remove with a slotted spoon and trim away any stringy tails with scissors. For best results, use fresh eggs. Do not add salt to the water while cooking, as this will toughen the white.*

Chicken Thighs with Nectarines

The nectarine is related to the peach, but is richer and often very juicy. Choose firm fruit and do not overcook; nectarines have a tendency to become mushy when exposed to too much heat. For this recipe, they should be glazed and warmed through, but not soft and shapeless. Look for the freestone variety rather than the clingstone. Fresh apricots could be used, too.

6 large nectarines (1¾ pounds)

2 tablespoons red wine vinegar

1 tablespoon sugar

2 tablespoons unsalted butter

2 tablespoons vegetable oil

6 large or 12 small chicken thighs

Salt and freshly ground black pepper

1. Remove the pits from the nectarines and cut into quarters. Place in a large bowl and sprinkle with the vinegar. Add the sugar and stir to coat. Set aside.

2. Melt the butter with the oil in a large skillet over medium-high heat. Season the thighs with salt and pepper. Cook the thighs, partially covered, until golden brown and cooked through, 10 to 12 minutes per side. Remove to a plate and cover with foil to keep warm.

3. Pour off all but 1 tablespoon of the fat. Add the nectarines, with the vinegar, sugar, and any juices that have accumulated, to the skillet and cook, turning often, until the fruit is slightly softened and lightly caramelized, 5 to 7 minutes. Baste frequently with pan juices. Arrange the nectarines attractively around the chicken and serve at once.

 Serves 6

Crunchy Cornflake Chicken Thighs like Jody's Mom Used to Make

Mr. Will Kellogg discovered, at the turn of the century, that flakes of rolled corn could be made into a cold breakfast cereal. His product changed the way Americans eat breakfast. Jody Weatherstone is a New York food writer whose mother was one of many who later discovered that cornflakes make a really crispy coating for chicken thighs. Serve this nostalgic chicken dish with another comfort food like macaroni and cheese or mom's mashed potatoes.

½ cup all-purpose flour

1 teaspoon salt

½ teaspoon freshly ground black pepper

2 large eggs

2 tablespoons water

1 cup crushed cornflakes

½ cup fresh bread crumbs

1½ teaspoons paprika

1½ teaspoons dry mustard

6 large or 12 small chicken thighs, skin removed

1 tablespoon unsalted butter

1. Preheat the oven to 350°F. Grease a baking sheet large enough to hold the chicken in one flat layer. In a large bowl or baking dish, combine the flour, salt, and pepper. Beat the eggs with the water in a small bowl. Toss the cornflake crumbs with the bread crumbs, paprika, and dry mustard in a separate bowl or dish for dipping.

2. Place the chicken in the flour mixture and turn to coat well. Shake to remove excess flour, then dip in the egg mixture. Drain slightly, then roll in the cornflake mixture to coat. Pat the crumbs gently against the flesh to adhere.

3. Place the chicken pieces skin side up on the baking sheet and bake until lightly browned, about 30 minutes. Cut butter into small pieces and use to dot the top of the chicken. Bake until the chicken is crisp and golden, 12 to 15 minutes longer.

 **Serves 6**

Thighs
Simply Sophisticated

Thanksgiving Chicken Thighs

Here is a simple, one-easy-dish Thanksgiving-esque meal that is good any time of the year! Serve with creamy mashed potatoes for comfort food at its best.

4 tablespoons (½ stick) unsalted butter

2 celery stalks, with leaves, finely chopped

1 medium onion, finely chopped

2 tablespoons finely chopped fresh sage

⅔ cup dried cranberries

1 cup finely chopped walnuts

12 boneless, skinless chicken thighs

1. Preheat the oven to 400°F. Melt 2 tablespoons of the butter in a large skillet over medium-high heat. Add the celery, onion, and sage. Cook, stirring often, until the onion and celery are softened, 3 to 4 minutes. Add the cranberries and walnuts. Transfer to a bowl and cool slightly.

2. Place the remaining 2 tablespoons butter in a baking dish large enough to hold the thighs in one flat layer. Transfer to the oven to melt. Pound the thighs between 2 pieces of parchment paper or plastic wrap to a thickness of ¼ inch. Spread 1 to 2 tablespoons of the stuffing on each thigh, pressing down slightly. Roll into a tight cylinder and secure with a couple of toothpicks. Lay the stuffed thighs seam side down in the hot, buttered dish and sprinkle with any remaining stuffing. Bake until the juices run clear when pierced with a fork, 45 to 50 minutes.

3. Remove the toothpicks and serve on a warmed platter. Spoon over any loose stuffing and pan juices.

 Serves 6

Chicken Thighs with Pasta, Ham, and Swiss Chard

A relative of the beet family, Swiss chard has leaves that are like spinach in taste and texture. Substitute green cabbage, kale, collard, mustard greens, or spinach if chard is not to be found. Lean, boiled ham is best for this pasta dish.

2 cups chicken stock

6 large or 12 small boneless, skinless chicken thighs

1 pound Swiss chard, stalks trimmed

1 pound penne or rigatoni pasta

2 tablespoons olive oil

1 small onion, finely chopped

2 garlic cloves, minced

1/2 cup diced ham or Canadian bacon (about 3 ounces)

1 1/2 teaspoons grated lemon zest

1/2 cup heavy cream

1/2 cup dry white wine

1 tablespoon all-purpose flour

Salt and freshly ground black pepper

1/2 cup grated Romano cheese

1. Bring the stock to a boil in a large skillet or saucepan. Add the chicken thighs and enough water to cover. Reduce the heat to a simmer and cook until just opaque, about 5 minutes.

Remove from the heat, cover, and let stand until the thighs are tender but not quite cooked, about 10 minutes. Remove the chicken from the liquid and cut into 1/2-inch dice.

2. Meanwhile, fill a large pot about 1 inch deep with salted water. Bring to a boil, add the chard, cover, and simmer over medium heat until tender, 3 to 4 minutes. Drain well and finely chop.

3. Bring another large pot of salted water to a boil. Add the pasta and boil rapidly until tender but still firm, 8 to 10 minutes. Drain the pasta well, return to the pot, and toss with 1 tablespoon of the oil.

4. Preheat the oven to 350° F. Heat the remaining tablespoon of oil in a large skillet over medium-high heat. Add the onion and cook, stirring, until slightly softened, about 2 minutes. Add the garlic and cook 1 minute longer. Add the ham, the diced chicken, 1 teaspoon of the lemon zest, the cream, and the wine. Simmer until reduced and slightly thickened, 3 to 4 minutes. Sprinkle over the flour, stir well to blend, and cook 1 to 2 minutes longer or until thick enough to coat the back of a spoon. Season to taste with salt and pepper.

5. Lightly oil a large baking dish. Spread half of the pasta over the bottom and top with half of the chicken mixture.

Top with half of the Swiss chard and sprinkle on half of the Romano cheese. Repeat these layers, ending with the cheese. Sprinkle over the remaining ½ teaspoon of lemon zest, cover with foil, and bake until steaming hot and bubbly, 20 to 25 minutes. Let stand for 5 minutes before serving.

 Serves 6

Thighs *en Papillote* with Apples and Raisins

*The rich, almost ducklike flavor of chicken thighs marries well with raisins and apples. It is important to use a good cooking apple, such as Golden Delicious, Cortland, Winesap, Rome, or Granny Smith. These stay firm when heated rather than turning soft. Serve these **papillotes** with wild rice flavored with orange and pecans—a great fall menu!*

6 large boneless, skinless chicken thighs

Salt and freshly ground black pepper

2 tablespoons unsalted butter, plus additional softened butter for brushing

1 small onion, finely chopped

½ cup golden raisins

3 large cooking apples (1½ pounds), peeled, cored, and cut into eighths

1. Preheat the oven to 375°F. Trim the thighs of fat; season with salt and pepper.

2. Melt 2 tablespoons of the butter in a small skillet over medium-high heat. Add the onion and raisins and cook, stirring, until the onion is softened, 3 to 5 minutes. Remove from heat and set aside.

3. Fold 6 large sheets of parchment paper in half and cut into large heart shapes. Make sure each side of the heart is at least 2 inches larger all around than the chicken thighs. Brush the insides of the hearts lightly with butter. Place a thigh in the center of one side of each of the hearts. Arrange 4 apple slices over the tops of each and spoon over a scant tablespoonful of the onion and raisin mixture. Season with salt and pepper.

4. Fold the other side of the heart over the chicken and, starting at the curve of the heart, crimp the edges together to form a tight seal. Place the packages on 2 large baking sheets. Bake until the paper is browned and puffed, 25 to 30 minutes. Serve on individual plates as soon as possible. (Be careful when opening the packages, from which steam will escape quickly, possibly harming unsuspecting guests.)

 **Serves 6**

Thighs Coq au Vin

*Some dishes require a little loving care in the preparation. Recipes like the following are best done over a few days, in incremental steps. Marinate one day, brown and cook the next day, sauté mushrooms and glaze onions later . . . then combine all in a large casserole and refrigerate until ready to heat and serve. Thighs make great **coq au vin.** They stand up well to long cooking and have lots of rich flavor. Serve with plain boiled potatoes and a crusty fresh baguette to help savor the sauce!*

FOR THE MARINADE

6 large chicken thighs

2 medium onions, quartered

3 medium carrots, peeled and coarsely chopped

2 celery stalks, coarsely chopped

1 tablespoon olive oil

Several sprigs fresh thyme, or 2 teaspoons dried

1 bottle hearty red wine

FOR THE STEW

½ pound slab bacon, cut into ¼-inch pieces

2 heaping tablespoons all-purpose flour

3 or 4 large tomatoes, peeled, seeded, and chopped, or 1 large can (28 ounces) peeled tomatoes, drained and chopped

3 tablespoons unsalted butter

2 tablespoons vegetable oil

10 to 12 large mushrooms

25 to 30 tiny pearl onions, peeled

2 teaspoons sugar

Salt and freshly ground black pepper

1 tablespoon chopped fresh parsley

1. For the marinade, trim the thighs of all fat and place in a large nonreactive bowl. Add the onions, carrots, celery, olive oil, and thyme. Blend well and pour over the wine. Cover and marinate for 30 minutes at room temperature or 2 hours in the refrigerator. (The thighs can marinate for up to 2 days, if desired.)

2. To prepare the stew, remove the chicken from the marinade and pat dry. Strain the marinade and reserve the solids and liquid separately.

3. Cook the bacon in a large Dutch oven or casserole over medium-high heat until browned, about 5 minutes. Remove the bacon with a slotted spoon and set aside. Brown the chicken in the hot bacon fat, about 5 minutes on each side. Remove to drain on paper towels and pour off all but 2 tablespoons fat. Add the onions, carrots, celery, and thyme from the marinade. Cook, stirring

often, over medium-high heat until the vegetables are slightly softened, 3 to 5 minutes. Sprinkle over the flour and stir to coat. Cook, stirring often, until the flour has been absorbed and begins to turn a light brown. Stir in the tomatoes and cook 1 minute longer. Pour in the wine from the marinade and stir to scrape up any cooking bits left on the bottom of the casserole. Return the thighs to the casserole, cover, and cook over medium heat until the thighs are tender, 25 to 30 minutes.

4. Meanwhile, melt 2 tablespoons of the butter with the oil in a small skillet over medium-high heat. Add the mushrooms and cook, stirring or tossing the skillet often, until lightly browned, 5 to 7 minutes. Drain on paper towels and set aside. Place the pearl onions in a heavy, medium saucepan and pour over enough cold water to cover. Add the remaining tablespoon of butter and the sugar, and season to taste with salt and pepper. Bring to a boil over high heat. Boil until all of the liquid has evaporated. Reduce the heat slightly. Stir and shake the pan constantly until the residue of sugar begins to caramelize the onions. Continue cooking, stirring constantly, until golden brown. Remove from heat and set aside.

5. Transfer the thighs to a large, deep, warmed serving platter and cover with foil. Strain the sauce into a small saucepan, discard the solids, and bring to a boil over high heat. Cook until reduced and concentrated in flavor, 5 to 10 minutes. Season with salt and pepper (see Note). Add the mushrooms, pearl onions, and reserved cooked bacon to the sauce. Season with salt and pepper. Pour the sauce over the chicken and serve at once, sprinkled with parsley.

 **Serves 6**

NOTE: *If the sauce is too thin at this point, mix equal amounts of butter and flour in a small bowl to make what is known as a **beurre manie**. Drop pea-size amounts of this thickening mixture into the hot liquid and whisk quickly to blend. If the sauce is too thick, thin with chicken stock. Use as much as is necessary of either thickener or thinner to reach the desired consistency. The sauce should be velvety and smooth, not thick and gloppy.*

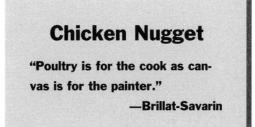

Chicken Nugget

"Poultry is for the cook as canvas is for the painter."

—Brillat-Savarin

Twice-Cooked Thighs with Lemon and Garlic

This recipe comes from an American friend who lives in Paris. Nora Carey is one of the finest cooks I know. Her attention to detail and quest for perfection turns something like simple chicken thighs into a memorable dish. These thighs take a little extra time and trouble but, boy, oh boy . . . the results are worth the effort. Serve with garlic mashed potatoes and a large, green salad.

12 small chicken thighs

3 tablespoons unsalted butter, softened

Salt and freshly ground black pepper

2 tablespoons olive oil

2 garlic cloves, unpeeled and crushed

2 tablespoons fresh lemon juice

1 tablespoon grated lemon zest

1. Preheat the oven to 400°F. Pat dry the thighs with paper towels. Slip a teaspoon or so of the butter under the skin of each thigh and rub all over with the remaining butter. Season well with salt and pepper. Place the thighs skin side up in a lightly buttered baking dish large enough to hold the thighs in one flat layer. Top with a buttered piece of heavy-duty foil, cover tightly, and bake for 45 minutes.

2. Heat the oil with the garlic in a large skillet over medium-high heat. Remove the baking dish from the oven. Carefully transfer the thighs to the hot skillet. Reserve all the cooking juices in the baking dish. Cook, turning often, until well browned, 7 to 10 minutes. Remove to a plate or platter and cover with foil to keep warm.

3. Pour off the fat from the skillet. Reduce the heat to low, and add the lemon juice and the zest. Cover and cook about 2 minutes.

4. Pour the reserved cooking juices from the baking dish into the skillet and bring to a boil. Boil until thickened and syrupy. Remove the garlic and discard. Season the sauce with salt and pepper. Spoon over the thighs and serve at once.

 Serves 6

Chicken Nugget

James Beard was a "dark meat man." Next to dark meat, his preference for chicken parts were the gizzards and hearts. All in all, chicken was one of his favorite foods.

Jamaican Jerk Chicken Thighs

Jerk chicken gets its name because the meat becomes so tender that it can be jerked right off the bone! It can be marinated for up to 24 hours if time permits. This recipe is a flavorful dish with plenty of heat but not as much as the traditional jerk, which can be overwhelming. If you want to experience sizzling heat, substitute Scotch bonnet chilies for the jalapeños as they do in Jamaica. Be sure to wear rubber gloves when handling them!

2 medium onions, quartered

2 to 3 jalapeño peppers, halved and seeded

2 garlic cloves, peeled

1 piece fresh ginger, 2 inches long, peeled

1 tablespoon grated lime zest

1 tablespoon salt

1 tablespoon freshly ground black pepper

2 tablespoons sugar

1 tablespoon chopped fresh thyme, or 2 teaspoons dried

1 tablespoon ground allspice

1 cup orange juice

1 cup white wine vinegar

½ cup soy sauce

6 large or 12 small chicken thighs

1. Combine the onions, jalapeño peppers, garlic, ginger, lime zest, salt, black pepper, sugar, thyme, and allspice in the bowl of a food processor. Puree until smooth. Blend the orange juice, vinegar, and soy sauce in a large measuring cup with a pour spout. Add this liquid to the processor with the motor running and process until smooth. (Add only half the amount of liquid if the capacity of your food processor is small. Transfer to a bowl and stir in the remaining liquid by hand.)

2. Place the chicken in a large, nonreactive baking dish or bowl. Pour over the marinade, turn to coat, cover, and leave at room temperature for ½ hour. (Refrigerate for up to 24 hours, if desired.)

3. Preheat the oven to 400° F. Remove the chicken from the marinade and place skin side up on a rack in a large roasting pan or baking dish. Brush the chicken with the marinade and bake until lightly browned and a fork inserted near the bone enters easily and there are no traces of pink, 40 to 45 minutes. Baste occasionally with the marinade. Remove from the oven and preheat the broiler. Transfer the pan to the broiler and broil 4 to 6 inches from the source of heat until crisp and lightly charred, 3 to 4 minutes. Watch carefully and turn often to prevent burning. Serve at once.

 Serves 6

Caribbean Plantain and Chicken Thigh Casserole

Plantain is the cooking banana found throughout Africa and the Caribbean. Green (unripe) bananas can be used, but they tend to loose their shape when cooked. If neither are available, sweet potatoes make a perfect substitute.

3 green plantains, peeled and cut into ¹/₂-inch slices

6 large boneless, skinless chicken thighs, cut into 1¹/₂-inch pieces

¹/₄ cup lime juice

2 garlic cloves, minced

2 tablespoons chopped fresh parsley

1 teaspoon salt plus to taste

¹/₂ teaspoon freshly ground black pepper plus to taste

2 tablespoons unsalted butter

2 medium onions, finely chopped

2 celery stalks, finely chopped

6 plum tomatoes, cored and cut into small dice

1 teaspoon sugar

2 large eggs, lightly beaten

2 cups grated Cheddar cheese

Salt and freshly ground black pepper

1. Bring a large pot of salted water to a boil. Add the plantain slices and cook rapidly until bright yellow and tender, 10 to 12 minutes. Drain well.

2. Combine the chicken, lime juice, garlic, parsley, salt, and pepper in a large bowl and toss well. Cover and marinate for 10 minutes.

3. Meanwhile, melt the butter in a large skillet over medium-high heat. Add the onions and celery and cook, stirring often, until softened, 3 to 5 minutes. Add the tomatoes and cook 4 to 5 minutes longer. Stir in the sugar and season to taste with additional salt and pepper.

4. Preheat the oven to 350° F. Lightly oil a large baking dish or casserole. Layer the bottom with half of the plantains. Remove the chicken from the marinade and arrange on top of the plantains. (Reserve the marinade.) Spread the tomato mixture over the plantains. Pour over the beaten eggs and sprinkle with half of the grated cheese. Top with the remaining plantains and drizzle over the chicken marinade. Sprinkle over the remaining cheese, cover with foil, and bake for 30 minutes. Remove the foil and bake 20 minutes longer or until bubbly and the cheese begins to brown. Remove from the oven and let stand 10 minutes before serving.

 Serves 6

Fajitas with Tequila-Marinated Thighs

Tortilla-wrapped fajitas made with various Tex-Mex ingredients originated in Texas and they have become very popular, probably because they're fun to eat and perfect for a party. These are made with thighs that have been marinated in tequila and lime juice. Now, that's a great way to get the party started!

- ⅔ cup tequila
- ⅓ cup lime juice
- ¼ cup chopped fresh cilantro
- ¼ teaspoon ground cumin
- 1 small jalapeño pepper, seeded and minced
- ½ teaspoon salt
- ½ teaspoon freshly ground black pepper
- 2 scallions (green onions), white part only, thinly sliced
- 12 flour tortillas, 10 inches in diameter
- 6 large boneless, skinless chicken thighs
- 2 cups diced tomatoes
- 4 cups thinly shredded lettuce
- 1 cup sour cream
- 1 cup finely chopped red onion

1. Combine the tequila, lime juice, cilantro, cumin, jalapeño, salt, pepper, and scallions in a large, nonreactive bowl or baking dish. Add the chicken and marinate, turning a few times, for 30 minutes at room temperature, or several hours refrigerated.

2. Wrap the tortillas in foil and keep warm in a low oven. Preheat a stove-top grill or heavy-bottomed skillet and brush lightly with oil. Remove the chicken from the marinade and grill or sauté over medium-high heat until cooked through, 6 to 7 minutes on each side. Spoon over some of the marinade at the beginning of cooking if desired. Allow the chicken to cool slightly and cut into ½-inch-wide strips.

3. To serve, place the chicken on a warmed platter. Serve the tomatoes, lettuce, sour cream, and red onion in individual bowls. Place the warmed tortillas in a basket lined with a clean towel. Allow each person to fill his or her own tortillas.

 Serves 6

Pan-Fried Chicken Croquettes

The rich, dark flesh and the juiciness of chicken thighs make it the perfect part for this recipe. There are a few steps that can be taken to ensure that these are the lightest, most delicate croquettes you'll ever have. The recipe works best if the ingredients are kept cold. Chill the bowl of the food processor, as well as the bowl the ground mixture is mixed in, and place a tray of ice on the work surface where the croquettes are formed, especially if it is a hot, humid day. Work quickly; warm hands can make the mixture sticky. Some chopped fresh herbs can be added to the ground chicken, if desired. Serve with Tomato Sauce (page 226).

3 slices white sandwich bread (3 ounces), torn into small pieces

½ cup milk

4 tablespoons (½ stick) unsalted butter

1 medium onion, finely chopped

1 large celery stalk, peeled and finely chopped

6 large boneless, skinless chicken thighs

1 large egg

1 teaspoon salt

½ teaspoon freshly ground black pepper

About 1 cup all-purpose flour

Salt and freshly ground black pepper

2 tablespoons vegetable oil

1. Place the bowl and blade of the food processor in the refrigerator to chill. Combine the bread and milk in a small bowl. Stir gently and allow to stand for a few minutes or until the liquid is absorbed.

2. Melt 2 tablespoons of the butter in a small skillet over medium-high heat. Add the onion and celery. Cook, stirring often, until softened, 3 to 4 minutes. Set aside to cool.

3. Cut the chicken into long strips and place in the chilled bowl of the processor. Process, scrapping the sides of the bowl often, until very smooth, about 2 minutes. Add the soaked bread and process about 1 minute longer or until well blended. (This procedure might have to be done in 2 batches depending on the capacity of the processor.) Transfer this mixture to a large bowl.

4. Add the cooked onion and celery, the egg, salt, and pepper to the bowl. Stir with a wooden spoon until blended. Do not overwork the mixture or it will be tough. Cover and chill until firm, about 30 minutes.

Thighs

5. Generously flour a large work surface. Use a ⅓ cup measure to scoop out 12 equal portions of the chicken mixture. Working with one portion at a time (keep the remaining portions refrigerated to facilitate forming the croquettes), make small cakes that measure about 3 inches wide and 1 inch thick. The mixture will be sticky, so do not be afraid to use as much flour as necessary to form the cakes. Handle carefully, as they will be fragile. Shift the formed cakes from hand to hand to remove excess flour. Place on a baking sheet lined with parchment paper and refrigerate until ready to prepare.

6. Season the croquettes with salt and pepper. Melt the remaining 2 tablespoons butter with the vegetable oil over medium-high heat in a large skillet. When the butter stops sizzling, add the croquettes. Cook, partially covered to prevent splattering, until well browned, about 10 minutes on each side. (Do not overcrowd the skillet or the croquettes will not properly brown. Fry in 2 batches if necessary.) Drain on paper towels, season with additional salt and pepper, and serve at once.

 Serves 6

Chicken Nugget

The Cinematic Chicken: **While the Marx Brothers gave us** *Duck Soup,* **the chicken has also been celebrated on the silver screen:**

- ***Chicken Every Sunday***—**This 1948 film stars Celeste Holm and a very young Natalie Wood.**
- ***The Chicken Chronicles***—**In 1977, this was Steve Guttenberg's first film.**
- ***The Egg and I***—**A 1957 film about chicken farming that stars Fred McMurray.**
- ***Chicken Wagon Family***—**This 1939 film stars Jane Withers and Leo Carrillo.**
- ***Dynamite Chicken***—**A 1971 film that features Richard Pryor, John Lennon, and Yoko Ono.**

Cuban Stewed Chicken Thighs with Tricolor Peppers

Use Italian sausage made with turkey, if desired, for a milder flavor and to reduce the fat. Serve with plenty of boiled rice and accompany with cold beer.

2 tablespoons olive oil

½ pound Italian sausage

½ cup hearty red wine

4 large chicken thighs, skin removed

1 large onion, thinly sliced

1 red bell pepper, seeded and thinly sliced

1 green bell pepper, seeded and thinly sliced

1 yellow bell pepper, seeded and thinly sliced

1 teaspoon chili powder

1 teaspoon dried oregano

½ teaspoon imported sweet Hungarian paprika

1 large can (28 ounces) peeled tomatoes, drained and coarsely chopped

Salt and freshly ground black pepper

1. Heat the oil in a large Dutch oven or casserole over medium-high heat. Add the sausage and cook, stirring and breaking into pieces, until browned, 4 to 5 minutes. Remove the sausage with a slotted spoon, pour off all but 1 tablespoon of the fat, and add half of the wine to the pot. Increase the heat to high and boil, scraping up the browned bits from the bottom of the pot, until almost all of the liquid has evaporated. Add the chicken and cook until lightly browned, 3 to 4 minutes per side.

2. Return the sausage to the casserole. Add the onion, bell peppers, chili powder, oregano, and paprika. Cover and cook over medium heat until the vegetables are slightly tender, about 5 minutes. Stir in the tomatoes, cover, and cook until there is no trace of pink near the center of the thighs, about 45 minutes. Remove the cover, increase the heat to medium high, and cook until the pan juices are slightly thickened, about 10 minutes. Stir in the remaining ¼ cup wine and season to taste with salt and pepper.

3. Pull the flesh off the bones of the thighs with 2 forks and discard the bones. Stir well to blend the stew and serve at once on a warmed platter.

 Serves 6

Chicken Thighs Stuffed with Feta Cheese and Spinach

The yogurt and flour coating called for here gives chicken thighs a deliciously crisp coating with a beautiful dark color. Serve with orzo or wide egg noodles tossed with butter.

- **3 tablespoons olive oil**
- **1 small onion, finely chopped**
- **1 teaspoon chopped fresh thyme, or ½ teaspoon dried**
- **1 garlic clove, minced**
- **1 pound fresh spinach, washed and coarsely chopped**
- **½ cup fresh bread crumbs**
- **½ cup crumbled feta cheese**
- **12 boneless chicken thighs, with or without skin**
- **1 cup plain yogurt**
- **½ cup all-purpose flour**
- **Salt and freshly ground black pepper**
- **Several sprigs fresh thyme, for garnish**

1. Heat 1 tablespoon of the oil in a large skillet over medium-high heat. Add the onion, thyme, and garlic. Cook, stirring often, until the onion is softened, 3 to 4 minutes. Shake off the excess water from the spinach but do not dry. Add to the skillet and cook, stirring constantly, until wilted, 1 to 2 minutes. Transfer to a bowl and cool. Stir in the bread crumbs and feta cheese.

2. Preheat the oven to 400°F. Pound the chicken between 2 pieces of parchment paper or plastic wrap to a thickness of about ¼ inch. Spread about 2 tablespoons of the stuffing over each thigh (not over the skin, if present) and roll into a tight cylinder. Secure with 1 or 2 toothpicks.

3. Place the yogurt and flour in separate bowls. Dip the chicken first in the yogurt, then roll in the flour. Heat the remaining 2 tablespoons oil in an oven-proof cast-iron skillet over medium-high heat. Add the chicken thighs and brown on all sides, 5 to 6 minutes. Leave the chicken in the skillet and transfer to the oven. Bake, turning occasionally, until the thighs are a dark, rich brown, 25 to 30 minutes.

4. Remove the toothpicks and transfer to warmed serving plates. Season with salt and pepper. Garnish with the sprigs of fresh thyme and serve at once.

 Serves 6

Soy-Marinated Chicken Thighs with Spicy Tahini Sauce

This is my own brand of fusion cooking. The Asian flavors of soy sauce, sake, ginger, and chilies mix with tahini, a sesame paste popular in Middle Eastern cooking. The blend makes the perfect match for the "meaty" thighs.

½ cup soy sauce

½ cup sake (rice wine)

1 piece fresh ginger, 1 inch long, peeled and minced

2 garlic cloves, minced

2 small, dried red chilies, coarsely chopped

1 tablespoon brown sugar

6 large or 12 small chicken thighs, skin removed

2 tablespoons peanut oil

⅓ cup tahini (sesame paste)

Dash of cayenne pepper

Dash of red pepper flakes

2 scallions (green onions), sliced into 1-inch pieces on a bias

1. Combine the soy sauce, sake, ginger, garlic, chilies, and brown sugar in a large bowl or baking dish. Trim the thighs of excess fat and place in the marinade. Turn a few times to coat. Cover and refrigerate for 30 minutes at room temperature, or several hours refrigerated.

2. Preheat the oven to 400° F. In a large, ovenproof, cast-iron skillet, preferably with raised ridges, heat the peanut oil over medium-high heat. Remove the chicken from the marinade and cook until browned, 3 to 4 minutes per side. Leave the chicken in the skillet and transfer to the oven. Bake, turning once, until a fork inserted near the bone enters the flesh easily and the chicken is cooked through, about 15 minutes.

3. Meanwhile, transfer the marinade to a small saucepan and bring to a boil. Reduce the heat to medium high and simmer until slightly thickened and reduced, about 5 minutes. Strain and discard the solids. Whisk in the tahini and season to taste with cayenne and red pepper flakes.

4. Transfer the cooked chicken to a warmed serving platter. Drizzle over a small amount of the sauce and serve the rest on the side. Scatter the scallions over the top and serve at once.

 **Serves 6**

Sesame Baked Chicken Thighs with Drizzled Honey

This is a great recipe to feature on a buffet table. Serve on a large platter and surround with watercress for garnish. No matter how you serve it, you'll find it to be a crowd-pleaser.

6 large or 12 small chicken thighs

Salt and freshly ground black pepper

3 large eggs

¼ cup milk

1 cup untoasted sesame seeds

1 cup fresh bread crumbs

½ cup honey

2 tablespoons lemon juice

1. Preheat the oven to 375° F. Lightly oil a baking sheet large enough to hold the thighs in one flat layer. Trim the thighs of excess fat and season both sides with salt and pepper.

2. In a large bowl or wide baking dish, beat the eggs with the milk until well blended. In a separate bowl, mix the sesame seeds with the bread crumbs. Dip the thighs in the egg mixture, drain slightly, then transfer to the sesame seed and bread crumb mixture. Turn to thoroughly coat on both sides. Place the coated thighs on the oiled baking sheet. Bake skin side up until golden brown and cooked through, 45 minutes to 1 hour.

3. Meanwhile, combine the honey and lemon juice in a small saucepan. Stir over very low heat until blended and smooth. Remove from heat and keep covered until ready to serve.

4. Remove the thighs from the oven and arrange on a warmed serving platter. Gently reheat the honey and lemon mixture and spoon a scant tablespoonful over each thigh while still hot. Serve at once.

 Serves 6

Chicken Nugget

Dealing in poultry has long been considered a separate trade to that of butchery. At the end of the thirteenth century, the Company of Poulters was active in London. Their shops were in an area close to the Bank of England, known as Poultry, and the industry come to be known for the location.

Sautéed Chicken Thighs with Madeira Sauce

Any fortified wine can be used in place of Madeira. Port, sherry, or even Cognac make good substitutes. Serve with almost any kind of potato dish and mounds of steamed spinach flavored with a touch of lemon.

6 large or 12 small chicken thighs

Salt and freshly ground black pepper

2 tablespoons unsalted butter

2 tablespoons vegetable oil

1 cup all-purpose flour

½ cup chicken stock

1 cup Madeira wine

1 tablespoon chopped fresh parsley

1. Trim the thighs of excess fat and season with salt and pepper. Melt the butter with the oil over medium-high heat in a large, heavy skillet. Place the flour in a large, deep bowl and dip the thighs in one at a time, turning a few times to thoroughly coat. Shake off the excess flour and place the thighs in the skillet, skin side down. Cook until golden brown, about 5 minutes per side. Transfer the chicken to a plate or platter.

2. Pour off all the fat from the skillet. Add the chicken stock, increase the heat to high, and bring to a boil. Cook rapidly, whisking to pick up any cooking bits in the bottom of the skillet, until reduced by half. Return the thighs to the skillet, reduce the heat to medium high, and cook, partially covered, until the thighs are tender when a fork is inserted close to the bone and cooked through, about 20 minutes. Remove the cooked thighs to a warmed serving platter and cover with foil to keep warm.

3. Skim any fat from the surface of the liquid in the skillet and increase the heat to high. Pour in the Madeira and boil, whisking often, until the liquid in the skillet has reduced by half and is thickened, about 3 minutes. Spoon the sauce over the thighs, sprinkle slightly with salt and pepper to taste, and garnish with the parsley just before serving.

 **Serves 6**

Lemongrass and Coconut Chicken Thigh Curry

Do not be alarmed if the sauce is thinner than what you might be used to. This is an authentic version of a true Asian classic. Serve lots of jasmine or basmati rice to soak up the flavorful sauce.

Almost any kind of fresh chilies can be used if serrano chilies are not available. Habanero or poblano are good substitutes. A pinch of red pepper flakes can be used in place of the red chilies, if desired.

4 stalks lemongrass

2 cups chicken stock

1 piece fresh ginger, 1 inch long, peeled and minced

½ lime

2 stems fresh cilantro, plus 1 chopped stem for garnish

2 small dried chilies, coarsely chopped

1 tablespoon brown sugar

1 tablespoon soy sauce

2 tablespoons peanut oil

4 shallots, thinly sliced

4 serrano chilies, seeded, deveined, and minced

6 large boneless, skinless chicken thighs, cut into 3 pieces

1 cup unsweeetened coconut milk

1. Discard the outer layers, tips, and roots of the lemongrass, leaving about 6 inches of stalks. Chop coarsely.

2. Combine the chicken stock, half of the chopped lemongrass, the ginger, lime, cilantro stems, and dried chilies in a medium saucepan. Bring to a boil over high heat, reduce the heat to medium, and simmer until reduced by half, about 15 minutes. Remove from the heat and stir in the brown sugar and soy sauce.

3. Heat the oil in a large, heavy skillet over medium-high heat. Add shallots, remaining lemongrass, and serrano chilies. Cook, stirring often, over medium-high heat until the shallots are softened, 3 to 4 minutes. Strain the chicken stock mixture into the saucepan, discarding solids. Bring the contents of the saucepan to a boil, then add the chicken and coconut milk. Reduce the heat to medium, cover loosely, and simmer, turning once, until the chicken is firm and cooked through, 20 to 25 minutes. Remove the chicken, increase the heat to high, and boil until the sauce is slightly thickened, about 5 minutes. Reduce the heat to medium low, return the chicken to the skillet, and cook for about 3 minutes to warm through. Serve over rice, garnished with the chopped cilantro.

 **Serves 6**

Oven-Baked Chicken Thighs with Beets and Fennel

Fresh beets are a must for this recipe. Canned beets are too soft and will not stand up to long cooking. The effect of this dish is unusual: the chicken basically roasts and the vegetables slightly caramelize. A large baking dish is essential. If the dish is too small, there will not be enough room to properly cook the ingredients. Serve with baked potatoes for a hearty meal.

6 small beets, greens removed

4 large fennel bulbs, trimmed

2 small onions, quartered

2 tablespoons olive oil

6 large or 12 small chicken thighs

Salt and freshly ground black pepper

1. Preheat the oven to 400°F. Use a paring knife to remove the roots and stem ends from the beets. Scrub clean with a vegetable brush and cut each beet into quarters. Cut the fennel into quarters and trim away some of the tough, inner core. (Leave enough of the core to hold the quarters together.) Place the beets, fennel, and onions in a large baking dish. Pour over the olive oil and toss or stir to thoroughly coat.

2. Place the thighs skin side up in the baking dish over the vegetables. Season the chicken and vegetables with salt and pepper. Bake in the oven until the vegetables are tender and the chicken is cooked through and the skin of the thighs is golden brown and crisp, about 1 hour. Use tongs to turn the vegetables and baste with a large spoon frequently during cooking.

3. Serve the chicken on a large warmed platter. Surround with the roasted vegetables.

 **Serves 6**

Braised Alsatian Chicken Thighs with Sauerkraut and Bacon

Choucroute is a personal favorite. All sorts of yummy pork products like ham, sausage, shanks, and bacon are cooked with sauerkraut and juniper berries for a traditional French-German dish that can't be beat. I've called for smoked slab bacon in this chicken thigh variation. It is worth seeking out for optimum flavor and effect. If not available, use ¼ pound sliced bacon and cut it into small pieces.

I love the gin flavor of juniper berries,

but they are unusual. If you or your guests are not used to them, you might want to tie the berries in a cheesecloth bundle that can be easily removed just before serving. The flavor will have permeated the dish during cooking, but the possibility of biting down on the whole berries, which are somewhat like mild peppercorns, will be eliminated.

This is a hearty dish. Serve with plain boiled potatoes and a green salad. Beer is the perfect accompaniment.

¼ pound smoked slab bacon, cut into ¼ × 1-inch pieces

1 tablespoon vegetable oil

12 small chicken thighs

Salt and freshly ground black pepper

2 large onions, thinly sliced

1 cup flat beer

1 pound packaged or canned sauerkraut, drained

1 tablespoon juniper berries

1. Combine the bacon with the oil in a large nonstick skillet. Cook over medium-high heat, stirring often, until the bacon is lightly browned and the fat is rendered, 3 to 5 minutes. Remove the bacon with a slotted spoon and set aside.

Season the thighs with salt and pepper, add to the skillet, and cook, turning often, until browned, 5 to 7 minutes. Transfer the chicken to a heavy, oven-proof casserole.

2. Preheat the oven to 375° F. Pour off and discard all the fat from the skillet. Add the onions and cook over medium-high heat, stirring often, until softened, 3 to 5 minutes. Pour in the beer, increase the heat to high, bring to a boil, and cook rapidly until the liquid has reduced by half. Stir constantly to pick up any cooking bits left in the bottom of the skillet. Stir in the sauerkraut, juniper berries, and cooked bacon.

3. Pour the contents of the skillet over the thighs, spreading the mixture so that the sauerkraut completely covers the chicken. Cover and cook in the oven until the chicken is very tender and cooked through, about 45 minutes. Serve the thighs on a large, warmed platter. Mound the sauerkraut over the top and surround with the bacon. Spoon over any juices in the bottom of the casserole and serve at once.

 Serves 6

Moroccan Spiced Chicken Thighs

Although the list of ingredients here appears to be a long one, most are probably already on your spice shelf. Preserved lemons are sometimes available in specialty stores that cater to a Middle Eastern clientele. They are quite easy to prepare at home (see Note).

¼ **teaspoon fennel seeds**

¼ **teaspoon cumin seeds**

4 **allspice berries**

10 **black peppercorns**

4 **whole cloves**

1 **cinnamon stick, 4 inches long**

¼ **teaspoon imported, sweet Hungarian paprika**

¼ **teaspoon ground ginger**

¼ **teaspoon turmeric**

2 **tablespoons raisins**

1 **small onion, finely chopped**

2 **preserved lemons (see Note)**

2 **tablespoons olive oil**

6 **large chicken thighs, trimmed of excess fat and skin**

2 **tablespoons chopped fresh parsley**

1. Combine the fennel, cumin, allspice, peppercorns, cloves, and cinnamon stick in a spice or coffee grinder and blend to a fine powder. Transfer to the bowl of a food processor and add the paprika, ginger, turmeric, raisins, and onion. Squeeze in the juice from the preserved lemons. Remove the zest from the lemons with a small, sharp knife or vegetable peeler and add to the bowl. (Avoid the bitter white pith.) Process the mixture until finely chopped, scraping down the sides of the bowl as necessary. With the motor running, add the olive oil in a slow stream until a paste forms.

2. Spread the paste on the chicken, coasting well on all sides. Cover and refrigerate for at least 20 minutes and up to 1 hour.

3. Preheat and oil a stove-top grill. Alternatively, heat and oil a cast-iron skillet. Place the chicken skin side down and cook over medium-high heat for about 10 minutes. Using a spatula, carefully turn the chicken over, being careful not to lose too much of the coating. Brush with any remaining spice mixture and cook until nicely browned and there are no traces of pink, 15 to 20 minutes. If the chicken begins to brown too fast, lower the heat and cover. Continue cooking until there are no traces of pink

near the bone. Remove the cover and brown a minute or two to crisp the coated skin. Garnish with a sprinkle of chopped parsley and serve at once.

 Serves 6

Chicken Nugget

Russia has gone crazy for chicken. After the fall of communism, the marina for American chickens became a windfall for large U.S. poultry concerns. *The New York Times* reported recently that, astoundingly, poultry accounts for one third of all American exports to Russia. Russian consumers favor American birds, which have become to symbolize quality, a new and growing demand in the modern state.

NOTE: *Preserved lemons are a staple of Moroccan cooking. Distinctive and delicious, they take a week to mature on the kitchen counter, but the result is well worth the effort. Preserved lemons add depth of flavor to salads, sauces, dressings, and soups. They keep up to two months in the refrigerator, once sealed with oil.*

To make preserved lemons: Sterilize a $1\frac{1}{2}$-quart jar. Wash and dry about 16 lemons. Cut 8 of the lemons in half, and then score the cut sides with an x so the base is still intact. Place the lemons in the jar, filling to the top. (You may need a few more or a few less lemons depending on the size of the lemons and the shape of the jar.) Add a couple of cinnamon sticks and a few whole cloves to the jar, if desired. Pour kosher salt into the jar to fill it. Squeeze the remaining 8 lemons and add their juice to the jar. Tightly cover the jar and keep at room temperature for 1 week, shaking the jar once a day.

After a week, the lemons are ready to use. To store, pour 1 inch of liquid off the top. Pour in enough olive oil to form a 1-inch layer. Store in the refrigerator until ready to use. Rinse the lemons with cool water before using.

Simply Sophisticated

Tuscan Stewed Chicken Thighs with White Beans and Olives

Dried beans are nutritious, inexpensive, and taste great. We use green olives here for flavor and color contrast. For a rustic presentation, serve this dish as is. If you prefer, remove and discard the bones from the meat and ladle into wide bowls. Either way, serve with lots of crusty bread to sop up the juices!

- **2 tablespoons olive oil**
- **4 large chicken thighs, skin and excess fat removed**
- **Salt and freshly ground black pepper**
- **1 medium onion, finely chopped**
- **1 large carrot, peeled and finely chopped**
- **2 celery stalks, thinly sliced**
- **2 garlic cloves, minced**
- **1 bay leaf**
- **1 teaspoon fresh thyme leaves, or $\frac{1}{2}$ teaspoon dried**
- **1 tablespoon chopped fresh rosemary**
- **1 pound (about 2 cups) dried cannellini or great northern beans, soaked overnight in cold water**
- **4 cups chicken stock**
- **$\frac{1}{2}$ cup chopped pitted green olives**
- **2 tablespoons chopped fresh parsley**

1. Heat the oil in a Dutch oven over medium-high heat. Season the chicken thighs with salt and pepper. Add to the Dutch oven and cook until lightly browned, about 4 minutes per side. Remove to a plate or platter. Add the onion, carrot, celery, and garlic. Cook, stirring often, until the onion is softened, about 5 minutes. Add the bay leaf, thyme, and rosemary. Stir in the beans, add the chicken stock, and raise the heat to high. Bring to a boil, add the chicken thighs, cover, and reduce the heat to medium. Cover and cook until the beans are tender and the chicken separates easily from the bone, 45 minutes to 1 hour.

2. Stir in the olives and parsley. Cover and simmer about 10 minutes longer or until most of the liquid is absorbed. Season to taste with salt and pepper and serve at once.

 **Serves 6**

Chicken Nugget

A 3.0 ounce (85 gram) serving of baked skinless chicken breast contains 24 grams of protein, only 1.5 grams of fat, and just 116 calories.

Drumsticks

The drumstick, the lower portion of the leg, is handy and fun to eat, but it seems to vary a lot in size. Two or three drumsticks usually constitute a serving. The following recipes were developed with drumsticks that weigh 4 to 6 ounces each.

Drumstick Tips

- Drumsticks should be plump, broad, and well fleshed. Avoid drumsticks that show signs of bad processing, like ripped skins, bruises, and excess blood.
- Drumsticks have more sinews and chewy tendons than other parts. It is impossible to remove these unless the drumsticks are boned, and even then it takes great effort to strip them clean. The flesh is tender and succulent, however, and certainly one of America's favorite ways to eat chicken.

Boning a Drumstick

1. Starting at the wide end, use a sharp knife to cut through the connective tissue all around the joint.
2. Place the knife edge perpendicular to the bone and begin scraping and pushing the flesh toward the narrow end of the drumstick. Once all the flesh is at the narrow end, put the knife down and carefully but firmly use your hand to push the flesh over the knuckle (like turning a shirt sleeve inside out).
3. Firmly grasp the loose flesh and pull it free of the knuckle. Trim away sinews and use your fingers to turn the flesh skin side out.

Drumsticks

Quick and Easy

Drumstick Packets with Cherry Tomatoes

Use small cherry tomatoes, if possible, or cut larger ones in half. Yellow cherry tomatoes have less flavor, but give a nice color contrast when mixed with red. Basil can be used in place of the savory, if desired. This is a great lazy-summer dish. I like to do this on the grill for a quick, easy-cleanup main course that makes good use of local produce.

12 medium to large drumsticks

Salt and freshly ground black pepper

30 to 36 small cherry tomatoes

12 sprigs fresh thyme

12 sprigs fresh savory

¾ cup dry white wine

1. Preheat the oven to 350°F. Alternatively, prepare a charcoal fire and allow the coals to burn to a gray ash.

2. Cut 6 squares of foil that measure 12 inches each. Brush each square lightly with olive oil and place 2 of the drumsticks, facing in opposite directions, in the center. Season with salt and pepper and surround with 5 or 6 tomatoes. Place one sprig of thyme and one sprig of savory on each drumstick. Spoon 2 tablespoons of white wine over each pair of drumsticks. Bring the opposite corners of the foil together and crimp the edges to seal.

3. Place the packets in the oven and bake until the chicken is tender and cooked through, 30 to 35 minutes. Or, place the packets on the hot charcoal grill, cover, and cook for the same amount of time. Open the packets carefully as the steam that escapes will be very hot.

 **Serves 6**

Pan-Fried Drumsticks with Quick Vegetable Ragoût

Fresh tomatoes are essential for this ragoût. Increasingly available are small zucchini and yellow squash about the size of small cigars. Their sweet, intense flavors are perfect for this recipe. Add a cup or two of corn kernels fresh from the cob and some chopped fresh basil for even more of a summer treat.

12 medium to large drumsticks

Salt and freshly ground black pepper

2 tablespoons unsalted butter

2 tablespoons vegetable oil

½ cup dry white wine

2 large tomatoes, peeled, seeded, and chopped

1 small yellow squash (about ¼ pound), cut into ½-inch dice

1 small zucchini (about ¼ pound), cut into ½-inch dice

½ pound haricots verts, or thin green beans, blanched in boiling salted water for 2 to 3 minutes

2 tablespoons finely chopped parsley

1. Season the drumsticks with salt and pepper. Melt the butter with the oil in a large, heavy skillet over medium-high heat. Add the drumsticks and cook partially covered, turning often, until well browned, crisp, and cooked through, about 30 minutes. Remove to a plate or platter, cover with foil, and keep in a warm oven while preparing the ragoût.

2. Pour off all the fat from the skillet. Return the skillet to high heat and pour in the wine. Boil, whisking often to pick up any cooking bits left in the bottom of the skillet, until reduced to only 1 tablespoon, about 5 minutes. Stir in the tomatoes and boil until thickened and pulpy, about 3 minutes. Add the yellow squash and zucchini. Reduce the heat to medium high, cover, and cook until the squash is tender, about 2 minutes. Stir in the haricots verts and cook until heated through. Season the mixture to taste with salt and pepper. Quickly stir in the parsley and transfer the ragoût to a large serving platter. Top with the chicken and serve at once.

 Serves 6

Poppy Seed Drumsticks

Sesame seeds can be used in place of the poppy seeds. I once had an awfully good chicken dish like this in Austria, served with spätzle (small, fresh flour dumplings), which inspired me to create this recipe. If you aren't familiar with spätzle, serve hot buttered noodles for a similar accompaniment.

12 medium to large drumsticks

Salt and freshly ground black pepper

2 cups all-purpose flour

2 cups fresh bread crumbs

¾ cup poppy seeds

3 large eggs

3 tablespoons melted, unsalted butter

1. Preheat the oven to 375° F. Oil a baking sheet large enough to hold the drumsticks in one flat layer.

2. Season the drumsticks with salt and pepper. Place the flour in a large bowl. Combine the poppy seeds and bread crumbs in a separate large bowl and mix well. Crack the eggs into a third bowl and beat lightly with a fork.

3. Dip the drumsticks in the beaten egg and turn several times to coat. Dredge in the flour and return to the beaten egg. Coat again with egg and immediately place in the bowl of bread crumbs and poppy seeds. Turn to coat and transfer to the baking sheet. Drizzle evenly with the melted butter and bake for 30 to 45 minutes or until cooked through and well browned and crisp.

 **Serves 6**

Chicken Nugget

Until the eighteenth century, French cooks would roast two chickens—one for meat and the second to make enough savory juices for a full-flavored gravy for the first bird. The second bird would be squeezed in a press to extract its juices for making gravy.

Lemon, Rosemary, and Roasted Garlic Drumsticks

Roasted garlic has a mellow, buttery taste that complements rosemary. Grill tender, young vegetables like zucchini or eggplant slices if you've opted for the barbeque method; quick sautéed seasonal vegetables if you're cooking in the oven.

6 large garlic cloves, roasted (see Note)

½ teaspoon coarse salt

½ teaspoon freshly ground black pepper

1 tablespoon chopped fresh rosemary

2 tablespoons lemon juice

12 medium to large drumsticks

Several sprigs fresh rosemary, for garnish

1. Prepare a charcoal fire and let coals burn to a gray ash. Lightly oil the grill. Alternatively, preheat the broiler and set an oiled broiling pan 6 inches from the source of heat.

2. Use your fingers to squeeze the pulp from the garlic into a mortar or large bowl. Add the salt, pepper, and chopped rosemary. With a pestle or with the back of a sturdy spoon, work the mixture into a rough paste. Stir in the lemon juice.

3. Spread the garlic mixture over the drumsticks to evenly coat. Place on a grill or broiling pan and cook, turning often, until cooked through, browned, and crisp, about 30 minutes. Serve hot on a large platter garnished with sprigs of fresh rosemary.

 Serves 6

NOTE: *To roast garlic, preheat the oven to 375°F. Place the garlic cloves in a large square of aluminum foil. Fold up the ends of the foil to meet in the middle and crimp tightly to seal. Bake the garlic until softened, 20 to 25 minutes. Remove the cooked garlic from the foil and set aside until cool enough to handle. (This can be done up to 2 days in advance.)*

Drumsticks Gremalata

Pan-roasting gives these drumsticks a rich, dark brown flavor. Gremalata is a classic garnish for the Italian favorite veal dish, osso buco. It seems like a natural for drumsticks. Add an extra garlic clove for more kick, if desired. Be sure to bake the gremalata long enough to give it crunchy texture. Add some chopped fresh tomatoes to instant couscous for a flavorful accompaniment.

12 medium to large drumsticks

Salt and freshly ground black pepper

2 tablespoons chopped fresh parsley

1 garlic clove, minced

2 tablespoons grated lemon zest

1. Preheat the oven to 375° F. Butter a baking dish large enough to hold the drumsticks in one flat layer. Place the drumsticks in the dish and season with salt and pepper. Bake, uncovered, until golden brown on one side, about 20 minutes. Turn and bake for 20 minutes longer, until cooked through.

2. Meanwhile, prepare the gremalata. In a small bowl, combine the parsley, garlic, and lemon zest. Mix well. (This can be done up to 2 hours in advance. Keep tightly covered with plastic wrap until ready to use.)

3. Sprinkle each drumstick with a heaping teaspoonful of the gremalata. Bake 5 minutes longer or until the lemon zest has darkened and the gremalata looks slightly dried. Serve at once.

 **Serves 6**

Chicken Nugget

Chicken was not always eaten as often as it is today. Considered a special treat, most country families kept only hens, and their eggs were too precious to the peasants' diets to use the birds for meat. Chickens were eaten only when too old to lay.

Drumsticks with Tarragon Butter

Do not attempt this recipe if fresh tarragon is not available; dried tarragon just will not give the same flavor. Double the amount of the tarragon butter and freeze it for future use. It works well with all sorts of grilled chicken and fish. Serve these drumsticks with breaded, grilled tomatoes.

12 medium to large drumsticks

Salt and freshly ground black pepper to taste

2 tablespoons finely chopped fresh tarragon

Several sprigs fresh tarragon, for garnish

4 tablespoons (½ stick) unsalted butter, softened

1 tablespoon lemon juice

1. Prepare a charcoal fire and let coals burn to a gray ash. Lightly oil the grill. Alternatively, preheat the broiler and set an oiled broiling pan 6 inches from the source of heat. Season the drumsticks with salt and pepper.

2. In a small bowl, combine the tarragon, butter, lemon juice, and salt and pepper. Use a fork to blend to a smooth paste. Set aside at room temperature until ready to serve the chicken. (The butter can be made up to 3 days in advance. Keep refrigerated until ready to use. Bring to room temperature before using.)

3. Place the drumsticks on the grill or broiling pan and cook, turning often, until browned and cooked through, about 30 minutes. Remove and, while still hot, spread the tarragon butter generously over the drumsticks. Serve at once on a large platter garnished with fresh sprigs of tarragon.

 Serves 6

Chicken Nugget

An entire chicken's cooked yield is just over one-half white meat and 47.5 percent dark meat.

Drumsticks with Smoky Bacon and Corn

*This recipe was inspired by a great test-kitchen cook, Marcia Keisel, who turns out wonderful ideas at **Food and Wine** magazine. I have learned a lot from her over the years. Use smoked ham if the bacon is impossible to find. (There is no need to cook the ham first, as is indicated for the bacon.) Be sure to season well with salt and lots of freshly ground black pepper. Serve with a salad of fresh tomatoes and Bermuda onions.*

2 ounces double-smoked slab bacon, cut into ½-inch pieces

2 tablespoons vegetable oil

12 medium to large drumsticks

Salt and freshly ground black pepper

½ cup dry white wine

4 cups fresh or frozen corn kernels (about 8 ears)

1 tablespoon chopped fresh parsley

1. Combine the bacon and oil in a large, heavy skillet. Cook, stirring often, over medium-high heat until the fat has been rendered and the bacon is browned, about 5 minutes. Remove the cooked bacon with a slotted spoon and set aside.

2. Season the drumsticks with salt and pepper. Add to the hot skillet and cook partially covered, turning often, until golden brown on all sides, about 20 minutes. Transfer the drumsticks to a large platter.

3. Pour off all the fat from the skillet and add the wine. Increase the heat to high and bring to a boil, stirring to pick up any cooking bits on the bottom. Boil until reduced by half.

4. Add the corn to the skillet. Stir well, place the drumsticks on top, and reduce the heat to medium. Cook until the corn is tender and the drumsticks are well done, about 10 minutes. Remove the drumsticks to a large serving platter. Add the cooked bacon to the corn and mix well. Surround the chicken with the corn and bacon. Season to taste with salt and pepper and serve at once, garnished with the parsley.

 **Serves 6**

Chicken Nugget

The domesticated chicken first appeared in about 2,000 B.C. in India, and was brought to America by Columbus in 1493.

Drumsticks with Fennel and Black Olives

Serve these drumsticks with a toss of roasted red and yellow peppers flavored with cumin. Follow with a green salad with goat cheese for a fabulous dinner.

4 fennel bulbs, trimmed

3 tablespoons olive oil

12 medium to large drumsticks

Salt and freshly ground black pepper

¼ cup dry white wine

1 tablespoon chopped fresh thyme

2 teaspoons grated lemon zest

⅓ cup chopped, pitted black olives (about 8 large olives)

1. Preheat the oven to 350° F. Halve each fennel bulb and remove the tough core. Thinly slice the halves and set aside. (If you do the fennel more than just a few minutes in advance, add vinegar or lemon juice to a large bowl of cold water. Keep the sliced fennel in this acidulated water to prevent discoloration. Drain before proceeding.)

2. Heat the oil in a large, ovenproof casserole over medium-high heat. Season the drumsticks with salt and pepper. Cook the drumsticks in the hot oil, turning often, until browned on all sides, about 10 minutes. Remove to a platter and set aside.

3. Pour off all but 1 tablespoon of the fat from the casserole. Add the fennel and cook for 2 to 3 minutes to heat through. Pour in the wine and stir vigorously to pick up any browned bits left on the bottom of the casserole. Stir in the thyme, lemon zest, and olives. Season with salt and pepper.

4. Return the drumsticks to the casserole, cover, and cook for 30 minutes or until the fennel is tender and the chicken shows no trace of pink when pierced near the bone. Transfer the drumsticks to a large serving platter. Season the fennel mixture with salt and pepper to taste and spoon over the chicken. Serve at once.

 **Serves 6**

Rum Raisin Drumsticks

Be careful when working with the rum here —it is very flammable. The rum must be warmed as is indicated, before it will ignite. So, stand back and make sure that there are no surrounding objects that could be affected by open flames when the match is struck. Dark rum gives a rich flavor, but light rum will work, too. I like to serve this dish with yellow rice mixed with tiny, diced, roasted red peppers.

½ cup raisins

2 tablespoons unsalted butter

2 tablespoons vegetable oil

12 medium to large drumsticks

Salt and freshly ground black pepper

1 cup dark rum

1 cup chicken stock

1. Place the raisins in a small bowl and add enough warm water to cover. Soak for 10 minutes to plump, then drain.

2. Melt the butter with the oil in a large, heavy skillet over medium-high heat. Season the drumsticks with salt and pepper and add to the skillet. Cook, turning often, until well browned on all sides, about 10 minutes.

3. Meanwhile, place the rum in a small saucepan and warm over low heat.

4. Pour off the fat from the skillet and pour the warmed rum over the drumsticks. Standing back, carefully ignite the rum with a match. Remove the skillet from the heat and shake until the flame subsides, 1 to 2 minutes. Return the skillet to the heat, add the stock, and scatter in the raisins. Cover and cook, turning often, until the drumsticks are very tender and cooked through, about 30 minutes. Transfer the drumsticks to a warmed platter and cover with foil to keep warm. Increase the heat to high and boil down the pan juices until thick and syrupy, 1 to 3 minutes. Pour the thickened pan juices and the raisins over the drumsticks and serve at once.

 Serves 6

Crunchy Fried Drumsticks with Peanut Dipping Sauce

This Indonesian-style recipe goes best with rice. I like to use the smaller grain, nutty-flavored basmati rice for full effect. Wheat germ gives the drumsticks a texture all its own. Use fresh bread crumbs if wheat germ is hard to find. This is a good recipe to include as part of a large buffet for special occasions. The quantities can be easily doubled.

½ cup smooth peanut butter

¼ cup soy sauce

2 tablespoons honey

¼ cup water

1 garlic clove

1 teaspoon Dijon mustard

2 tablespoons red wine vinegar

2 tablespoons Asian sesame oil

⅛ teaspoon red pepper flakes, or to taste

Vegetable oil, for deep-frying

1½ cups wheat germ

¾ cup all-purpose flour

Salt and freshly ground black pepper

2 large eggs

12 large drumsticks

1. Combine the peanut butter, soy sauce, honey, water, garlic, mustard, and vinegar in the bowl of a food processor. Process until smooth. With the motor running, add the oil in a slow stream until incorporated. Transfer to a bowl, stir in the red pepper flakes, and set aside.

2. Fill a heavy, deep Dutch oven or deep-fat fryer with 2 inches of vegetable oil. Heat to 375°F. (If you do not have a thermometer, heat the oil over medium-high heat. Add a small cube of fresh bread to the hot oil. If the bread turns browns in 40 seconds, it is ready.)

3. In a wide, shallow bowl, combine the wheat germ and flour with salt and pepper. In a separate bowl, beat the eggs lightly with 2 tablespoons of cold water. Dip the drumsticks first in the egg, then in the wheat germ mixture. Turn to coat well. Add the chicken to the hot oil and cook, turning occasionally, until well browned and crisp, 12 to 15 minutes. (Do not overcrowd the pan. Do it in 2 batches, if necessary, or the chicken will not brown properly.) Drain on paper towels and season to taste with additional salt and pepper, if desired.

4. Arrange the drumsticks on a large platter and drizzle over a small amount of the peanut sauce. Serve the remaining sauce on the side.

 Serves 6

Drumsticks with Fennel and Pears

Green apples could be used in place of the pears. Serve with oven-roasted potatoes and glazed pearl onions.

12 medium to large drumsticks

Salt and freshly ground black pepper

2 tablespoons unsalted butter

2 tablespoons vegetable oil

2 large fennel bulbs, trimmed of fronds, cored, and thinly sliced

3 large, ripe but firm Anjou pears, peeled, cored, and thinly sliced

½ cup chicken stock

1 teaspoon caraway seeds

1. Preheat the oven to 425°F. and lightly butter a large, heavy, oven-to-table casserole. Season the drumsticks with salt and pepper. Melt the butter with the oil in a large, heavy skillet. Add the drumsticks and cook, turning often, over medium-high heat until browned on all sides, about 10 minutes. Transfer to the buttered casserole.

2. Pour off the fat from the skillet. Add the fennel and cook, stirring often to pick up any browned bits on the bottom, until slightly tender, about 5 minutes. Add the sliced pears and stir gently to combine. Pour in the chicken stock and increase the heat to high. Boil rapidly for 1 minute to slightly thicken, scraping up any browned bits on the bottom. Stir in the caraway seeds and season to taste with salt and pepper. Scatter the fennel and pear mixture over the drumsticks, cover the casserole, and cook in the oven for 30 to 40 minutes, or until the chicken shows no trace of pink when pierced at its thickest point and the fennel is tender.

 **Serves 6**

Spanish Drumsticks

Drained, canned chickpeas can be used in place of the cranberry beans for convenience. Just add to the skillet in the last step.

12 medium to large drumsticks

Salt and freshly ground black pepper

2 tablespoons unsalted butter

2 tablespoons vegetable oil

1 medium onion, finely chopped

1 red or yellow bell pepper, finely chopped

1 cup chicken stock

2 large tomatoes, peeled, seeded, and diced

12 pitted black olives, preferably oil-cured, finely chopped

1 cup shelled cranberry beans

10 large basil leaves, thinly sliced

1. Season the drumsticks with salt and pepper. Melt the butter with the oil in a large skillet over medium-high heat. Add the drumsticks and cook, turning often, until well browned on all sides, about 10 minutes. Remove to a plate or platter.

2. Pour off all but 1 tablespoon of the fat from the skillet. Add the onion and bell pepper. Cook, stirring often, until softened, about 3 minutes. Pour in the stock and increase the heat to high. Boil until reduced by half.

3. Stir in the tomatoes and olives. Return the chicken to the skillet and reduce the heat to medium. Cover and cook, turning occasionally, until the drumsticks are very tender and cooked through, 30 to 35 minutes.

4. Meanwhile, bring a large saucepan of salted water to a boil. Add the cranberry beans and cook until tender, about 15 minutes. Drain.

5. Place the drumsticks on a large serving platter and cover with foil to keep warm. Add the drained beans to the skillet, increase the heat to high, and boil until the pan juices are thickened and the beans are heated through, about 5 minutes. Stir in the basil and season to taste with salt and pepper. Spoon the juices, vegetables, and beans over the chicken and serve at once.

 Serves 6

Quick Barbecued Drumsticks

Really in a hurry? Simply use one of the many fine bottled sauces on the market in place of this ketchup-molasses–lemon juice mixture. In either case, add bottled hot sauce to taste if a more fiery effect is desired.

1 cup ketchup

2 tablespoons molasses

2 teaspoons lemon juice

1 tablespoon vegetable oil

12 medium to large drumsticks

Salt and freshly ground black pepper

1. Prepare a charcoal fire and let the coals burn to a gray ash. Oil the grill. Alternatively, preheat the broiler and oil the broiling pan.

2. Blend the ketchup, molasses, lemon juice, and oil together in a small bowl.

3. Season the drumsticks with salt and pepper. Place in a large bowl and pour over the ketchup mixture. Turn several times to coat well. Remove the drumsticks and grill or broil 4 to 6 inches from the source of heat until dark amber in color and tender, 30 to 45 minutes. Baste often with the ketchup mixture.

 **Serves 6**

Drumsticks with Corn and Cranberry Beans

Cream-colored cranberry beans are easy to shell. The pods are large and paper thin. Fresh black-eyed peas would work nicely, too. Alternatively, drained and rinsed canned black-eyed peas or even kidney beans would work as a shortcut. Serve with a salad of romaine lettuce with large, garlicky croutons.

2 cups shelled cranberry beans

12 medium to large drumsticks

Salt and freshly ground black pepper

2 tablespoons unsalted butter

2 tablespoons vegetable oil

1 large tomato, peeled, seeded, and chopped

4 cups fresh corn kernels (from 4 ears), or 2 packages (10 ounces each) thawed frozen corn

2 tablespoons chopped fresh parsley

1. Place the beans in a medium saucepan and pour in enough cold water to cover. Bring to a boil over high heat, reduce the heat to medium, and simmer until tender, 15 to 20 minutes. Season with salt at the end of cooking and keep covered until ready to serve the dish. (The beans can be prepared up to 1 hour in advance. Do not drain until the last minute to prevent them from drying out.)

2. Meanwhile, season the drumsticks with salt and pepper. Melt the butter with the oil in a large, heavy skillet over medium-high heat. Cook the chicken partially covered, turning often, until browned on all sides and there are no traces of pink in the juices when the flesh is pierced at its thickest part, about 20 minutes. Remove to an ovenproof serving platter and keep warm in a slow oven. (Do not crowd the skillet or the drumsticks will not properly brown; do in 2 batches if necessary, adding additional oil and butter as needed.)

3. Pour off the fat from the skillet. Return the skillet to the heat and add the tomato. Increase the heat to high and cook, stirring to pick up any cooking bits left in the bottom, until thick and pulpy, about 5 minutes. Add the corn and stir well. Reduce the heat to medium, cover, and cook, stirring often, for 3 minutes or until the corn is tender.

4. Drain the beans and add to the skillet. Cook until heated through. Stir in all but 1 teaspoon of the parsley. Season with salt and pepper.

5. Surround the chicken with the corn and bean mixture. Garnish with the remaining teaspoon of parsley and serve at once.

 **Serves 6**

Garlicky Drumsticks with Broccoli Rabe

Kale, collard greens, mustard greens, or turnip greens could be substituted for the broccoli rabe. Fresh garlic works best for this recipe; older heads of garlic often become strong and bitter with age. Serve with gingered sweet potatoes and hot buttered rolls.

12 medium to large drumsticks

Salt and freshly ground black pepper

2 tablespoons unsalted butter

2 tablespoons vegetable oil

5 garlic cloves, peeled and thickly sliced

½ cup dry white wine

1 bunch broccoli rabe (about 1 pound), thoroughly cleaned and tough stems removed

2 tablespoons olive oil

1. Preheat the oven to 350° F. Season the drumsticks with salt and pepper. Melt the butter with the oil in a large skillet over medium-high heat. Add the drumsticks and cook, turning often, until well browned on all sides, 7 to 9 minutes.

Place the browned drumsticks on a large baking dish and cook in the oven until there is no trace of pink when the flesh is pierced at its thickest point, 25 to 30 minutes.

2. Add the garlic to the skillet and cook, stirring constantly, over medium-high heat just until golden brown. Do not over cook or the garlic will be bitter. Remove with a slotted spoon and set aside.

3. Pour off all the fat from the skillet. Pour in the wine and set the skillet over high heat. Boil, whisking to pick up any browned bits on the bottom, until reduced by half. Add the broccoli rabe and cover. Cook, turning often with tongs, until wilted but still crunchy, 5 to 7 minutes. Season well with salt and pepper.

4. Arrange the broccoli rabe in the center of a large, warmed serving platter. Drizzle over the olive oil. Place the drumsticks around the broccoli rabe and serve at once, sprinkled with the browned garlic.

 **Serves 6**

Stove-Top Drumsticks with Lemon and Celery

This is a simple recipe with a surprising amount of flavor. Celery leaves could be used to garnish the chicken. Add a teaspoon of grated lemon zest while the drumsticks cook for added flavor. Mashed potatoes make a great side dish, or peeled, cubed celery root, cooked with the potatoes and put through a ricer or food mill, makes a nice variation. For a super-quick version, simply pour over the sauce without straining.

12 large drumsticks

1 cup all-purpose flour

1 teaspoon salt

½ teaspoon freshly ground black pepper

2 tablespoons unsalted butter

2 tablespoons vegetable oil

1 cup finely chopped celery

1 cup finely chopped onion

1 cup chicken stock

Juice of 1 lemon (about 3 tablespoons)

1. Trim the drumsticks of excess fat. Place the flour, salt, and pepper in a large brown paper bag. Add the drumsticks, close tightly, and shake well to thoroughly coat.

2. Melt the butter with the oil in a large, heavy skillet over medium-high heat. Remove the drumsticks from the bag and shake off excess flour. Cook the legs, turning often, until well browned, about 10 minutes. Drain on paper towels.

3. Pour off all but 1 tablespoon of the fat. Add the celery and onion to the skillet and cook, stirring often, until softened, about 3 minutes. Pour in the stock, increase the heat to high, and boil until slightly reduced, about 2 minutes. Return the drumsticks to the skillet, pour over the lemon juice, reduce the heat to medium, cover, and simmer until tender and cooked through, 30 to 35 minutes.

4. Remove the drumsticks to a warmed platter. Increase the heat to high and boil the contents of the skillet until reduced and thickened. Strain the juices over the drumsticks, discarding the solids, and serve at once.

 **Serves 6**

Drumsticks with Tomato, Corn, and Basil

This simple dish can be made with canned tomatoes and frozen corn for a quicker rendition, but I do not recommend this. What makes the recipe special is the freshness of the ingredients. The red wine gives an unusual tartness and deep purple color, or use white wine for a different taste. Serve with zucchini and yellow squash sautéed together quickly in olive oil.

12 medium to large drumsticks

Salt and freshly ground black pepper

2 tablespoons unsalted butter

2 tablespoons vegetable oil

½ cup red wine

9 or 10 small Italian plum tomatoes (1½ pounds), peeled, seeded, and chopped

4 cups fresh corn kernels (from 6 medium ears)

10 large basil leaves, sliced into thin shreds (about ½ cup loosely packed)

6 very small whole leaves of basil, for garnish

1. Season the drumsticks with salt and pepper. Melt the butter with the oil in a large skillet over medium-high heat. Add the drumsticks and cook, turning often, until browned on all sides, 8 to 10 minutes. Remove the drumsticks to a plate or platter, pour off the fat in the skillet, and increase the heat to high. Return the skillet to the heat and pour in the wine. Boil rapidly until reduced by half, whisking often to pick up any cooking bits on the bottom. Stir in the tomatoes, reduce the heat to medium, return the drumsticks to the skillet, and cover. Cook, turning occasionally, until the chicken is very tender and cooked through, about 45 minutes.

2. Remove the chicken to a plate or platter. Increase the heat to high and boil the pan juices, stirring often, until thickened, about 5 minutes. Stir in the corn and basil. Cook, stirring constantly, until the corn is tender, about 3 minutes. Season with salt and pepper.

3. Return the drumsticks to the skillet, reduce the heat to medium high, and cover. Cook until the chicken is heated through and the corn is very soft, 5 to 10 minutes. Serve at once garnished with small leaves of basil.

 **Serves 6**

Union Square Summer Drumsticks

The farmers' market at Union Square in New York City is a sight to behold in mid-summer. Farmers from New York state, New Jersey, and Pennsylvania bring in some of the finest produce there is to be found in the country. The inspiration for this dish came after a Wednesday morning visit in mid-July. Peppers, tomatoes, cranberry beans, and basil are combined with everyday drumsticks for a dish that celebrates the fruits of the good earth.

12 medium to large drumsticks

Salt and freshly ground black pepper

2 tablespoons unsalted butter

2 tablespoons vegetable oil

1 medium onion, finely chopped

1 red or yellow bell pepper, finely chopped

1 cup chicken stock

2 large tomatoes, peeled, seeded, and diced

12 to 15 pitted black olives, preferably oil-cured, finely chopped

1 cup shelled cranberry beans

10 large basil leaves, thinly sliced

1. Season the drumsticks with salt and pepper. Melt the butter with the oil in a large skillet over medium-high heat. Add the drumsticks and cook, turning often, until well browned on all sides, 8 to 10 minutes. Remove to a plate or platter. Pour off all but 1 tablespoon of the fat from the skillet. Add the onion and bell pepper. Cook, stirring often, until softened, about 3 minutes. Pour in the stock and increase the heat to high. Boil until reduced by half.

2. Stir in the tomatoes and olives. Return the chicken to the skillet and reduce the heat to medium. Cover and cook, turning occasionally, until the drumsticks are cooked through and very tender, 30 to 45 minutes.

3. Meanwhile, bring a large saucepan of salted water to a boil. Add the cranberry beans and cook until tender, about 15 minutes. Drain.

4. Place the drumsticks on a large serving platter and cover with foil to keep warm. Add the beans to the skillet, increase the heat to high, and boil until the pan juices are thickened and the beans are heated through, about 5 minutes. Stir in the basil and season with salt and pepper. Spoon the juices, vegetables, and beans over the chicken and serve at once.

 **Serves 6**

Drumsticks

· ·

Simply Sophisticated

Pistachio Drumsticks

Watch these carefully during the last few minutes of cooking. Nuts vary in their oil content, depending on their age and the way that they have been stored. Some cook more quickly than others. Serve with sweet potatoes flavored with orange juice and zest and a seasonal green vegetable.

1 cup finely chopped pistachios

½ cup all-purpose flour

½ cup fine cornmeal

⅛ teaspoon cayenne pepper, or to taste

1 cup buttermilk

12 large drumsticks

4 tablespoons (½ stick) unsalted butter, melted

Salt and freshly ground black pepper

1. Preheat the oven to 400°F. Lightly oil a large baking sheet.

2. Combine the pistachios, flour, cornmeal, and cayenne in a wide, shallow bowl. Mix well. Pour the buttermilk into a separate bowl for dipping. Add the drumsticks to the buttermilk, lift to drain slightly, then dip into the pistachio mixture. Turn to coat well on all sides.

3. Arrange the drumsticks in one flat layer on the baking sheet. Bake until lightly browned on top, about 15 minutes. Turn the drumsticks with tongs and drizzle with the melted butter. Bake until crisp and uniformly browned and cooked through, about 15 minutes longer. Season to taste with salt and pepper while hot. Serve at once.

 **Serves 6**

Grilled Drumsticks with Peppers on Mesclun

Mesclun, an old Niçois word for "mixture," is traditionally a combination of assorted young shoots and leaves of wild plants used to make a salad. Mesclun has come to mean just about any mixture of young salad greens. It is often sold in fancy produce markets and in some large supermarkets already washed and ready to be served. Crispy grilled drumsticks and roasted peppers provide texture and flavor, making this a wonderful recipe for a summer lunch or light supper. Serve with chewy olive bread, available at many bread counters and bakeries these days.

¼ cup soy sauce

2 tablespoons peanut or vegetable oil

2 teaspoons honey

2 tablespoons sherry vinegar

12 medium to large drumsticks

Salt and freshly ground black pepper

⅓ cup homemade vinaigrette or bottled salad dressing

8 to 10 cups loosely packed mesclun salad

1 roasted red bell pepper, peeled, seeded, and cut into thin strips (see page 5)

1 roasted yellow bell pepper, peeled, seeded, and cut into thin strips (see page 5)

4 ounces fresh goat cheese, crumbled (about 1 cup)

10 to 12 large basil leaves, thinly sliced (about ½ cup)

1. Preheat the broiler and lightly oil a broiling pan. Alternatively, light a charcoal fire and let the coal burn down to a gray ash.

2. Combine the soy sauce, oil, honey, and vinegar in a small bowl. Mix well to blend. Brush the drumsticks with this mixture and season with salt and pepper. Broil or grill the drumsticks 6 to 8 inches from the source of heat, turning often, until dark brown on all sides and cooked through, 20 to 25 minutes. Brush from time to time with the marinade.

3. Meanwhile, put the vinaigrette in the bottom of a large bowl. Place the mesclun on top. Add the peppers, cheese, and basil leaves. Toss well and spread out evenly on a large serving platter.

4. Remove the chicken from the oven or the grill and let cool slightly. Arrange attractively on top of the tossed greens and serve at once.

 **Serves 6**

Parsleyed Chicken "Meatballs"

The rich, dark meat of drumsticks is good for making these "meatballs." Serve with rice or a small pasta like orzo. Finely diced red pepper makes a nice garnish.

12 medium to large drumsticks, boned and skin removed

½ cup chopped fresh parsley leaves

¼ cup fresh bread crumbs

1 small onion, finely chopped

¼ teaspoon ground cumin

½ teaspoon salt

½ teaspoon freshly ground black pepper

2 cups chicken stock

2 tablespoons unsalted butter

3 tablespoons all-purpose flour

Salt and freshly ground black pepper

1. Remove the skin from the drumsticks. Cut the drumsticks into large pieces. In the bowl of a food processor, combine the chicken, parsley, bread crumbs, onion, cumin, salt, and pepper. Process until the mixture forms a solid mass around the blades, scraping down the sides as necessary.

2. In a medium skillet, combine the stock with enough cold water to form a 1- to 2-inch layer of liquid. Bring the mixture to a boil over high heat. Form the meatballs from the chicken mixture by briskly rolling heaping teaspoonfuls between the palms of your hands. Add to the boiling stock, reduce the heat to medium, and cook, turning often, until firm, 7 to 10 minutes. Remove the meatballs with a slotted spoon and measure the cooking liquid. You should have 2 cups. Add more stock to measure this amount if necessary. Pour off any excess if too much liquid.

3. Melt the butter in a small, heavy saucepan. Stir in the flour, blend well, and cook until bubbling and lemon colored. Pour in the measured liquid from the meatballs and increase the heat to high. Boil, stirring constantly, until thickened, about 3 minutes. Season to taste with salt and pepper and return the meatballs to the sauce. Reduce the heat to medium and cook for 2 to 3 minutes, or until heated through.

 **Serves 6**

Drumsticks with Italian Plums

Dark purple plums, no bigger than small eggs, are plentiful in the summer. This recipe makes good use of this tart, flavorful fruit. Black Friar plums work well, too, but are hard to pit. I find that port wine adds a particularly nice color to this dish, but any fortified wine or brandy will add dimension. Serve with corn on the cob and a salad of seasonal greens with roasted red peppers and goat cheese.

1¾ pounds small Italian plums (30 to 35 plums), halved and pitted

1 tablespoon lemon juice

1 teaspoon sugar

12 medium to large drumsticks

Salt and freshly ground black pepper

2 tablespoons unsalted butter

2 tablespoons vegetable oil

½ cup port wine or Madeira

1. Combine the plums, lemon juice, and sugar in a large bowl. Set aside at room temperature, stirring occasionally, while preparing the chicken. Preheat the oven to 200° F.

2. Season the drumsticks with salt and pepper. Melt the butter with the oil in a large, heavy skillet over medium-high heat. Add the chicken and cook partially covered, turning often, until well browned and cooked through, 30 to 45 minutes. Remove to a plate or platter and keep warm in a slow oven until ready to serve.

3. Pour off the fat from the skillet. Increase the heat to high and add the port or Madeira. Stir with a whisk to pick up any cooking bits left in the bottom of the skillet. Boil until reduced to about 1 tablespoon, 3 to 5 minutes. Stir in the plums and any juices that have accumulated in the bowl. Reduce the heat to medium, cover, and cook, stirring often, until the plums are tender but not mushy, about 3 minutes.

4. Arrange the chicken on a large, warmed serving platter. Spoon over the plums and all pan juices. Serve at once.

 Serves 6

Chicken Nugget

"What is sauce for the goose may be sauce for the gander, but it is not necessarily sauce for the chicken (or the duck, the turkey or the Guinea hen)."

—Alice B. Toklas

Drumsticks with Rice, Golden Raisins, and Pine Nuts

Use Italian pine nuts if you can find them. They have a more profound flavor than the omnipresent Chinese variety. Currants or regular raisins can be substituted for the golden raisins. This is comfort food at its best!

½ cup golden raisins

¼ cup brandy

2 tablespoons unsalted butter

2 tablespoons vegetable oil

12 medium to large drumsticks

Salt and freshly ground black
    pepper

1 medium onion, finely chopped

2 cups rice

4 cups chicken stock

½ cup toasted pine nuts

1. Preheat the oven to 350°F. Place the raisins in a small bowl, add the brandy, and pour over enough warm water to cover (about ½ cup). Set aside to plump for about 10 minutes. Drain.

2. Meanwhile, melt the butter with the oil in a large, heavy skillet over medium-high heat. Season the drumsticks with salt and pepper. Cook, turning often, until browned on all sides, 8 to 10 minutes. Transfer the drumsticks to a heavy casserole or Dutch oven.

3. Pour off all but 1 tablespoon of the fat from the skillet. Add the onion and cook, stirring often, until softened, about 3 minutes. Stir in the rice and cook until glossy, about 2 minutes. Pour in the stock, increase the heat to high, and bring to a boil. Stir constantly to pick up any cooking bits in the bottom of the skillet. Season to taste with salt and pepper.

4. Pour the rice mixture and all the liquid over the chicken in the casserole. Cover and bake for about 45 minutes or until the rice is tender and the chicken is falling off the bone.

5. Transfer the cooked chicken to a large, warmed serving platter and cover with foil to keep warm. Pat the raisins dry with paper towels. Stir the raisins and pine nuts into the rice. Surround the chicken with the rice and serve at once.

 **Serves 6**

Paul's Jerk Chicken Drumsticks

*I met Paul Chung at **Food and Wine** magazine. A wonderful cook of Jamaican and Chinese ancestry, Paul's jerk chicken has almost a cult following among some of New York's foodies. The secret ingredient is the Scotch bonnet peppers, increasingly available in large farmers' markets and in some specialty food stores. Use jalapeños or small dried red peppers if Scotch bonnets are not to be found. This is a slight variation on the Jamaican Jerk Chicken Thighs recipe on page 123. Serve with homemade cole slaw and chunky potato salad.*

- **1 large onion, finely chopped**
- **2 Scotch bonnet peppers, seeded and chopped**
- **2 garlic cloves, minced**
- **1 teaspoon ground allspice**
- **1 teaspoon coarsely ground black pepper**
- **½ teaspoon ground cinnamon**
- **½ teaspoon freshly grated nutmeg**
- **½ teaspoon salt**
- **½ cup soy sauce**
- **1 tablespoon vegetable oil**
- **12 large drumsticks**

1. Prepare a charcoal fire, and let the coals burn to a gray ash. Lightly oil the grill. Alternatively, preheat the broiler and set an oiled broiling pan 6 inches from the source of heat.

2. Combine the onion, peppers, garlic, allspice, black pepper, cinnamon, nutmeg, and salt in the bowl of a food processor. Process until the mixture forms a paste. With the blade in motion, add the soy sauce and vegetable oil. Scrape down the sides of the bowl and puree until smooth.

3. Cut slashes about ¼ inch deep over 2 sides of the drumsticks to score. Arrange on the bottom of a large baking dish in one flat layer. Spoon the jerk mixture over the legs and turn with tongs until thoroughly coated. (The chicken can be marinated for up to 24 hours. Keep refrigerated and turn often for best flavor.)

4. Place the drumsticks on a grill or broiling pan and cook, turning often, until browned and cooked through, about 30 minutes.

 **Serves 6**

Drumsticks with Fresh Chutney

Serve with couscous and fried green bananas (plantains) for an exotic, colorful dinner.

1 orange

Zest and juice of 2 limes

4 medium mangos, peeled, seeded, and cut into ½-inch dice

2 small onions, finely chopped

½ cup raisins

1 piece fresh ginger, 1 inch long, peeled and finely chopped

1 jalapeño pepper, seeded and finely chopped

1 cup firmly packed brown sugar

1 tablespoon mustard seeds

1 cinnamon stick, 3 inches long

1 cup white wine vinegar

2 tablespoons vegetable oil

12 large drumsticks

Salt and freshly ground black pepper

1 tablespoon chopped fresh cilantro

1. Zest the orange and remove the pulp in sections, discarding the pits and membranes. Zest the limes and juice them.

2. Combine the mangos, onions, raisins, orange zest and pulp, lime zest and juice, ginger, jalapeño, brown sugar, mustard seeds, cinnamon stick, and vinegar in a large saucepan. Bring to a boil, reduce the heat, and simmer, stirring occasionally, until thickened and bubbly, about 10 minutes. (The chutney can be prepared several days in advance. Keep refrigerated until ready to serve.)

3. Heat the oil in a large skillet over medium-high heat. Season the drumsticks with salt and pepper and add to the skillet. Cook, turning often, until lightly browned on all sides, 5 to 7 minutes. (Do not crowd the pan; do it in 2 batches, if necessary, or the drumsticks will not brown properly.)

4. Pour off any extra cooking fat, reduce the heat to medium high, and add the mango chutney. Cover and simmer, stirring often, until the chicken is tender and cooked through, 15 to 20 minutes. Remove the cover and increase the heat to high. Cook rapidly for about 5 minutes to thicken the pan juices.

5. Arrange the chutney over the bottom of a warmed, large platter. Top with the drumsticks, sprinkle with the cilantro, and serve at once.

 **Serves 6**

Drumsticks with Portobello Mushrooms

Portobello mushrooms, with their rich flesh and dark earthy color, are sometimes describes as "beefy." Here, they are paired with drumsticks that are the most "beefy" part of the chicken. Serve with thyme-roasted potatoes and blanched tender green beans tossed in a little butter.

3 large portobello mushrooms, stems removed

Salt and freshly ground black pepper

1 tablespoon olive oil

1 garlic clove, minced

2 tablespoons unsalted butter

2 tablespoons vegetable oil

12 medium to large drumsticks

½ cup dry white wine

1 cup chicken stock

1 tablespoon chopped fresh parsley

1. Preheat the oven to 350°F. Place the mushrooms on an oiled baking sheet and season with salt and pepper. Brush the tops lightly with olive oil and sprinkle with the garlic. Bake the mushrooms until dark around the edges and tender in the center, about 20 minutes. (The mushrooms can be done several hours in advance. Wrap in plastic and keep at room temperature until ready to finish the dish.)

2. Meanwhile, melt the butter with the oil in a large skillet over medium-high heat. Season the drumsticks with salt and pepper. Cook, turning often, until browned on all sides, 7 to 10 minutes. (Do not crowd the pan. Cook the drumsticks in 2 batches if necessary.) Transfer to an ovenproof baking dish and place in the oven, uncovered, for 25 to 30 minutes or until there is no trace of pink when the flesh is pierced at its thickest point. Remove the chicken to a large, warmed serving platter and cover to keep warm.

3. Pour off the fat from the skillet. Place the skillet over high heat and pour in the wine. Cook, whisking to pick up any browned bits, until reduced to about 1 tablespoon. Pour in the chicken stock and bring to a boil. Boil until reduced to about ¼ cup.

4. Cut the mushrooms into long, thin strips. Add to the skillet and season with salt and pepper. Spoon the mushrooms with all of the pan juices over the chicken and serve at once, sprinkled with the parsley.

 **Serves 6**

Boned Drumsticks with Cornbread Stuffing

This recipe is worth the time involved in its preparation. The drumsticks can be filled with a variety of stuffings and they cook quickly. Cornbread stuffing is one of my favorites. Add a few toasted pecans for even more flavor and texture.

3 tablespoons unsalted butter

1 small onion, finely chopped

1 large celery stalk, peeled and thinly sliced

1 tablespoon chopped fresh thyme

2 cups crumbled, cooked cornbread, preferably stale

½ cup chicken stock

Salt and freshly ground black pepper

12 large drumsticks, boned and skin removed (see page 142)

1. Melt 2 tablespoons of the butter in a large, heavy skillet over medium-high heat. Add the onion and celery. Cook, stirring often, until very soft, about 5 minutes. Add the thyme and cook 1 minute longer. Stir in the cornbread, mix well, and pour in the stock. Season with salt and pepper. (Makes about 1¾ cups stuffing. The stuffing can be made up to 2 days in advance. Keep refrigerated, tightly covered, until ready to fill the drumsticks.)

2. Preheat the oven to 375°F. Butter a baking dish large enough to hold the drumsticks in one flat layer. Fill each boned drumstick with 1 tablespoon of the stuffing. Gently form into original shapes and arrange the drumsticks snugly in the dish. Dot with the remaining tablespoon butter and sprinkle with salt and pepper. Bake for 30 to 40 minutes, or until golden brown and cooked through.

 Serves 6

Chicken Nugget

American breeds are called dual purpose because they are suited for both meat and egg production. Major breeds are the Rhode Island Red, the Plymouth Rock (of which there are several varieties), and the New Hampshire.

Drumsticks *en Papillote* with Tomato and Saffron

I like to serve this with garlic mashed potatoes. Simply add a few peeled cloves to the potatoes while they are cooking and work them right through the ricer or food mill with the cooked potatoes. Use only fresh, ripe tomatoes for this recipe. Powdered saffron could be used in place of the threads. Use a little less than ⅛ teaspoon powdered saffron for each pair of drumsticks.

- **12 medium to large drumsticks**
- **Salt and freshly ground black pepper**
- **1 teaspoon saffron threads**
- **4 medium tomatoes, peeled, seeded, and chopped**
- **1 teaspoon grated lemon zest**
- **6 tablespoons heavy cream**

1. Preheat the oven to 375°F. Tear off 6 large pieces of foil or parchment paper and lightly oil one side of each of the pieces. Arrange 2 drumsticks snugly together in the center of the bottom half of each piece. Season the drumsticks on all sides with salt and pepper.

2. Top each drumstick with a thread or two of saffron. (Be judicious with the saffron; a thread will give exotic flavor, more than that will leave a medicinal taste that overpowers the dish.) Spoon over equal amounts of the chopped tomato, add a pinch of lemon zest, and spoon on a tablespoonful of cream.

3. Fold the top part of the pieces of foil or paper over the bottom to enclose the drumsticks. Crimp the edges to form a tight seal. Place the packages on 2 large baking sheets. Cook for 30 minutes, until puffed. (The parchment, if used, will be well browned.) Break or cut open the packages at the table, being careful to avoid the escaping steam.

 Serves 6

Chicken Nugget

There are 44 standard breeds and 225 varieties of large chickens, and 23 breeds and 107 varieties of small chickens, called bantams.

Drumsticks Country Captain

Country Captain was a festive dish served mostly at wedding rehearsal dinners, cotillion parties, and other celebrations when I was growing up in Georgia. It still conjures up memories of close family and friends gathering to share good food. This version uses only drumsticks, which have that extra-rich, dark meat flavor. Crisp, chopped bacon, chopped hard-boiled eggs, mango chutney, and chopped onions are usually served on the side as condiments. Accompany with plenty of plain white rice.

- **½ cup golden raisins**
- **2 tablespoons unsalted butter**
- **2 tablespoons vegetable oil**
- **12 large drumsticks**
- **Salt and freshly ground black pepper**
- **1 medium onion, finely chopped**
- **2 celery stalks, peeled and thinly sliced**
- **1 green bell pepper, seeded and finely chopped**
- **1 red bell pepper, seeded and finely chopped**
- **2 garlic cloves, minced**
- **1 tablespoon curry powder**
- **2 large ripe tomatoes, peeled, seeded, and chopped**
- **½ cup toasted, slivered almonds**
- **1 tablespoon chopped fresh parsley**

1. Preheat the oven to 350° F. Pour enough hot water over the raisins to cover. Set aside until plump, at least 10 minutes. Drain and dry on paper towels.

2. Melt the butter with the oil in a large, heavy skillet over medium-high heat. Season the drumsticks with salt and freshly ground black pepper and add to the hot oil. Cook, turning often, until golden brown, 7 to 10 minutes. (Do not crowd the pan. Cook in 2 batches, if necessary.) Transfer to a large, oven-to-table baking dish and set aside.

3. Pour out all but 2 tablespoons of fat from the skillet. Add the onion, celery, peppers, and garlic and cook, stirring often, until softened, 5 to 7 minutes. Add the curry powder and stir constantly for 1 minute to remove the raw taste of the spice. Stir in the tomatoes and cook until they begin to give off liquid, about 3 minutes. Season to taste with salt and pepper. Spoon this mixture over the drumsticks. Bake, uncovered and turning often, until the drumsticks show no trace of pink at their thickest point, 40 to 45 minutes.

4. Sprinkle the raisins, almonds, and parsley over the cooked chicken and serve at once.

 Serves 6

Boned Drumsticks with Liver and Prunes

Duck, liver, and prunes reign supremely in the southwest of France, where my good friend, Daniele, has a farm. An excellent cook, who once was the personal chef of the president of France, Daniele is the inspiration for this recipe. Serve with a butter-enriched cabbage puree and caramelized onions for a special meal that friends and family won't soon forget.

12 small pitted prunes

½ cup brandy or Cognac

2 tablespoons unsalted butter

1 small onion, very finely chopped

1 pound chicken livers

Salt and freshly ground black pepper

12 large drumsticks, boned and skin removed (see page 139)

1. Place the prunes in a small bowl and pour over the brandy. Soak at room temperature for at least 10 minutes and up to several hours. Drain and reserve the liquid.

2. Melt 1 tablespoon of the butter in a large, nonstick skillet over medium-high heat. Add the onion and cook, stirring often, until softened but not browned, about 3 minutes. Add the livers, season with salt and pepper, and cook, carefully turning often with tongs, until firm, 5 to 7 minutes. Use a slotted spoon to transfer the livers to a plate and set aside. Pour the reserved brandy into the pan that the livers have cooked in and stir to pick up any cooking bits in the bottom of the skillet. Increase the heat to high. Carefully avoiding exposure to flames, boil the brandy until slightly reduced, thick, and syrupy. Remove from the heat and reserve.

3. Preheat the oven to 375° F. Butter a large baking dish. Use your fingers to open up and form deep pockets in the boned drumsticks. Cut the livers into large pieces. Fill each drumstick with a piece of liver and a prune. (Cut the livers small enough to fit snugly in the cavities without breaking. Reserve any leftover liver for another use.) Form the filled drumsticks into triangular shapes similar to their original form.

4. Place drumsticks in the baking dish and top each with a bit of the reduced brandy mixture. Dot the drumsticks with the remaining tablespoon of butter. Bake 30 to 40 minutes, or until golden brown and cooked through. Baste with the pan juices from time to time to prevent drying.

 **Serves 6**

Drumsticks with Leeks, Acorn Squash, and Bacon

Most good butchers have double-smoked bacon. If it is not available, however, any bacon will do. Use a sharp knife and caution while peeling the acorn squash, which is tricky because of its tough rind and grooved surface. Sweet potatoes could be substituted for the squash, and onions could replace the leeks. This recipe requires a very large pan; you could, however, make this in two batches.

- ¼ **pound bacon, preferably double-smoked, cut into small pieces**
- **1 tablespoon vegetable oil**
- **12 large or 24 small drumsticks**
- **Salt and freshly ground black pepper**
- **3 medium leeks (1½ pounds), trimmed of greens and sliced ¼ inch thick**
- **1 cup chicken stock**
- **2 large acorn squash (2½ pounds), peeled, seeded, and sliced about ½ inch thick**

1. Combine the bacon and oil in a large, heavy skillet. Cook over medium-high heat, stirring often, until the bacon is browned and the fat is rendered. Remove the bacon with a slotted spoon and set aside.

2. Season the drumsticks with salt and pepper. Add to the skillet and cook, turning often, until well browned on all sides, 7 to 10 minutes. Remove to a plate or platter.

3. Pour off the fat from the skillet. Add the leeks and cook, stirring, until slightly softened, 3 to 5 minutes. Add the stock and stir to pick up any browned bits on the bottom of the skillet.

4. Arrange the drumsticks in one flat layer on top of the leeks. Spread the squash in a thick layer over the chicken. Sprinkle over the bacon and cover tightly. Reduce the heat to medium and cook, shaking the pan from time to time, until the chicken shows no trace of pink when pierced at its thickest part and the squash is very tender, 30 to 40 minutes. Arrange the chicken on a large, warmed platter. Spoon over the squash, leeks, and bacon, along with any cooking juices. Serve at once.

 Serves 6

Chicken Nugget

China is the world leader in poultry meat production, followed by the United States.

Irish Drumsticks in a Clay Pot

Cooking in a clay pot is an ancient technique. Special pots are readily available and come with specific instructions. It takes a little longer to cook in clay than in, say, a covered casserole (mostly because the process starts in a cold oven), but the results are excellent. Serve these drumsticks with good bread and a crisp, seasonal salad.

12 medium to large drumsticks

Salt and freshly ground black pepper

1 head green cabbage (1½ to 2 pounds), quartered, cored, and thinly sliced

3 medium all-purpose potatoes (1½ pounds), peeled and thickly sliced

2 medium green apples, such as Granny Smith, peeled and thickly sliced

½ cup dry white wine

1 tablespoon chopped fresh parsley

1. Soak a large clay pot designed for cooking in cold water for 10 to 15 minutes, or as directed by the manufacturer's instructions. Season the drumsticks with salt and pepper.

2. Spread half of the sliced cabbage in the bottom of the clay pot. Arrange half of the potatoes on top of the cabbage and top with half of the apples. Season liberally with salt and pepper between the layers. Arrange the drumsticks on top of the apples. Place the remaining apples on top of the drumsticks, spread the remaining potatoes on top of the apples, and top with the remaining cabbage. Season well between the layers. Pour over the wine and cover.

3. Place the clay pot in a cold oven and turn the oven on to 425°F. Cook, basting occasionally with any accumulated pan juices, until the chicken shows no sign of pink when pierced at its thickest point and the potatoes are very tender, about 1 hour. Arrange the chicken on a large, warmed platter and surround with the cabbage, potatoes, and apples. Sprinkle with parsley and serve at once.

 Serves 6

Chicken Nugget

Chicken-fried steak is not a chicken at all but a beefsteak that has been tenderized by pounding, coated with flour or batter, and fried. It gets its name from the style of cooking, which is similar to Southern fried chicken.

Whole Legs

■■

Many poultry sections sell whole legs, the unseparated drumstick and thigh without the back portion. Grocery stores sell many packages of this all-dark-meat segment of the bird, and the free-range packagers seem to sell this part in lieu of individual thighs and drumsticks. Therefore, a few recipes need to be included.

Whole legs provide large portions. Look for smaller ones for smaller portions, if desired, but most of these recipes are so good you won't want to cut back at all! And cold, cooked chicken is always welcome the next day.

Whole Leg Tips

- Whole legs are great for grilling. They are easy to stuff with a savory filling tucked up under their generous skin cover and make for crispy, hearty eating. Use a drip pan for best results. The fattiness of this part makes for repeated flame-ups on the grill, which will char the flesh. Grill the whole legs skin side up to begin and turn often with tongs—not a fork, which will pierce the skin and create unnecessary loss of juices.

- Whole legs are also well suited to long cooking in liquid. Baked, stewed, and braised legs are moist and succulent. It is difficult to dry out the texture of this chicken part by overcooking.

- Most producers of free-range chickens sell only whole birds. However, whole legs (and sometimes breasts) are the only parts that are sometimes sold separately. This is good news for chicken lovers with discriminating palates! Free-range whole legs are often reasonably priced.

Whole Legs

Quick and Easy

Grilled Legs with Honey Mustard and Bourbon Glaze

If time permits, the legs can be marinated in the honey mustard mixture for up to two days. Honey mustard is an increasingly popular condiment found in some large grocery stores and many specialty food shops. If not available, use an equal amount of a good-quality Dijon mustard and increase the sugar in the below ingredients list by 2 tablespoons. Serve with garlicky mashed potatoes or cheesy polenta.

6 whole chicken legs

Salt and freshly ground black pepper

¼ cup honey mustard

½ cup bourbon

2 tablespoons olive oil

2 tablespoons brown sugar

1. Prepare a charcoal fire and let coals burn to a gray ash. Lightly oil the grill. Alternatively, preheat the broiler and set an oiled broiling pan 4 to 6 inches from the heat source. Season the legs with salt and pepper.

2. In a small bowl, combine the mustard, bourbon, oil, and brown sugar. Whisk to blend well. Generously brush the legs on both sides with the mustard mixture.

3. Grill or broil the legs, turning often, until well browned and glazed and there is no trace of pink in the juices when a sharp knife is pierced into the thickest part of the flesh, 30 to 45 minutes. Baste with the mustard mixture frequently as the chicken cooks.

 **Serves 6**

Grilled Pesto Chicken Legs

If you add the pesto before grilling or broiling, the chicken turns a dark color and loses some flavor. I like to brush on the pesto liberally at the end of cooking, as indicated. Homemade pesto is easy to make and keeps for months in the freezer.

6 whole chicken legs

Salt and freshly ground black pepper

¼ cup lemon juice

2 tablespoons olive oil

¼ cup homemade or bottled pesto (see Note)

1. Prepare a charcoal fire and let coals burn to a gray ash. Lightly oil the grill. Alternatively, preheat the broiler and set an oiled broiling pan 4 to 6 inches from the source of heat. Season the legs with salt and pepper.

2. In a small bowl, mix the lemon juice with the oil until blended. Grill or broil the legs, turning often, until browned and there is no trace of pink in the juices when a sharp knife is pierced into the thickest part of the flesh, 30 to 45 minutes. Brush often with the lemon and oil mixture.

3. Turn all of the legs skin side up on the grill. (If broiling, brush the skin side of the chicken with the pesto and return the chicken, skin side down, to the broiler for 2 minutes to heat the pesto.) Brush the cooked chicken with equal amounts of the pesto while still hot. Remove from the grill and serve at once.

 Serves 6

NOTE: *To make the pesto, combine 2 cups tightly packed, clean basil leaves, 10 peeled garlic cloves, and ⅔ cup toasted pine nuts in the bowl of a food processor. Process until the mixture forms a smooth puree. With the blade in motion, slowly add 1½ cups olive oil. (The pesto can be made and kept in the freezer for up to 6 months at this point. Thaw before continuing.) Then stir 2 cups grated Parmesan cheese into the pesto and season with salt and freshly ground black pepper to taste just before serving. Makes about 3 cups.*

Quick and Easy

Chicken Nugget

"I don't know which is more discouraging, literature or chickens."

—From a letter to Stanley Hart White from E. B. White, in January 1929

Stove-Top Braised Chicken Legs with Potatoes and Fennel

Some varieties of potatoes hold up better to long cooking than others. (Like Golden Delicious apples used for making pies.) Yukon Gold potatoes will stay firm and keep their shape in a dish like this one. Floury potatoes like Russets will disintegrate and turn to mush. The right ingredients make a difference!

6 whole chicken legs

Salt and freshly ground black pepper

2 tablespoons unsalted butter

2 tablespoons vegetable oil

1½ pounds Yukon Gold potatoes, peeled and cut into 1-inch cubes

1 fennel bulb, trimmed, cored, and thinly sliced

1 cup chicken stock, preferably homemade

2 tablespoons chopped fresh parsley

1. Season the legs well with salt and pepper. Melt the butter with the oil in a large skillet. Brown over medium-high heat, turning often, 7 to 10 minutes. Remove to a plate or platter and pour off all but about 1 tablespoon of the fat from the skillet.

2. Add the potatoes to the skillet and stir constantly until lightly browned, about 2 minutes. Add the fennel and cook 1 minute longer. Pour in the stock, arrange the chicken legs on top, season with salt and pepper, cover, and cook until tender and cooked through, 20 to 25 minutes. Remove the cover during the last 10 minutes and increase the heat to high. The cooking liquid will reduce to thicken the consistency and concentrate the flavors.

3. Remove the legs to a warmed serving platter. Use a slotted spoon to surround the chicken with the potatoes and fennel. Pour any accumulated pan juices over the chicken. Sprinkle with the chopped parsley and serve at once.

 Serves 6

Whole Legs

Simply Sophisticated

Grilled Legs Stuffed with Black Olives and Goat Cheese

Use soft, fresh goat cheese and oil-cured olives if possible here. Older goat cheese and olives cured in brine tend to make this filling too salty. Cream cheese could be used in place of the goat cheese for a milder flavor. Serve with grilled tomatoes and corn on the cob.

6 whole chicken legs

Salt and freshly ground black pepper

1 cup pitted black olives

4 ounces fresh goat cheese

1 tablespoon chopped fresh parsley

1 garlic clove, minced

Olive oil, for brushing

1. Prepare a charcoal fire and let the coals burn to a gray ash. Lightly oil the grill. Alternatively, preheat the broiler, oil a broiling pan, and set the rack about 6 inches from the source of heat.

2. Use fingers to probe deeply under the skin of the legs to separate it from the meat without tearing to form a pocket for filling. Season the legs with salt and pepper.

3. Combine the olives, goat cheese, parsley, and garlic in the bowl of a food processor. Process until smooth. Use your fingers to force the filling into the deep pockets of each leg. Cover as much of the surface as possible without tearing the skin. (Reserve any leftover filling for another use; it freezes well.)

4. Brush the legs lightly with olive oil. Arrange skin side up on a grill or skin side down on a broiling pan. Cook until the filling has set, about 20 minutes. Turn and cook the skin side until golden brown, about 10 minutes longer. Serve at once.

 **Serves 6**

Legs *Grand-mère* with Portobello Mushrooms

*It is important to use the right potato for this recipe. If too starchy, it will fall apart and turn to mush during cooking. Firm-fleshed yellow potatoes, such as Yukon Gold are virtually foolproof! Any bacon will do here, but the smoky slab kind gives a flavor that **Grand-mère** would certainly approve of.*

¼ pound smoky bacon, cut into small pieces

1 tablespoon vegetable oil

6 whole chicken legs

Salt and freshly ground black pepper

12 to 15 medium, firm, yellow-flesh potatoes, such as Yukon Gold (2½ to 3 pounds), peeled and cut into 1-inch pieces

3 medium onions

2 portobello mushrooms, caps only, sliced about ¼ inch thick

1. Preheat the oven to 425°F. Combine the bacon and oil in a large, heavy oven-proof casserole or Dutch oven. Cook on top of the stove over medium-high heat, stirring often, until the bacon is golden brown and the fat is rendered, about 5 minutes. Remove the bacon with a slotted spoon and set aside.

2. Season the chicken with salt and pepper. Add to the casserole and cook, turning often, until well browned, about 10 minutes. (Cook the chicken in batches if necessary to ensure proper browning. Do not crowd the casserole.) Remove the legs and pour off all but 1 tablespoon of the fat.

3. Add the potatoes and onions to the casserole and cook, stirring often, until the onions have slightly softened, 5 to 7 minutes. Season with salt and pepper and stir in the cooked bacon. Return the chicken to the casserole and scatter the mushrooms over the top. Cover tightly and cook in the oven until the potatoes are tender, and the juices of the chicken show no sign of pink when the leg is pierced at its thickest point, 30 to 45 minutes.

 **Serves 6**

Chicken Legs with Pumpkin and Green Apples

Small sugar pumpkins have a lot of flavor and are plentiful in the early fall. This dish can be made with sweet potatoes with almost equally satisfying results. (Canned pumpkin will not work for this recipe, as it is precooked.) Be sure to keep the chicken uncovered in the oven to keep the skin crisp. You can keep the skillet partially covered during the browning to prevent splattering. Serve with crisp, oven-roasted potatoes flavored with fresh thyme.

6 whole chicken legs

Salt and freshly ground black pepper

2 tablespoons unsalted butter

2 tablespoons vegetable oil

½ cup Calvados, apple jack, or dry white wine

1 small sugar pumpkin (about 2 pounds), peeled, seeded, and cut into ½-inch dice

3 medium green apples, such as Granny Smith, peeled, cored, and cut into ½-inch pieces

1 tablespoon chopped fresh parsley

1. Preheat the oven to 300°F. Season the legs with salt and pepper. Melt the butter with the oil in a large, heavy skillet over medium-high heat. Cook the legs in the hot skillet until well browned, about 15 minutes per side. Transfer the legs to a large baking sheet and bake, uncovered for 15 to 20 minutes, or until cooked through.

2. Meanwhile, pour off the fat from the skillet. Carefully pour in the Calvados or wine and increase the heat to high. Boil rapidly, stirring with a wire whisk to pick up any browned bits on the bottom of the skillet, until the liquid has reduced by half. Add the pumpkin and apples, reduce the heat to medium high, and cover. Cook, stirring often, until the apples have given off juices and the pumpkin is slightly tender, 15 to 20 minutes. Remove the cover and stir until the liquid has evaporated and the pumpkin is very tender, about 5 minutes longer. Season to taste with salt and pepper.

3. Arrange the chicken on a large, warmed serving platter and surround with the pumpkin and apples. Sprinkle with the parsley and serve at once.

 **Serves 6**

Poached Chicken Legs with Peach Chutney

This makes a nice feature for a summer buffet, since it is served chilled or at room temperature. It can be done in stages over a few days and put together at the last minute. If you make the chutney in advance, add the cilantro and scallions at the last minute. They tend to wilt, darken, and loose flavor if left in the chutney for a long time.

6 whole chicken legs

2 bay leaves

1 medium onion, quartered

1 tablespoon black peppercorns

12 small peaches, peeled, pitted, and cut into 1/2-inch dice (see Note)

1/4 cup dry white wine

2 tablespoons sherry vinegar

1/4 cup finely chopped scallions (green onions)

1/2 cup chopped fresh cilantro

1/2 cup golden raisins

Salt and freshly ground black pepper

Several sprigs fresh cilantro, for garnish

1. Place the legs in a skillet large enough to hold them in one flat layer. Add the bay leaves, onion, and peppercorns. Pour in enough cold water to cover and bring to a boil over high heat. Reduce the heat to medium, cover, and poach the legs until tender and cooked through, 30 to 45 minutes. Remove the skillet from the heat and allow the legs to cool in the liquid. Place the legs on a large plate or platter. Cover and refrigerate for several hours or overnight. Strain the liquid and reserve for another use. (The chicken can be cooked up to 3 days in advance. Keep tightly covered in the refrigerator until ready to serve.)

2. Combine the peaches, wine, vinegar, scallions, cilantro, and raisins in a large bowl. Season to taste with salt and pepper. Cover and refrigerate until ready to serve. Can be made up to a day in advance (makes about 4 cups).

3. Arrange the cold chicken on a large serving platter. Garnish with the fresh cilantro sprigs. Serve the chutney on the side, chilled or at room temperature.

 Serves 6

NOTE: *Peeling peaches is a cinch. With a sharp knife, make a small incision on the opposite side from the stem end in the form of an* X. *Drop the peaches into rapidly boiling water. Bring back to a boil, then immediately drain and rinse under cold water. Pull back the skin where the* X *was made. It should come right off. If the peaches are not completely ripe, you might need to leave them in the boiling water for a minute or two longer.*

Chicken Legs with Celery Root

Celery root gives legs a nice flavor during cooling and the puree is soul-satisfying fare at its best. Serve with glazed carrots and blanched sugar snap peas.

6 whole chicken legs

Salt and freshly ground black pepper

2 tablespoons unsalted butter

2 tablespoons vegetable oil

1 medium onion, halved lengthwise and thinly sliced

2 cups chicken stock

2 medium celery roots (2¾ pounds), trimmed, peeled, and cut into 1-inch cubes

3 medium all-purpose potatoes, peeled and cut into 1-inch cubes

1 tablespoon finely chopped fresh parsley

1. Season the legs with salt and pepper. Melt the butter with the oil in a large, heavy casserole over medium-high heat. Add the legs and cook, turning often, until well browned, about 10 minutes. (Do it in 2 batches if necessary. Do not crowd the casserole or the legs will not brown properly.) Remove the legs with tongs and set aside.

2. Pour off all but 1 tablespoon of the fat from the casserole. Add the onion and cook, stirring often, until softened, about 3 minutes. Pour in the stock and increase the heat to high. Bring to a boil, stirring to pick up any browned bits in the bottom. Return the chicken legs to the casserole and lower the heat to medium. Arrange the celery roots and potatoes on top of the chicken. Cover and cook until the potatoes and celery roots are tender and the legs show no trace of pink when pierced at the thickest point, about 40 minutes.

3. Remove the legs and cover with foil to keep warm. Strain the contents of the casserole in a large colander. (Reserve the liquid for another use, if desired. It makes a good base for soups or sauces.) Transfer the solids to a food processor and process until very smooth. Return the puree to the casserole and stir over medium-high heat for 3 to 5 minutes or until very hot. Season well with salt and pepper.

4. Spoon the puree over the bottom of a warmed, deep serving platter. Arrange the legs on top and sprinkle over the parsley. Alternatively, serve the puree in a separate bowl on the side. Serve at once.

 **Serves 6**

Stewed Legs with Spinach and Chickpeas

This recipe can be done up to several days in advance and reheated in a hot oven or on top of the stove. Serve with couscous and curried diced carrots for a colorful, complete meal.

2 tablespoons unsalted butter

2 tablespoons vegetable oil

6 whole chicken legs

Salt and freshly ground black pepper to taste

1 medium onion, thinly sliced

1 garlic clove, minced

½ cup dry white wine

5 medium tomatoes (1½ pounds), peeled, seeded, and chopped, or 1 large can (28 ounces) plum tomatoes, drained and chopped

2 sprigs fresh thyme, or 1 teaspoon dried

1 tablespoon chopped fresh oregano, or 1 teaspoon dried

2 cups cooked or canned chickpeas, drained and rinsed

12 cups fresh spinach leaves (about 3 pounds unstemmed), or 2 packages (10 ounces each) frozen spinach leaves, thawed and squeezed of excess moisture

1. Preheat the oven to 375°F. Melt the butter with the oil in a large, heavy casserole or Dutch oven over medium-high heat. Season the legs with salt and pepper and cook, turning often, until browned, about 10 minutes. Remove the legs and pour off all but 1 tablespoon of the fat.

2. Add the onion to the casserole and cook, stirring often, until slightly softened, about 3 minutes. Add the garlic and cook 1 minute longer. Increase the heat to high and pour in the wine. Boil rapidly, stirring with a whisk to pick up any browned bits from the bottom, until the liquid has reduced by half. Return the browned legs to the casserole and add the tomatoes, thyme, and oregano. Cover and cook in the oven until the legs are very tender and cooked through, 30 to 40 minutes.

3. Remove the legs to a warmed serving platter and cover with foil to keep warm. Remove and discard the sprigs of thyme, if necessary. Add the chickpeas and spinach. Return the casserole to the oven, cover, and cook, stirring deep from the bottom every minute or so to ensure that the spinach cooks evenly, until the spinach is tender and the chickpeas are warmed through, 5 to 7 minutes. Season to taste with salt and pepper. Surround the chicken with the spinach and chickpea mixture and serve at once.

 Serves 6

Wings

● ●

Chicken wings are always a good buy. We think of them mainly as finger food—tasty morsels best enjoyed in a casual setting, when you can pick them up and nibble. But happily wings are surprisingly versatile and can be served in a variety of ways.

Wing Tips

- The meatier portion of the wing is called the drumette. It is the ultimate finger food to be served at parties and with drinks before dinner—perfect for dipping.
- The wing flat, or mid-joint, is a tender part of the chicken. However, they are a little difficult to eat, so a sharp knife and a little practice is important. Learn how to cut the wings quickly and easily with a knife and fork when serving the whole wing. Remember that the joint is easy to cut through with just a little pressure.
- Always remove the skinny third part or wing tip, which has no meat and serves no purpose. To do so, cut down between the soft connective joint. Discarding the tips will make for a more attractive presentation and facilitate preparation as well.
- Wings make excellent stock. I like to buy them on sale and make a huge pot of stock for using right away and for freezing.

Cutting Wings into Drumettes

1. Flatten the wing on a large work surface with the skin side down. Cut off and discard the tip.
2. Cut through the remaining joint, leaving as much skin as possible on the drumette. Save the wider, flatter part for another use, such as making stock.

Wings

Quick and Easy

Mexican Grilled Chicken Wings

Olé! These wings can be as hot as you like. Just add as much hot sauce as desired—the sky is the limit! Chili powder packs varying degrees of hot punch, too. I prefer the rich flavor of the mild chili powders, but if you like heat, use one of the more intense varieties.

4 pounds chicken wings

Salt and freshly ground black pepper

½ cup olive oil

2 tablespoons lemon juice

2 garlic cloves, minced

1 tablespoon tomato paste

2 teaspoons sugar

2 teaspoons mild chili powder

1 teaspoon finely chopped and seeded fresh jalapeño pepper

Several drops of bottled hot sauce, or to taste

1. Trim away and discard the wing tips. Season the remaining wings with salt and pepper.

2. Combine the oil, lemon juice, garlic, tomato paste, sugar, chili powder, and jalapeño in a small bowl. Add hot sauce. Mix well. Lay the wings out on a large work surface and use a pastry brush to thoroughly coat the wings with the sauce.

3. Prepare a charcoal fire and let the coals burn to a gray ash. Lightly oil the grill. Alternatively, preheat the broiler and set an oiled broiling pan 6 inches from the source of heat. Grill the wings, turning often, until dark amber–colored and firm to the touch, 25 to 30 minutes.

 **Serves 6**

Beer Batter Wings with Tartare Sauce

Use the smallest wings you can find for this recipe. The trick is to cook the chicken without burning the thick coating. Flat beer works best for the batter. Be sure to hold the dipped wing parts in the air briefly to drain a little before submerging in the hot oil. The batter should coat well and not be too thick. Cool slightly before serving the wings on a large platter with the sauce in the center for dipping. Additional fresh herbs can be added to the tartare sauce, if desired.

2 cups mayonnaise

2 tablespoons finely chopped sour pickles

2 tablespoons drained, chopped capers

1 tablespoon chopped fresh parsley

Salt and freshly ground black pepper

3 pounds small chicken wings

2 cups all-purpose flour

1 teaspoon salt

1 cup beer

1 large egg

Vegetable or peanut oil, for deep-frying

2 large egg whites

1. Combine the mayonnaise, pickles, capers, and parsley in a medium bowl and stir well to combine. Season to taste with salt and pepper, cover, and refrigerate until ready to serve. (The sauce can be made up to 2 days in advance.)

2. Remove the wing tips and discard. Separate the remaining wing parts by cutting neatly between the joint that holds them together. Season with salt and pepper.

3. Combine the flour and the 1 teaspoon salt in a large bowl and make a well in the center. Combine half the beer and the whole egg in the well and mix with a fork to blend. Slowly draw in the flour, mixing to form a smooth batter. Stir in the remaining beer and cover. Let sit for at least 15 minutes and up to 1 hour.

4. Heat a large amount of oil in a deep-fat fryer to 350°F. Beat the egg whites until firm and fold into the beer batter. Dip the wings in the batter, a few at a time, and submerge in the hot oil. Fry in batches until golden brown, about 10 minutes. Drain on paper towels and season with salt and pepper. Serve with the tartare sauce on the side.

 Serves 6 as an appetizer

Drumettes with Honey and Peanuts

Some of the peanuts will fall off the mini-drumsticks as they are turned, and these loose nuts will be very dark at the end of cooking. Do not be alarmed; the peanuts that adhere to the chicken will not burn as easily. Watch carefully, however, during the last few minutes. The peanuts should be very dark but not burned and bitter.

36 chicken wings (6 to 8 pounds)

Salt and freshly ground black pepper

2 cups roasted, salted peanuts

½ cup honey

1 tablespoon lemon juice

1. Preheat the oven to 425° F. and line a large baking sheet with parchment paper. Trim away and discard the wing tips. Cut the remaining wing parts in half by cutting through the connective joint. Reserve the wide middle joint for another use. Trim the mini-drumsticks or drumettes of excess fat. Season to taste with salt and pepper.

2. Place the peanuts in the bowl of a food processor. Process in several quick pulses to coarsely grind—no more than 10 to 15 seconds. Pour into a large, shallow bowl for dipping.

3. Combine the honey and lemon in a small bowl and mix well. Brush each drumette with the honey mixture. Dip into the peanuts and roll, pressing the nuts to adhere. Arrange on the baking sheet and bake in the upper part of the oven for 12 minutes. Turn carefully and bake 10 to 12 minutes longer or until the chicken is firm and the peanuts are well browned. Cool slightly before serving.

 Serves 6 as an appetizer

Chicken Nugget

"To get a better piece of chicken, you'd have to be a rooster."
    —Slogan from Mickey Mantle's Country Cookin' (restaurant)

Coconut Party Wings

Coconut milk imparts great flavor and tenderizes these party wings. The coconut doesn't adhere too easily to the milk-soaked drumettes, but enough will stick to give full effect. Handle them gingerly after rolling to keep as much of the coconut on as possible. Turn gently for the same reason, and watch carefully during cooking. The coconut burns easily, especially the flakes that fall off onto the pan. The coconut should be dark brown and very toasted but not blackened. Unsweetened, flaked coconut is available in many health food stores. I've done this recipe with sweetened, flaked coconut and found it to be too sweet for my taste. Take the time to search out the unsweetened kind for best results.

36 chicken wings (6 to 8 pounds)

2 cans (15 ounces each) unsweetened coconut milk

2 cups unsweetened, flaked coconut

2 tablespoons unsalted butter, melted

2 tablespoons lemon juice

Salt and freshly ground black pepper

1. Trim off the wings tips and discard. Cut the remaining wing parts in half by slicing down between the joint that connects them. Reserve the wide middle joint part for another use. Trim the mini-drumsticks of excess fat and place in a large, shallow dish. Pour over the coconut milk, cover, and set aside for 15 minutes at room temperature. (The wings can soak in the coconut milk for up to 24 hours, covered and refrigerated.)

2. Preheat the oven to 375°F. Lightly oil 2 large baking sheets and place the coconut in a large bowl for dipping. Remove the mini-drumsticks from the coconut milk and roll in the flaked coconut to coat. Arrange about 1 inch apart on the baking sheets.

3. Mix the butter with the lemon juice and spoon about ½ teaspoonful over each chicken piece. Bake for 15 minutes, carefully turn over, and bake 15 minutes longer, or until the coconut is dark brown and the chicken is cooked through. Season lightly with salt and pepper and cool for 5 minutes before serving.

 Serves 6 as an appetizer

Buttermilk-Dipped Fried Wings

Serve these fried wings at room temperature as part of an informal picnic or summer buffet. A cold salad of black beans with fresh corn and cilantro makes a nice accompaniment. Wings with cole slaw and potato salad wouldn't make a bad menu, either!

4 pounds chicken wings

1 quart buttermilk

2 cups all-purpose flour

1 teaspoon salt

½ teaspoon freshly ground black pepper

½ teaspoon red pepper flakes, or to taste

3 large eggs

1 teaspoon water

4 cups fresh bread crumbs

Vegetable or peanut oil, for deep-frying

Salt and freshly ground black pepper

1. Remove and discard the wings tips and place the wings in a large, shallow bowl. Pour over the buttermilk and set aside, covered, at room temperature for at least 15 minutes. (Soak the wings overnight in the refrigerator if time allows. The buttermilk flavor will be even more pronounced and the flesh will be super-tender.)

2. Combine the flour, 1 teaspoon salt, and ½ teaspoon pepper in a large dish for dipping. Lightly beat the eggs with the water and place in a separate bowl for dipping. Arrange the bread crumbs in a large bowl for the final dipping.

3. Heat a large amount of oil in a deep-fat fryer to 370° F. Drain the wings and roll, one at a time, in the flour mixture. Dip next into the egg mixture and immediately transfer to the bread crumbs. Turn well to thoroughly coat, then place in the hot fat. Fry the wings, in batches, until golden brown and crisp, 6 to 9 minutes. Drain on paper towels and season to taste with salt and pepper.

 Serves 6 as an appetizer

Sautéed Wings with Spicy Yogurt Sauce

The inspiration for this party wing recipe with a spicy sauce comes from the Moosewood Restaurant in Ithaca, New York. I had this sauce over a baked potato, and made a mental note to try it as a dipping sauce. I have altered it slightly to go with sautéed wings. You'll find it a great dish to serve with drinks before dinner or as part of a large cocktail party buffet. This recipe is pretty fiery to my taste, but increase the amount of pepper flakes if you want even more intense flavor.

36 chicken wings (6 to 8 pounds)

2 bunches (12 to 14) fresh scallions (green onoins), white part only

½ teaspoon red pepper flakes, or to taste

¼ cup olive oil

2 teaspoons ground cumin

2 teaspoons mild curry powder

2 large ripe tomatoes, peeled, seeded, and chopped

1 tablespoon all-purpose flour

2 cups plain yogurt

Salt and freshly ground black pepper

2 tablespoons unsalted butter

2 tablespoons vegetable oil

1. Trim away and discard the wing tips. Cut the remaining parts in half by cutting through the connective joint. Reserve the wide middle joint for another use. Trim the mini-drumsticks or drumettes of excess fat.

2. Slice the scallions in half lengthwise, thinly slice crosswise, and place in a small saucepan. Add the red pepper flakes, olive oil, cumin, and curry powder. Cook, stirring often, over medium-high heat until the scallions are tender, about 3 minutes. Stir in the tomatoes and flour. Stir constantly until the mixture is smooth and heated through, about 2 minutes. Add the yogurt and immediately remove from the heat. Stir in the saucepan until warmed and combined. (Do not allow the yogurt to become too hot or it will curdle.) Season the sauce to taste with salt and pepper and set aside at room temperature (makes about 2½ cups sauce).

3. Melt the butter with the oil in a large, heavy skillet over medium-high heat. Season the drumettes with salt and pepper. Cook, turning often, until well browned on all sides, 15 to 20 minutes. Drain on paper towels. Season with additional salt and pepper if desired.

4. Serve the drumettes on a large platter. Pour the sauce into a decorative bowl and place near the platter for dipping.

 Serves 6 as an appetizer

Maple-Brushed, Bacon-Wrapped Party Wings

Use a deep-sided baking sheet when cooking these wings; otherwise, the bacon fat will spill over the sides onto the oven floor. Turn the wings often to ensure even browning, but do so carefully so that the bacon stays wrapped around the chicken.

36 chicken wings (6 to 8 pounds)

½ cup maple syrup

½ pound thinly sliced bacon

Salt and freshly ground black pepper

1. Preheat the oven to 425°F. and line 2 large, 1-inch-deep baking sheets with foil. Trim away and discard the wing tips. Cut the remaining parts in half by cutting through the connective joint. Reserve the wide middle joint for another use. Trim the mini-drumsticks or drumettes of excess fat.

2. With a pastry brush, lightly coat each drumette with a small amount of syrup. Cut each bacon slice in half crosswise and wrap a piece securely around each drumette. (There should be no need to secure the bacon. It will adhere to the chicken as it cooks.) Season lightly with salt and lots of pepper. Arrange 1 inch apart on the baking sheets. Place the sheets in the oven and bake until the bacon is golden brown and crisp, about 25 minutes. Use tongs to carefully turn the drumettes from time to time.

3. Remove to drain on paper towels. Cool for several minutes then pass on a serving tray with plenty of napkins.

 Serves 6 as an appetizer

Balsamic-Glazed Wings

Balsamic vinegar has become so popular, and many food companies have come out with inferior products in an attempt to imitate the real thing. Good basalmic vinegar from Modena, Italy, is more expensive than other vinegars, but worth every penny. Because it is so intense in flavor, a little goes a long way, as in this recipe. Serve these wings on a bed of cooked linguini tossed in olive oil with tiny slivers of fresh garlic. Remember—quality products always make a difference!

4 pounds chicken wings

Salt and freshly ground black pepper

¼ cup balsamic vinegar

¼ cup honey

1 tablespoon olive oil

1 tablespoon chopped fresh thyme leaves

1. Preheat the oven to 425°F. and heavily butter 1 or 2 baking dishes large enough to hold the wings in a flat layer. Remove and discard the wing tips and season the remaining parts well with salt and pepper.

2. Combine the vinegar, honey, oil, and thyme in a small bowl. Stir until the honey is dissolved. Use a pastry brush to thoroughly coat the wings on all sides with the balsamic mixture. Arrange the wings flat in the dish or dishes and bake, basting often, until the wings are glazed and cooked through, about 30 minutes. Remove to a large, warmed platter and pour over any pan juices from the baking dish or dishes.

 **Serves 6**

Chicken Nugget

Buffalo wings: This famous chicken appetizer does, indeed, come from Buffalo, New York. It was created in 1964 at the city's Anchor Bar, where you can still sample the spicy wings today.

Quick and Easy

Sautéed Wings with Herbed Dipping Sauce

The dipping sauce is great for grilled wings, too. The fresh flavor of the herbs balances the hotter flavors of the red pepper and ginger.

36 chicken wings (6 to 8 pounds)

1 cup rice wine vinegar

2 tablespoons sugar

¼ teaspoon red pepper flakes, or to taste

½ red bell pepper, cut into tiny dice

1 piece fresh ginger, 2 inches long, peeled and grated

½ tablespoon chopped fresh cilantro

½ tablespoon chopped fresh mint

2 tablespoons unsalted butter

2 tablespoons vegetable oil

Salt and freshly ground black pepper

1. Trim away and discard the wing tips. Cut the remaining parts in half by cutting through the connective joint. Reserve the wide middle joint for another use. Trim the mini-drumsticks or drumettes of excess fat.

2. Combine the vinegar, sugar, red pepper flakes, bell pepper, and ginger in a small saucepan. Bring to a boil over high heat. Reduce the heat slightly to medium high and simmer until reduced by half. Remove from the heat, cool, and stir in the cilantro and mint. Pour the sauce into a bowl for dipping and set aside at room temperature.

3. Melt the butter with the oil in a large, heavy skillet over medium-high heat. Season the drumettes with salt and pepper. Cook, turning often, until well browned on all sides and firm, 15 to 20 minutes. Drain on paper towels. Season with additional salt and pepper, if desired.

4. Serve the drumettes on a large platter. Pass the platter with the dipping sauce and let guests serve themselves.

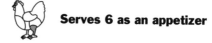 **Serves 6 as an appetizer**

Chicken Nugget

Chickens have been domesticated for at least 4,000 years, but not until the beginning of the nineteenth century did the meat and eggs start to become mass-production commodities.

Indoor-Barbecued Chicken Wings

Add a half-teaspoon (or more!) red pepper flakes for a hotter version. Serve barbecued wings with glazed sweet potatoes and sautéed bitter greens. Cornbread would be nice, too!

2 tablespoons olive oil

1 large onion, finely chopped

1 celery stalk, thinly sliced

2 garlic cloves, minced

10 medium tomatoes (2 pounds), peeled, seeded, and chopped, or 1 large can (28 ounces) plum tomatoes, drained and chopped

¼ cup brown sugar

¼ cup vinegar

2 tablespoons soy sauce

1 tablespoon tomato paste

2 teaspoons ground ginger

Salt and freshly ground black pepper

4 pounds chicken wings

1. Trim away and discard the wing tips. Heat the oil in a large saucepan over medium-high heat. Add the onion and celery and cook, stirring often, until soft, about 5 minutes. Add the garlic and cook 1 minute longer. Add the tomatoes, brown sugar, vinegar, soy sauce, tomato paste, and ginger. Stir well to blend and simmer, stirring often, until the sauce is thickened and smooth, about 30 minutes. Season to taste with salt and pepper. (The sauce can be made up to 3 days in advance. Keep refrigerated until ready to use.)

2. Preheat the oven to 425°F. Place the wings in a single layer in 1 or 2 large baking dishes, season with salt and pepper, and pour over the sauce. Bake uncovered, stirring and turning the wings often, until dark brown and cooked through, 25 to 30 minutes. Add small amounts of water as needed if the sauce begins to burn on the bottom(s) of the pan or pans. Transfer the wings to a large serving platter and pour over any sauce that remains in the pan or pans.

 Serves 6 as an appetizer

Quick and Easy

Wings with Ginger Carrots

Serve with couscous mixed with toasted pine nuts and currants that have been plumped in Madeira or Port.

2 pounds (12 to 15) carrots, trimmed, peeled, and sliced ¼ inch thick

2 tablespoons unsalted butter

2 tablespoons vegetable oil

4 pounds chicken wings

Salt and freshly ground black pepper

½ cup Madeira or port wine

1 piece fresh ginger, 2 inches long, peeled and finely grated

1 cup thinly sliced scallions (green onions)

1. Trim away and discard the wing tips. Bring a large pot of salted water to a boil. Add the carrots, bring back to a boil, and cook rapidly for 2 minutes to blanch. Drain and rinse under cold, running water.

2. Melt the butter with the oil in a large, heavy skillet over medium-high heat. Season the wings with salt and pepper. Cook the wings until golden brown, about 10 minutes on each side. (Do it in 2 batches if necessary. Do not crowd the pan.) Remove the wings and pour off the fat from the skillet.

3. Return the skillet to the heat and pour in the Madeira. Stir with a wire whisk to pick up any browned bits on the bottom of the skillet. Increase the heat to high and boil until the liquid has reduced by half. Add the carrots, ginger, and half of the scallions. Stir well and reduce the heat to medium.

4. Return the wings to the skillet. Cover and cook, stirring occasionally, until the carrots are tender and the wings show no trace of pink when pierced at the larger of the 2 joints, about 10 minutes. Transfer the wings to a large, heated platter. Stir the remaining scallions into the carrot and ginger mixture. Spoon the carrots and sauce over the wings and serve at once.

 Serves 6 as an appetizer

Stewed Wings with Tomato and Herbs

Simple, quick, and oh-so-flavorful when made with great tomatoes, this is a dish that is hard to beat. Substitute two thinly sliced medium leeks for the onion, if desired. Serve with a puree of white beans enriched with a little cream.

3 to 4 pounds chicken wings

Salt and freshly ground black pepper

2 tablespoons unsalted butter

1 large onion, halved lengthwise and thinly sliced

5 medium plum tomatoes (1 pound), peeled, seeded, and chopped, or 1 large can (28 ounces) peeled plum tomatoes, drained and chopped

1 tablespoon chopped fresh basil

1 tablespoon chopped fresh thyme leaves, or 1 teaspoon dried

1 tablespoon chopped fresh oregano leaves, or 1 teaspoon dried

1. Preheat the oven to 425° F. and heavily butter 2 large baking pans. Remove the wing tips and discard. Season the wings with salt and pepper and arrange in a flat layer in the baking pans.

2. Melt the butter in a large, heavy skillet over medium-high heat. Add the onion and cook, stirring often, until wilted and slightly softened, about 5 minutes. Stir in the tomatoes, basil, thyme, and oregano. Season with salt and pepper and spoon equal amounts over the chicken.

3. Bake in the upper part of the oven, stirring often, until the wings are very tender and the onion is soft, 30 to 45 minutes. Serve on a large, warmed platter.

 Serves 6 as a first course

Tomato-less Barbecued Wings

These are excellent done on the grill, too!

1 cup dry white wine

¼ cup red wine vinegar

⅔ cup olive oil

1 tablespoon Dijon mustard

¼ cup tightly packed, shredded basil leaves

1 tablespoon chopped fresh thyme leaves, or 1 teaspoon dried

1 tablespoon chopped fresh oregano, or 1 teaspoon dried

2 garlic cloves, minced

4 pounds chicken wings

Salt and freshly ground black pepper

1. Trim away and discard the wing tips. Preheat the oven to 425°F.

2. Combine the wine, vinegar, oil, mustard, basil, thyme, oregano, and garlic in a blender. Blend for several seconds or until very smooth. Arrange the wings flat in 1 or 2 large baking dishes, season with salt and pepper, and pour over the sauce. Bake uncovered, stirring and turning the wings often, until golden brown, 25 to 30 minutes. Add small amounts of water as needed if the sauce begins to evaporate and burn the bottom of the pan.

3. Transfer the wings to a large, warmed serving platter. Pour over any sauce that remains in the pan or pans. Serve at once with plenty of napkins!

 **Serves 6 as an appetizer**

Chicken Nugget

Chicken mushrooms: Hen-of-the-woods *(Grifola frondosa)* and chicken-of-the-woods *(Polyporus sulphureus)* are not poultry but wild mushrooms that grow on tree trunks and stumps. Hen-of-the-woods gets it name from its curling clusters that resemble a fowl's tail feathers. When small and succulent, the flavor of chicken-of-the-woods is said to be like chicken.

Pepper Jelly Wings

Use a hot pepper jelly for this recipe. Some of the heat seems to dissipate during cooking, so a mild variety doesn't impart much flavor. These are sticky and very messy to eat. Enjoy with family or very good friends who don't mind watching one another lick their fingers. Serve as a main course with cole slaw and potato salad.

4 pounds chicken wings

Salt and freshly ground black pepper

1 cup homemade or store-bought pepper jelly

2 tablespoons red wine vinegar

1. Trim away and discard the wing tips. Preheat the oven to 425° F. Line 1 or 2 large baking sheets with heavy-duty foil; lightly oil the foil. Arrange the wings in a flat layer and season with salt and pepper.

2. Combine the jelly with the vinegar in a small, heavy saucepan. Stir over medium-high heat until the jelly has melted, 3 to 5 minutes. Use a pastry brush to thoroughly coat the wings.

3. Bake the wings, turning and brushing with the remaining jelly often, until sticky and golden brown, 25 to 30 minutes. Let cool slightly before serving.

 Serves 6

Drumettes with Honey and Poppy Seeds

Robert Carmack, an American food writer living in Australia, is the inspiration for this recipe. Robert has long served these attractive, tasty mini-drumsticks with drinks. Some of the poppy seeds will fall off as the wings are turned during cooking. You can sprinkle on a few more as replacements while they are still hot, if desired.

36 chicken wings (6 to 8 pounds)

Salt and freshly ground black pepper

½ cup honey

1 tablespoon lemon juice

3 to 4 tablespoons poppy seeds

1. Preheat the oven to 425° F. and line a large baking sheet with parchment paper. Trim away and discard the wing tips. Cut the remaining wing parts in half by cutting through the connective joint. Reserve the wide middle joint for another use. Trim the mini-drumsticks or drumettes of excess fat. Season to taste with salt and pepper.

2. Combine the honey and lemon in a small bowl and mix well. Brush each drumette all over with the honey mixture. Sprinkle about ¼ teaspoon of poppy seeds all over each of the drumettes. Arrange on the baking sheet and cook in the upper part of the oven, turning often, until dark brown and firm, 20 to 25 minutes. Cool slightly before serving.

Serves 6 as an appetizer

Chicken Nugget

When settlers arrived in America, only the wealthy could afford chicken. The birds multiplied rapidly and within fifty years, there were some on almost every farm. As hunting killed off more and more wild birds, the colonists ate more and more domesticated chicken.

Wings

Wings
Simply Sophisticated

Grilled Teriyaki Chicken Wings

For a quick dipping sauce to go with these wings, mix equal parts soy sauce and rice wine vinegar in small bowls. Pass the wings on a tray with dipping sauce on the side.

36 chicken wings (6 to 8 pounds)

½ cup olive oil

¼ cup soy sauce

2 tablespoons white vinegar

2 teaspoons brown sugar

1 piece fresh ginger, 2 inches long, peeled and grated

¼ teaspoon ground ginger

2 garlic cloves, minced

2 tablespoons sherry

1. Trim away and discard the wing tips. Cut the remaining parts in half by cutting through the connective joint. Reserve the wide middle joint for another use. Trim the mini-drumsticks or drumettes of excess fat.

2. Combine the oil, soy sauce, vinegar, brown sugar, fresh ginger, ground ginger, garlic, and sherry in a small bowl. Stir well to mix. Pour over the wings and marinate, turning often, for 30 minutes at room temperature. (The wings can marinate for up to 24 hours, covered and refrigerated.)

3. Prepare a charcoal fire and let the coals burn to a gray ash. Lightly oil the grill. Alternatively, preheat the broiler and set an oiled broiling pan 6 inches from the heat source. Remove the drumettes from the marinade and grill or broil, turning often, until the wings are dark amber–colored and firm to the touch, about 20 minutes. Brush with the marinade while cooking.

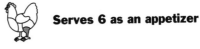 **Serves 6 as an appetizer**

Baked Wings with Dried Cherries, Orange, and Scallions

Dried cherries are found in many specialty food stores and catalogs. They can be ordered directly from Chuckar Cherries (1-800-624-9544), or the King Arthur Flour Company (1-800-877-6836). Raisins or halved dried apricots can be substituted, if desired.

1½ cups pitted dried tart cherries

Salt and freshly ground black pepper

4 pounds chicken wings

2 tablespoons unsalted butter, at room temperature

2 medium seedless oranges

½ cup dry white wine

½ cup very thinly sliced scallions (green onions), white parts only

1. Soak the dried cherries in warm water to cover for 10 minutes. Drain.

2. Preheat the oven to 425°F. Remove and discard the wings tips. Season the remaining parts with salt and pepper. Spread the butter over the bottoms and sides of a large baking dish. Arrange the wings in a single flat layer. (You may need 2 dishes if there is not enough room to lay the wings flat. In this case, use the same amount of butter to spread over the second dish.)

3. Grate the zest from the oranges, avoiding the bitter white pith. (You should have about 1 tablespoon. If not, use another orange to obtain this amount.) Sprinkle the grated zest over the chicken. Remove the entire rind and pith from the oranges. Cut down between the membranes of the stripped oranges to extract whole sections. Place the sections in a small bowl and set aside.

4. Sprinkle the cherries over the chicken and pour over the wine. (Use an extra ½ cup wine if a second dish is necessary). Cover the dish or dishes tightly with foil and place in the oven. Bake, turning several times, until the wings are golden brown and cooked through and the cherries are slightly plumped, 25 to 30 minutes. (Remove the foil during the last 10 minutes if the wings are not beginning to brown. Watch carefully and add a spoonful of water if the liquid starts to burn the bottom of the dish or dishes.) Transfer the wings and cherries to a large, warmed serving platter. Pour over any juices that have accumulated in the dish or dishes. Garnish with the orange sections and scatter over the scallions. Serve at once.

 **Serves 6 as an appetizer**

Apricot and Mustard–Glazed Wings

These wings take on a mellow orange color as they cook. Line the baking pans with heavy-duty foil to help in the clean-up process. Try these wings cold, too. They add color and flavor to any picnic spread.

4 pounds chicken wings

Salt and freshly ground black pepper

½ pound dried apricots

2 cups chicken stock

2 tablespoons Dijon mustard

1. Remove and discard the wing tips. Season the remaining parts with salt and pepper.

2. Preheat the oven to 425°F. and butter a baking dish large enough to hold the wings in a single flat layer. (Use 2 dishes, if necessary.)

3. Place the apricots in a small saucepan and pour over the chicken stock. Bring to a boil over high heat, reduce the heat to medium, and cook, uncovered, until the apricots are very tender, about 10 minutes.

4. Transfer the apricots and stock to a food processor. Process until completely pureed, about 30 seconds. Place the puree in a small bowl and stir in the mustard.

5. Brush the wings liberally with the apricot mixture on all sides. Arrange the brushed wings on the baking dish or dishes and cook, turning and brushing often with the apricot mixture, until lightly browned and glazed and cooked through, about 30 minutes. Serve on a large, warmed platter.

 Serves 6 as an appetizer

Chicken Nugget

Chicken soup a cold remedy? Studies show that chicken soup— and other hot drinks—can help alleviate cold symptoms by increasing the flow of nasal secretions. The taste and aroma of chicken soup may be part of the therapy.

Simply Sophisticated

Braised Wings with Morel Mushrooms

Any dried mushroom works well in this recipe. Dried porcini would be a particularly good substitute. Serve with a puree of half potatoes and half cauliflower blended with a little butter. Tender, young sautéed brussels sprouts would make a nice side dish, too.

4 pounds chicken wings

Salt and freshly ground black pepper

2 carrots, peeled and thinly sliced

1 large onion, finely chopped

1 celery stalk, thinly sliced

1 cup dried morel mushrooms (about 1 ounce)

½ cup dry white wine

1 cup chicken stock

2 teaspoons coarsely chopped fresh parsley

1. Preheat the oven to 425°F. and heavily butter 2 large baking pans. Remove the wing tips and discard. Season the remaining parts with salt and pepper and arrange in one single flat layer over the bottoms of the baking pans. Scatter the carrots, onion, and celery over the chicken. Place the pans in the oven and cook uncovered, stirring often, until the wings are golden brown and cooked through and the vegetables are softened,

about 30 minutes. Remove the wings to a large serving platter and cover with foil to keep warm.

2. Meanwhile, place the mushrooms in a bowl and cover with about 1 cup warm water or enough water to completely cover. Soak until softened, about 10 minutes. Drain well and reserve the soaking liquid. Line a sieve with a double layer of cheesecloth and pour the soaking liquid through to filter out any grit. Measure out ½ cup of this filtered liquid and set aside. Reserve any excess for another use. Rinse the mushrooms under cold running water to remove any remaining sand. Squeeze out excess moisture, finely chop the mushrooms, and set aside.

3. Place both baking pans with the softened vegetables over high heat on top of the stove. Pour ¼ cup wine in each of the pans and stir with a whisk to pick up any browned bits from the bottoms. Boil until the liquid has reduced to 2 tablespoons in each pan. Scrape the contents of both pans into a sieve and strain into a small saucepan, pressing down on the solids to extract all the juices. Pour the ½ cup reserved mushroom soaking liquid and the chicken stock into the saucepan. Boil over high heat until the juices are slightly thickened and reduced to about ½ cup. Add the chopped mushrooms and cook about 30 seconds longer to warm through. Season the

sauce with salt and pepper and spoon over the wings. Garnish with parsley and serve at once.

 Serves 6

Sautéed Chicken Wings with Clams

This dish must be eaten with your fingers, so be sure to serve finger bowls and lots of napkins! Serve as a separate course with soup spoons to enjoy the delicious broth. Crusty bread and a salad of orange sections, arugula, and red onions would make an exquisite lunch. Chilled white wine would nicely round out the meal. Mussels could be used in place of the clams. Use the same amount as for clams, and be sure to remove the beards from the mussels when cleaning.

4 pounds chicken wings

Salt and freshly ground black pepper

2 tablespoons unsalted butter

2 tablespoons vegetable oil

1 cup chicken stock

1 garlic clove, minced

1 tablespoon chopped fresh parsley

2 pounds cherrystone or littleneck clams (24 to 30 medium), scrubbed

1. Remove the wing tips and discard. Season the remaining parts with salt and pepper. Melt the butter with the oil in a large saucepan or Dutch oven over medium-high heat. Add the wings and cook, turning often, until well browned, 7 to 10 minutes. Remove and set aside.

2. Pour off all the fat from the pan and add the stock. Increase the heat to high and bring to a boil. Boil rapidly, stirring with a whisk to pick up any browned bits from the bottom, until the liquid has reduced by half.

3. Add the garlic and half of the parsley and reduce the heat to medium. Add the browned wings and cover. Cook, stirring often for 10 minutes. Add the clams and cook for about 10 minutes longer, or until the clams have opened and the wings are firm and opaque.

4. Line a large sieve with a double layer of cheesecloth. Using a slotted spoon, divide the clams and wings among 6 warmed, shallow serving bowls. Pour the broth from the pan into the lined sieve and strain to remove any sand or grit. Ladle a half cupful or so of the broth over each serving of wings and clams. Sprinkle with a pinch of the remaining parsley and serve at once.

 **Serves 6 as a first course**

Chicken Wings Casserole with Chickpeas, Tomatoes, and Rice

There is a fellow at my farmers' market who sells sweet organic chickpeas like I've never had before. They take only a little while to cook and are easy to peel. Canned chickpeas work just fine, though, and there are some excellent brands in most supermarkets. A romaine lettuce salad with garlicky dressing would be all that this hardy dish needs to be a complete meal.

4 pounds chicken wings

Salt and freshly ground black pepper

2 tablespoons unsalted butter

2 tablespoons vegetable oil

1 medium onion, finely chopped

1½ cups rice

3 medium tomatoes, peeled, seeded, and chopped, or 1 can (16 ounces) plum tomatoes, drained and chopped

2 cups cooked or canned chickpeas, drained and rinsed

2½ tablespoons finely chopped fresh parsley

2 cups chicken stock

1. Remove and discard the wing tips. Cut the remaining wings in half by slicing down between the connective joint. Season on all sides with salt and pepper.

2. Melt the butter with the oil in a large, heavy casserole over medium-high heat. Add the wings and cook, turning often, until well browned on all sides, about 10 minutes. Remove the wings and pour off all but 1 tablespoon of the fat.

3. Add the onion to the casserole and cook, stirring often, until just softened, about 3 minutes. Stir in the rice and cook until it glistens, 2 to 3 minutes. Add the tomatoes, chickpeas, and 2 tablespoons of the parsley. Stir well to pick up any browned bits from the bottom of the casserole. Pour in the chicken stock, return the wings, cover, and cook until the rice is tender, 25 to 30 minutes. Remove the cover, stir gently with a fork to fluff the rice, and cover again. (Add a few spoonfuls of water or stock if the rice looks dry at this point.) Cover again and cook 5 minutes longer or until the rice is soft and the wings are cooked through.

4. Turn the contents of the casserole onto a large, warmed serving platter. Sprinkle with the remaining parsley and serve at once.

 **Serves 6**

Wing Ragoût with Leeks and Potatoes

One cup of cream in a recipe that serves six people works out to less than a few tablespoons per serving. And what flavor that little bit of cream gives! Serve the ragoût very hot, with a simple sautéed green vegetable, such as broccoli, green beans, or just-wilted spinach.

4 pounds chicken wings

Salt and freshly ground black pepper

2 tablespoons unsalted butter

2 tablespoons vegetable oil

10 medium mushrooms, quartered

3 large leeks (1¾ pounds), white part only, cleaned and thinly sliced

½ cup dry white wine

12 to 15 small, firm-fleshed potatoes (2 pounds), preferably Yukon Gold, peeled and sliced about ¼ inch thick

1 cup heavy cream

2 teaspoons chopped fresh parsley

1. Remove and discard the wing tips. Cut the remaining parts in half by slicing down between the connective joint. Season on all sides with salt and pepper.

2. Melt the butter with the oil in a large, heavy casserole over medium-high heat. Add the wings and cook, turning often, until browned on all sides, about 10 minutes. (Do it in 2 batches, if necessary. Do not crowd the casserole or the wings will not brown properly.)

3. Remove the wings, add the mushrooms, and increase the heat to high. Season with salt and pepper and cook, stirring often, until browned, about 4 minutes. Remove the mushrooms with a slotted spoon and set aside.

4. Pour off all but 1 tablespoon of the fat from the casserole. Add the leeks to the casserole and cook, stirring often, until just tender, about 3 minutes. Add the wine and stir to pick up any browned bits in the bottom. Boil until the liquid has reduced by half. Stir in the potatoes and cream. Season to taste with salt and pepper.

5. Return the browned wings and the mushrooms to the casserole. Reduce the heat to medium, cover, and cook, stirring often, until the potatoes are tender and the wings are cooked through, about 25 minutes. Season well with salt and pepper. Serve on a large, warmed platter and sprinkle over the parsley.

 **Serves 6**

Stewed Chicken Wings with Lentils and Tomato

When friends ask me what they can bring from France, I always say lentils. The small, green variety from a village named LePuy have a pronounced flavor and a superior texture. Happily, these imported legumes are increasingly available here. Lentils, like dried beans, can vary in cooking time according to how old they are and how they have been stored. You might need to add a little additional stock to this dish before serving if they look dry. For a little zip, add a couple of tablespoons of good red-wine vinegar to the final seasoning, if desired. Steamed white rice makes this a homespun dish to remember.

4 pounds chicken wings

Salt and freshly ground black pepper

2 tablespoons unsalted butter

2 tablespoons vegetable oil

4 or 5 medium mushrooms, quartered

1 cup dry white wine

5 large tomatoes, peeled, seeded, and chopped, or 1 large can (28 ounces) plum tomatoes, drained and chopped

2 cups lentils (about 1 pound), preferably imported (LePuy)

2 cups chicken stock

1 tablespoon chopped fresh rosemary, or 1 teaspoon dried

Several sprigs fresh thyme, or 1 teaspoon dried

1. Trim and discard the wing tips. Season the wings with salt and pepper. Melt the butter with the oil in a large, heavy casserole over medium-high heat. Add the wings and cook, turning often, until well browned, 7 to 10 minutes. (Do it in batches, if necessary. Do not crowd the casserole or the chicken will not brown properly.) Remove the wings and set aside. Add the mushrooms to the casserole and cook, stirring, until lightly browned, about 3 minutes. Remove with a slotted spoon and set aside.

2. Pour off the fat from the casserole. Add the wine and increase the heat to high. Boil rapidly, stirring with a wire whisk to pick up any browned bits from the bottom, until the amount of liquid has reduced by half. Stir in the tomatoes and lentils. Stir well to combine. Pour over the chicken stock and add the rosemary and thyme. Return the browned wings to the casserole. Lower the heat to medium, cover, and cook, stirring often, until the lentils are very tender and the chicken is falling off the bone, about 1 hour. Remove the thyme and season to taste with salt and pepper.

 Serves 6

Chicken Wings Baked with Plum Sauce

Bottled plum sauce is often available in the Asian section of large supermarkets. It works just fine for this recipe, but nothing beats the flavor of homemade sauce made with luscious Italian plums. Serve these wings with rice studded with toasted, slivered almonds or Chinese cellophane noodles with bamboo shoots.

1¾ pounds small Italian plums (30 to 35), halved and pitted

1¼ cups dry white wine

2 tablespoons red wine vinegar

2 tablespoons soy sauce

2 tablespoons honey

4 pounds chicken wings

Salt and freshly ground black pepper

1. Combine the plums, wine, vinegar, and soy sauce in a small, heavy saucepan. Place the pan over medium heat, cover, and cook, stirring often, until the plums are very tender, 15 to 20 minutes. Remove from the heat and stir in the honey. Strain the mixture through a sieve, pressing down hard on the solids to extract as much pulp as possible. (This makes about 1½ cups sauce. The sauce can be made up to 3 days in advance. Keep tightly covered in the refrigerator until ready to prepare the wings.)

2. Preheat the oven to 425°F. Remove the wing tips and discard. Heavily butter a baking dish large enough to hold the wings in one flat layer. (Use 2 dishes if necessary.) Season the wings with salt and pepper on both sides. Place the wings flat in the baking dish and brush each wing with an equal amount of the plum sauce on all sides. Transfer the baking dish to the oven and bake the wings, turning often, until they are glazed and cooked through, about 30 minutes. Watch carefully toward the end of cooking; add several tablespoonfuls of water at a time if the sauce begins to burn off and scorch the bottom of the dish or dishes. Serve the wings hot on a large, warmed platter.

 Serves 6

Stewed Wings with Tuscan White Beans

Use cooked, dried navy or great northern beans or imported canned cannellini beans for best results. Rice and a large green salad would make this a memorable meal.

4 pounds chicken wings

Salt and freshly ground black pepper

2 tablespoons unsalted butter

2 tablespoons vegetable oil

2 garlic cloves, minced

1 cup dry white wine

4 cups cooked or canned white beans, drained and rinsed

2 tablespoons tomato paste

2 tablespoons chopped fresh thyme leaves

1 tablespoon chopped fresh parsley

1. Remove the wing tips and discard. Season the remaining parts with salt and pepper. Melt the butter with the oil in a large casserole or Dutch oven over medium-high heat. Add the wings and cook, turning often, until well browned, about 10 minutes. (Do it in batches, if necessary. Do not crowd the casserole or the wings will not brown properly.)

2. Pour off and discard all but 1 table-spoon of the fat from the casserole. Return the casserole to the heat and add the garlic. Cook, stirring constantly, until the garlic is softened but not browned, about 2 minutes. Pour in the wine, increase the heat to high, and bring to a boil. Boil, using a wire whisk to pick up any browned bits from the bottom, until the liquid has reduced by half.

3. Puree half of the beans in a food processor until smooth. Stir the puree into the casserole with the wine and garlic. Add the remaining beans, tomato paste, and thyme. Stir well and season with salt and pepper. Return the wings to the casserole and pour in enough cold water to cover.

4. Cook over medium-high heat until the bean mixture is thickened and the wings show no trace of pink at the joint, 30 to 40 minutes. (Remove the cover and allow some of the liquid to cook off if the mixture looks too soupy. The beans should be smooth and creamy, looking like the sauce for a stew. Add water as is necessary if the mixture looks too dry.) Stir the casserole often, being careful to keep the wings in one piece. Season to taste with salt and pepper. Serve at once, sprinkled with the parsley.

 **Serves 6**

Wings with Cornbread and Pecan Coating

Cornbread is so easy to prepare. I like to make extra and keep it in the freezer (see Note). For this recipe, cut a large square of it into cubes and let it stand at room temperature for at least a few hours or overnight. When cooking the wings, be careful to keep the temperature of the oil at no more than 370°F. (It is always best to use a deep-fat fryer or a good thermometer when frying.) Pecans burn easily and can result in a bitter taste.

4 pounds chicken wings

Salt and freshly ground black pepper

2 cups all-purpose flour

3 large eggs

1 teaspoon water

2 cups stale cornbread crumbs (see Note)

1 cup shelled pecans

Vegetable or peanut oil, for deep-frying

1. Remove and discard the wing tips. Cut the remaining parts in half, cutting between the connective joint. Season the wings with salt and pepper. Place the flour in a large dish for dipping. Lightly beat the eggs with the water and place in a separate bowl for dipping.

2. Combine the cornbread crumbs with the pecans in the bowl of a food processor and process until the nuts are very finely ground, about 30 seconds. Empty into a large dish for coating.

3. Heat a large amount of oil in a deep-fat fryer to 370°F. Roll the wings, one at a time, in the flour, then dip into the egg mixture. Transfer to the cornbread and pecan mixture and turn to thoroughly coat. Fry the wings in batches until golden brown and crisp, 6 to 9 minutes. Drain on paper towels and season to taste with salt and pepper.

 Serves 6 as a first course

NOTE: *To make cornbread, preheat the oven to 425°F. and oil an 8 × 8-inch baking pan. Combine 1 cup all-purpose flour, 1 cup cornmeal, 1 tablespoon baking powder, and 1½ teaspoons salt in a large bowl. Beat 2 large eggs with 1 cup milk in a separate bowl. Stir the wet ingredients into the dry ingredients just to combine and moisten. Do not work the batter too much or it will be tough. Fold in 2 tablespoons melted, unsalted butter and pour into the pan. Bake for about 15 minutes or until golden brown on top and a toothpick inserted in the center comes out clean. Cool on a wire rack.*

Roasted Wings with Tricolored Peppers and Portobello Mushrooms

The mixture of peppers makes this a particularly colorful dish. You can omit the mushrooms if time is a factor, but they do add a wonderful, earthy flavor to the dish. Serve with garlic mashed potatoes followed by a green salad with homemade croutons.

1 large red bell pepper

1 large yellow bell pepper

1 large green bell pepper

3 portobello mushrooms

1 tablespoon olive oil

1 garlic clove, minced

Salt and freshly ground black pepper

4 pounds chicken wings

1 large onion, thinly sliced

1 tablespoon chopped fresh parsley

1. Bring a large pot of salted water to a boil. Cut each of the bell peppers in half lengthwise and remove the membrane and all seeds. Cut the halves into long, thin strips about ¼ inch wide. Plunge the strips into the boiling water and bring back to a boil. Boil for 1 minute, then drain and rinse under cold, running water. Lay the blanched strips out on paper towels to dry.

2. Preheat the oven to 425° F. Remove the stems from the mushrooms and reserve for another use. Clean the caps by wiping with damp paper towels. Place the caps on an oiled baking sheet and brush each lightly with olive oil. Sprinkle a pinch of the garlic over each cap and season well with salt and pepper. Bake for 20 minutes, or until the garlic is golden and the mushrooms are softened. Remove the mushrooms to a large work surface, and when cool enough to handle, cut into long, thin strips.

3. Remove and discard the wing tips. Cut the wings in half by slicing down between the connective joint. Heavily butter a baking dish large enough to hold the wings in a single flat layer.

Sprinkle the onion over the bottom of the dish. Spread over half of the pepper strips and add the wings, placing them about 1 inch apart over the peppers. Season with salt and pepper, then scatter over the strips of mushrooms. Spread the remaining pepper strips over the mushrooms and season again with salt and pepper. Place the dish in the oven and roast, turning often, until the wings are lightly browned and the peppers are very tender, 30 to 35 minutes. Serve in a large, warmed dish, sprinkled with the parsley.

 Serves 6

Chicken Nugget

Will a chicken by any other name taste the same? It depends on how you prepare it: *Poulet* **(French),** *pollo* **(Spanish and Italian),** *frango* **(Portuguese),** *chi* **and** *gai* **(Chinese),** *murgh* **(Indian),** *ayem* **(Indonesian),** *ayam* **(Malaysian),** *kai* **(Thai), and** *hünchen* **(German).**

Simply Sophisticated

Chicken Wing Tetrazzini

Named for an Italian opera singer, Luisa Tetrazzini, this classic dish is soothing and comforting fare of the best kind. Usually made with leftover chicken or turkey, here I've adapted it using wings for a surprisingly good casserole that can be prepared in advance. A half-cup of heavy cream could be added to the sauce for enrichment, if desired. I like to use spaghetti, but wide noodles work well, too. Serve with a cold, crisp salad and follow with a light dessert.

2½ to 3 pounds chicken wings

Salt and freshly ground black pepper

2 tablespoons unsalted butter

2 tablespoons vegetable oil

12 medium mushrooms, halved or quartered

1 small onion, finely chopped

1 celery stalk, thinly sliced

3 tablespoons all-purpose flour

3 cups chicken stock

6 cups drained, cooked spaghetti (about ¾ pound, uncooked)

1 cup fresh bread crumbs

1 cup freshly grated Parmesan cheese

2 tablespoons melted, unsalted butter

1. Preheat the oven to 375° F. Butter a very large baking dish (or use 2 smaller ones) and set aside. Remove the wing tips and discard. Cut the wings in half by slicing through the connective joint. Season well with salt and pepper.

2. Melt the butter with the oil in a large skillet over medium-high heat. Add the wings and cook, turning often, until well browned, about 10 minutes. Transfer the wings to the buttered baking dish. Add the mushrooms to the skillet and cook, stirring often, until browned, about 5 minutes. Use a slotted spoon to transfer the mushrooms to the baking dish.

3. Add the onion and celery to the skillet and cook, stirring often, until tender, about 3 minutes. Stir in the flour, reduce the heat to medium, and cook until smooth and well blended, about 2 minutes. Add the stock to the skillet and stir to pick up any browned bits from the bottom. Increase the heat to high and bring to a boil, stirring constantly. Boil until the sauce is thickened and smooth. Season with salt and pepper.

4. Spread the cooked spaghetti over the wings and mushrooms in the baking dish and strain the sauce over through a colander, discarding the solids. Combine the bread crumbs and cheese in a small bowl. Sprinkle this mixture evenly over the top of the baking dish and drizzle

Wings

with the melted butter. (The dish can be made up to 2 days in advance at this point. Keep tightly covered in the refrigerator until ready to bake. Bring to room temperature before heating if time permits.) Bake for about 30 minutes or until the top is golden brown, the chicken is cooked through, and the sauce is bubbly. Serve at once.

 Serves 6

Cuban-Style Chicken Wing Stew with Black Beans

Serve this one-dish-meal with yellow rice, roasted red peppers, and lots of cornbread. Have plenty of hot sauce on hand for those who have no fear! Ice cold beer is hands-down the beverage of choice.

2 tablespoons olive oil

2 large carrots, peeled, halved lengthwise, and thinly sliced

1 large red or Bermuda onion, finely chopped

1 celery stalk, thinly sliced

1 garlic clove, minced

2 large tomatoes, peeled, seeded, and chopped

½ cup loosely packed chopped fresh parsley

4 cups cooked or canned black beans, drained and rinsed

2 teaspoons ground cumin

3 pounds chicken wings

3 to 4 cups chicken stock

Salt and freshly ground black pepper

1. Place the olive oil in a large, heavy casserole or Dutch oven. Add the carrots, onion, and celery. Cook over medium-high heat, stirring often, until slightly softened, about 5 minutes. Add the garlic and cook 1 minute longer. Stir in the tomatoes and half of the parsley. Cook, stirring often, until the tomatoes have given off their liquid, about 5 minutes. Stir in the beans and cumin.

2. Cut off and discard the wings tips. Cut the remaining parts of the wings in half by cutting through the connective joint that holds them together. Add these wing parts to the beans and pour in enough stock to barely cover. Bring to a simmer over medium-high heat. Reduce the heat to medium and cook uncovered, stirring often, until the stew is thickened and the chicken is falling off the bones, about 45 minutes. Season well with salt and pepper.

 Serves 6

Roasted Wings and Fennel

Save some of the fronds from the fennel bulbs to use as a garnish. Serve these roasted wings and fennel with creamy polenta sprinkled with Parmesan cheese. The longer cooking time allows the fennel to infuse the wings with their flavor.

4 pounds chicken wings

2 medium carrots, peeled, halved lengthwise, and finely sliced

1 large onion, finely chopped

1 celery stalk, thinly sliced

4 small fennel bulbs, trimmed of fronds, quartered, and cored

Softened unsalted butter, as needed

Salt and freshly ground black pepper

1. Preheat the oven to 425° F. Remove the wing tips and discard. Cut the remaining parts in half by slicing down between the connective joint. Generously butter a baking dish large enough to hold the wings in a single flat layer.

2. Scatter the carrots, onion, and celery over the bottom of the dish. Arrange the quarters of fennel all around and add the wings. Season well with salt and pepper and dot the wings and fennel with butter as desired.

3. Place the dish in the oven. Roast the wings and fennel, turning often to ensure even cooking, until well browned, about 1 hour. Transfer the entire contents of the dish to a warmed platter and serve at once.

 Serves 6

A Few Recipes for Liver Lovers

Plump and tasty chicken livers, creatively cooked, are one of the best parts a chicken has to offer. They are rich in iron, phosphorous, and vitamin A. Unfortunately, many folks have early memories of badly prepared liver dishes, or they think of livers only in that soggy sack of innards pushed into the cavity of whole chickens. Others may have fond memories of chopped chicken liver on Ritz crackers. In any event, liver dishes have intense flavor and can work well as either a first course or a main entrée.

Liver Tips

- When purchasing livers, try to find a specialty food store or local butcher who sells free-range birds. Even at premium prices, free-range livers are a bargain and worth the extra time and trouble. Owing to increased demand, many mass-market chickens today are fed a diet enriched with fat to bring them to market earlier. Therefore, livers are sometimes flabbier, more mushy, and yellow or orange in color from the increased fat deposits. Free-range chickens are more likely to be fed a leaner diet, resulting in a solid, tighter-textured liver. Good livers should be firm, shiny, and dark red or brown. Avoid discolored, splotchy livers that have been exposed to air from sloppy packaging.

- Livers are more perishable than other chicken parts. It is best to watch the "sell by" dates on packages and to use them within 1 or 2 days of buying. Do not freeze for more than three months. Keep livers tightly wrapped in plastic or in an airtight container and store in the coldest part of the refrigerator. Remove just before preparation.

- Overcooked livers tend to dry out and toughen. Try to keep them pink in the middle. While no more susceptible to disease or contamination than any other chicken part, livers should be cooked to an internal temperature of 160° F. to kill any potentially harmful bacteria.

- Livers are rich. I find that a small amount goes a long way. Several of the recipes that follow are for first-course dishes. I prefer a small amount of good liver as a first course, and find that more appetizing than a large amount served as a main course. Adjust the recipes to fit your appetite needs if the quantities look skimpy.

Preparing Livers for Cooking

1. Trim away any green left from the bile sack that might not have been cut off in the production process. It is extremely bitter.

2. Cut off the connective tissue that holds the lobes together. Like all gristle, it tends to become tough when cooked.

Liver

∙∙

Quick and Easy

Cajun Dirty Rice

The name for this Cajun classic comes from the color that the liver turns the rice, brown. While it makes a wonderful, economical main dish, it is usually served as a side dish with cooked meats or chicken. Use as much or as little of the red pepper flakes as desired to achieve the level of heat you want. Of course, most Cajuns keep the ubiquitous bottle of hot sauce on the table to liven up any and every dish deemed too tame!

2 tablespoons unsalted butter

1 large celery stalk, thinly sliced

1 small onion, finely chopped

1 green pepper, halved, seeded, and chopped

¾ pound chicken livers

2 tablespoons finely chopped fresh parsley

½ teaspoon red pepper flakes, or to taste

Salt and freshly ground black pepper

3 cups cooked white rice

1. Melt the butter in a large skillet over medium-high heat. Add the celery, onion, and green pepper. Cook, stirring often, until softened, 3 to 5 minutes.

2. Meanwhile, trim the livers of all membrane and place in a food processor. Puree the livers until smooth, about 30 seconds, and add to the skillet. Stir in the parsley and red pepper flakes. Season with salt and pepper.

3. Just before serving, stir the rice into the skillet and mix well. Season again with salt and pepper, add additional red pepper flakes if desired, and stir over medium heat until warmed through, about 5 minutes. Serve at once in a warmed bowl.

Serves 6 as a side dish

Curried Chicken Livers

Serve this spicy dish as a first course with a small amout of basmati rice and mango chutney. Adjust the seasoning to suit your own taste.

- **1 pound chicken livers**
- **Salt and freshly ground black pepper**
- **1 cup all-purpose flour**
- **2 tablespoons unsalted butter**
- **2 tablespoons vegetable oil**
- **1 small onion, finely chopped**
- **1 celery stalk, thinly sliced**
- **2 teaspoons mild curry powder, or to taste**
- **1 cup chicken stock**
- **1 cup heavy cream**

1. Trim the livers of all gristle and separate the lobes. Season well with salt and pepper. Roll the livers in the flour to coat. Shake off the excess flour from the livers.

2. Melt the butter with the oil in a large nonstick skillet over medium-high heat. Add the livers and cook until well browned, about 2 minutes on each side. Remove the livers to a large plate or platter and cover with foil to keep warm.

3. Pour out all but 1 tablespoon of the fat from the skillet. Add the onion, celery, and curry powder. Stir well to blend. Cook until the onion is tender, about 2 minutes. Pour in the stock, increase the heat to high, and bring to a boil. Boil, stirring often, until reduced by half. Add the cream and boil again until reduced to a thick, syrupy sauce. Strain the contents of the skillet into a large saucepan, pushing down hard on the solids to extract as much flavor as possible.

4. Bring the sauce to a boil over medium-high heat. Taste for seasoning and add salt, pepper, and additional curry powder as needed. Return the liver to the sauce and cook for 3 to 5 minutes, or until firm and very hot.

Serves 6 as a first course

Liver

Judy Witt's Crostini

This recipe comes from an American friend who teaches cooking in Florence. Judy likes to serve these crostini with drinks before dinner. The recipe could be done in a food processor, but I like the coarse texture that chopping by hand gives to this incredibly tasty and easy recipe.

8 chicken livers (¾ pound)

5 tablespoons unsalted butter, softened

1 small onion, finely chopped

¼ cup hearty red wine (preferably Chianti)

2 tablespoons capers

2 tablespoons anchovy paste

Salt and freshly ground black pepper

1 French baguette, cut into ¼-inch-thick slices

1. Trim the livers of all gristle and cut into large pieces.

2. Melt 3 tablespoons of the butter in a medium skillet over medium-high heat. Add the onion and cook, stirring often, until softened, about 3 minutes. Add the livers and cook, stirring gently, until they have just lost all signs of pink, about 2 minutes. Add the wine and increase the heat to high. Cook, stirring constantly, until all of the liquid has evaporated and the livers are firm. Turn the livers out onto a large work surface and cool.

3. Add the capers to the livers. Using a large, sharp knife, finely chop to form a chunky paste. Transfer to a small saucepan and add the anchovy paste. Cook over low heat, stirring constantly, for 1 minute to blend. Add an additional tablespoon or so of wine if the mixture looks too dry. Remove from the heat and stir in the remaining softened butter. Mix well and season to taste with salt and pepper.

4. Spread a teaspoonful or so of the liver mixture on the bread slices and serve at once, topped with a coarse grind or two of black pepper.

Serves 6 as hors d'oeuvres

Quick and Easy

Bacon-Mushroom-Liver Skewers

This makes a wonderful first course when served on a small mount of hot rice, couscous, or polenta; serve with Tomato Sauce (page 226) and garnish with thin slices of red onion. Double the recipe if serving as a main course.

5 or 6 whole chicken livers (about ½ pound)

½ pound thinly sliced bacon

6 to 12 whole white mushrooms

2 to 3 tablespoons olive oil

Salt and freshly ground black pepper

1. Preheat the broiler and set a rack about 8 inches from the heat source. Line a large broiling pan with foil and set aside.

2. Trim away all gristle from the livers and cut into 1½- to 2-inch pieces. Cut the bacon strips in half crosswise. Use half a strip to wrap around each piece of liver.

3. Trim away the ends of the mushrooms and wipe clean with a damp paper towel. Cut each into halves or quarters, depending on size.

4. Thread 4 halves or quarters of mushrooms on each of 6 metal skewers, alternating with 3 of the wrapped livers, beginning and ending with mushrooms. Place the skewers on the broiling pan. Brush the mushrooms with olive oil and season the skewers with salt and pepper.

5. Broil the skewers until the mushrooms are golden brown and the bacon is crisp around the edges, about 7 minutes on each side. Turn the skewers carefully and brush occasionally with the accumulated pan juices to prevent the mushrooms from drying out. Serve at once.

Serves 6 as a first course

Liver

Quick Liver Sauté with Soy and Ginger

This incredibly easy, quick stir-fry of livers is surprisingly versatile. Serve over rice, with Chinese noodles, or even over a bed of fresh salad greens tossed with a small amount of dressing. Sherry wine vinegar gives depth of flavor and a mellow yet tart taste that marries well with the rich liver. If not on hand, use any good-quality vinegar and add a splash of sherry just before serving for a similar effect.

1 pound chicken livers

¼ cup soy sauce

¼ cup sherry wine vinegar

3 tablespoons olive oil

½ cup chopped, fresh, peeled ginger

Salt and freshly ground black pepper

¼ cup thinly sliced scallions (green onions)

1. Trim the livers of all gristle and cut into separate lobes. Combine the soy sauce, vinegar, and 1 tablespoon of the olive oil in a small bowl. Add the livers, turn gently, and set aside to marinate for 10 minutes at room temperature.

2. Heat the remaining 2 tablespoons olive oil in a wok over medium-high heat. Strain the livers in a large sieve and reserve the liquid. Pat the livers dry, add to the wok, and cook, stirring often, until golden brown on all sides, about 5 minutes.

3. Remove the livers and add the marinade liquid and ginger to the wok. Cook, stirring constantly, until the ginger is softened, about 2 minutes. Return the livers to the wok and cook, stirring often, until firm to the touch, 3 to 5 minutes. Season well with salt and pepper. Serve at once, garnished with the sliced scallions.

Serves 6

Chicken Nugget

U.S. consumption of chicken jumped from 9 pounds person in 1950 to 37 pounds in 1970, then skyrocketed to 69 pounds in 1993. Projected growth rates put the per capita level as high as 73 pounds in 1995, and over 84 pounds in the year 2000!

Chicken Liver Ragoût with Pasta

The shallots give this simple dish a wonderfully subtle flavor, but onions could be used if desired. Balsamic vinegar is mellow and goes well with the liver, but good-quality red wine would work, too. If the large pieces of liver are off-putting, they could be cut into smaller pieces. However, remove them with a slotted spoon and cut them after they have cooked for best texture. This is a rich dish that needs nothing more than a salad to make a very satisfying meal.

- **1 pound tubular pasta (such as ziti, penne, or rigatoni)**
- **2 tablespoons unsalted butter**
- **5 shallots, minced**
- **1 pound chicken livers, trimmed**
- **¼ cup balsamic vinegar**
- **¾ cup Rich Chicken Stock (page 227)**
- **2 tablespoons chopped capers**
- **2 tablespoons finely chopped fresh parsley**
- **Salt and freshly ground black pepper**

1. Prepare the pasta according to package directions.

2. Melt the butter in a large saucepan over medium-high heat. Add the shallots and cook, stirring often, until softened but not browned, about 3 minutes. Cut the livers in half by slicing through the connective part of the lobes. Add the liver to the saucepan. Cook, stirring gently, until the pink exteriors of the livers have turned brown all over, about 3 minutes.

3. Pour the vinegar and stock into the saucepan, and increase the heat to high. Bring to a boil, then reduce the heat to medium high. Simmer, uncovered, until the liquid thickens to a saucelike consistency and the livers are firm, 5 to 7 minutes. Keep warm until ready to serve.

4. Drain the pasta well and turn out into a large, warmed serving bowl. Add the livers with all of the sauce, then add the capers and parsley. Toss well and season to taste with salt and pepper. Serve at once.

Serves 6

Chicken Livers with Apples and Vidalia Onions

The tart apples give the rich livers an inviting contrast of taste and texture. Sweet Vidalia onions add depth, but any onion will do if these are not available. Use brandy, Cognac, or dry white wine if Calvados or apple jack are hard to come by. Serve very hot with buttered noodles for best results.

1 pound chicken livers

Salt and freshly ground black pepper

2 tablespoons unsalted butter

2 tablespoons vegetable oil

1 cup all-purpose flour

1 large Vidalia onion, finely chopped

2 large Granny Smith apples, peeled, seeded, cored, and cut into ¼-inch pieces

¼ cup Calvados or apple jack

½ cup chicken broth

1. Trim the livers of all gristle and cut each into separate lobes. Season well with salt and pepper. Melt the butter with the oil in a large nonstick skillet over medium-high heat. Place the flour in a large bowl and add the livers. Toss well to coat, shake off the excess, and add to the skillet. Cook until well browned, about 2 minutes on each side. Remove to drain on paper towels.

2. Add the onion to the skillet and cook until tender, stirring often, about 3 minutes. Add the apples and cook 2 minutes or until warmed through. Add the Calvados and increase the heat to high. Boil until the liquid has reduced by half. Add the broth and boil again until the juices are thickened and slightly syrupy, 2 to 3 minutes.

3. Return the livers to the skillet and reduce the heat to medium high. Cook, turning carefully to prevent the livers from breaking, until firm and warmed through, 3 to 5 minutes. Season to taste with salt and pepper and serve at once.

Serves 6

Quick and Easy

Liver

Simply Sophisticated

Chicken Livers in Piquante Sauce

This is an adaptation of a regional classic in Burgundy. Serve with lots of rice and additional chutney on the side.

2 tablespoons unsalted butter

1 small onion, finely chopped

¼ cup (2 to 3 slices) finely chopped bacon

1 cup all-purpose flour

1 pound chicken livers

Salt and freshly ground black pepper to taste

3 or 4 large mushrooms, trimmed and thinly sliced

1 cup homemade or canned beef stock

1 tablespoon tomato paste

1 teaspoon Dijon mustard

1 tablespoon bottled chutney (preferably Major Grey mango chutney)

1 teaspoon sugar

1 tablespoon finely chopped fresh parsley

1. Melt the butter in a large skillet over medium-high heat. Add the onion and the bacon. Cook, stirring often, until the onion has softened, 2 to 3 minutes.

2. Place the flour in a large bowl. Trim the livers of all gristle and cut into separate lobes. Season with salt and pepper. Place the livers in the bowl with the flour and roll to coat. Add to the skillet. Cook until the livers are browned, about 2 minutes on each side.

3. Add the mushrooms, stock, tomato paste, mustard, chutney, and sugar to the skillet. Season with salt and pepper, cover the skillet, and reduce the heat to medium. Simmer until the sauce is slightly thickened, about 20 minutes. Sprinkle with parsley.

Serves 6

Baked Chicken Liver "Cake"

*This is an adaptation of a recipe that we used to do in the cooking school that I attended in France. I have attempted to simplify the process while keeping its essential character. I call it a "cake" because in French it is called a **gâteau de foies de volaille**. While it might **sound** better in French, it tastes wonderful in any language. Serve as a first course with plenty of Tomato Sauce. For an attractive presentation, try spooning a bit of the sauce on the plate and spreading it thinly with a spatula or the back of a spoon. Place the wedge of the "cake" on top and sprinkle with chopped fresh parsley.*

¼ cup all-purpose flour

½ pound chicken livers

1 small garlic clove, crushed

4 large eggs, slightly beaten

2 large egg yolks

1 cup milk

Pinch of freshly grated nutmeg

Salt and freshly ground black
    pepper to taste

1 recipe Tomato Sauce (page
    226)

1. Lightly oil an 8-inch round cake pan and line the bottom with parchment or wax paper. Oil the paper. Preheat the oven to 325° F.

2. Combine the flour, livers, garlic, eggs, egg yolks, milk, nutmeg, and salt and pepper in the bowl of a food processor. Process until very smooth, then work through a fine-mesh strainer. Discard any solids that will not go through the strainer. Pour the mixture into the cake pan and gently move the pan to and fro to settle any air bubbles on the surface.

3. Place the cake pan in a baking pan large enough to hold it flat. Pour enough boiling water into the baking pan to come up the sides of the cake pan almost to the top. Bake the mold in this water bath for about 40 minutes or until a skewer inserted in the center comes out clean.

4. Run the tip of a knife around the circumference of the pan to dislodge the sides. Invert onto a large serving platter and remove the paper. Heat the Tomato Sauce until very hot and pour over the "cake." Serve warm with additional tomato sauce on the side, if desired.

Serves 6 as a first course

Potato Pancake with Onion and Chicken Liver

I served this at a recent breakfast with cold applesauce on the side. What a winner! It might sound odd, but don't knock it until you've tried it!

6 medium Yukon gold potatoes (1½ pounds)

1 medium onion

¼ cup chopped fresh parsley

Salt and freshly ground black pepper to taste

2 tablespoons unsalted butter

½ pound chicken livers

1. Peel the potatoes and coarsely grate them into a large bowl. Grate the onion and add to the potatoes. Fill the bowl with enough cold water to cover. Soak for 10 minutes.

2. To drain the potatoes, line a large colander with a double layer of cheesecloth or a clean linen kitchen towel. With your hands or with a slotted spoon, gently lift the grated potatoes and onion from the bowl of water and transfer to the lined colander. (Be sure to save and set aside the soaking water.) Lift the corners of the cheesecloth or towel and twist to wring out excess moisture from the potatoes.

3. Slowly pour out the water from the soaking bowl, being careful to save the small amount of residual starch left in the bottom. Return the potatoes and onion to the bowl, add the parsley, and stir with a fork to blend, incorporating the starch. Season with salt and pepper.

4. Melt the butter in a medium nonstick skillet with sloping sides over medium-high heat. Add half the potato mixture and flatten on the bottom of the skillet to form a pancake.

5. Trim the livers of all gristle and cut into separate lobes. Cover the surface of the potatoes with the liver, placing them over as evenly as possible. Season the livers with salt and pepper. Spread the remaining potato mixture over the liver and smooth to form the top of the pancake. Cook, lifting the edges with a spatula and shaking the pan often to prevent sticking, until a crust has formed on the bottom, about 15 minutes. To flip and cook the top, gently slide the pancake out onto a large plate, place the empty skillet over the uncooked side, and turn over, allowing the pancake to fall back into the skillet. Cook the flip side for 15 minutes longer or until crisp. Slide out onto a cutting board and cut into wedges. Serve warm.

Serves 6

Liver

The Basics

Here are a few basic recipes referred to throughout the book. Many of these can be doubled and frozen for future use. For best results, use only top-quality, fresh ingredients.

Poultry Terms

- **Bantam:** A small domestic bird, often a miniature of a member of a standard breed.
- **Broiler:** A young bird of either sex, up to 10 weeks of age and weighing up to 6 pounds; used interchangeably with "fryer."
- **Capon:** A castrated male chicken, fatter, with especially tender meat.
- **Chick (poussin):** A sexually immature chicken of either sex.
- **Cock:** An adult male chicken; rooster.
- **Cockerel:** A young male chicken.
- **Pullet:** A young female chicken.

Tomato Sauce

2 tablespoons olive oil

1 medium onion, finely chopped

3 or 4 ripe medium tomatoes (about 1 pound), peeled, seeded, and chopped, or 1 large can (28 ounces) tomatoes, drained and chopped

1 tablespoon chopped fresh thyme, or 1 teaspoon dried

Salt and freshly ground black pepper to taste

1. Heat the oil in a large saucepan over medium-high heat. Add the onion and cook, stirring often, until softened, about 3 minutes. Stir in the tomatoes and reduce the heat to medium. Add the thyme, salt, and pepper. Simmer partially covered, stirring often, until the tomatoes are pulpy and thickened, about 15 minutes.

2. Transfer the sauce to a food processor or blender and puree. Wipe out the saucepan and return the sauce to it. Gently warm over medium heat and season again with salt and pepper.

Makes 2 cups

Savory Pastry

1 cup (2 sticks) unsalted butter

2½ cups all-purpose flour

1 teaspoon salt

¼ to ½ cup ice water

1. Cut the butter into small pieces and keep very cold until ready to make the pastry. Combine the flour and salt in the bowl of a food processor and pulse several times to blend. Add the cold butter and process, pulsing, until the mixture resembles the texture of coarse meal, about 10 seconds.

2. With the blade in motion, slowly pour in the water and process until the dough forms a solid mass around the blades. Turn out onto a floured surface and knead gently into a tight ball. Cover with plastic wrap and refrigerate for at least 1 hour before using. (The pastry can be made up to 2 days in advance.) This is enough dough to line two 9-inch pie plates, or make a double-pie crust. Any leftover dough can be frozen for up to a month, tightly wrapped.

Makes two 9-inch crusts or 1 double crust

Chicken Stock

3 to 4 pounds meaty chicken backs, necks, or wings

2 medium onions, quartered

2 medium carrots, thickly sliced

2 celery stalks, thickly sliced

2 bay leaves, crumbled

10 whole black peppercorns

3 to 4 quarts water

1. Combine the chicken with the onions, carrots, celery, bay leaves, and peppercorns in a large stockpot. Pour in water to cover by 1 inch and bring to a boil over high heat, skimming off any scum that rises to the top. Reduce the heat to medium and simmer, skimming often, for 3 to 4 hours.

2. Line a sieve with a double layer of damp cheesecloth. Strain the stock and discard the solids. Skim off any fat that rises to the top. If not used immediately, let the stock come to room temperature. Pour into a tightly covered container and refrigerate until ready to use.

Makes 2 to 3 quarts

RICH CHICKEN STOCK: *Use at least 4 pounds chicken parts, trimmed of excess fat, and replace the water with 3 to 4 quarts of home-made or canned (reduced-sodium) chicken stock. The stock will be quite concentrated and velvety. Makes about 1½ quarts.*

White Sauce

2 cups whole milk

3 tablespoons unsalted butter

3 tablespoons all-purpose flour

Small pinch of freshly grated nutmeg

Salt and freshly ground white pepper to taste

1. Place the milk in a medium saucepan and bring to a boil. Reduce the heat to medium and keep warm while preparing the roux.

2. Melt the butter in a large saucepan over medium-high heat. Stir in the flour and cook until foaming, about 1 minute. Remove the pan from the heat and pour in the hot milk.

3. Return the pan to high heat and bring back to a boil, stirring constantly until thickened. Season with nutmeg, salt, and pepper. Reduce the heat to medium and simmer for 2 minutes longer.

Makes 2 cups

The Basics

Index

Conversion Chart

Equivalent Imperial and Metric Measurements

American cooks use standard containers, the 8-ounce cup and a tablespoon that takes exactly 16 level fillings to fill that cup level. Measuring by cup makes it very difficult to give weight equivalents, as a cup of densely packed butter will weigh considerably more than a cup of flour. The easiest way therefore to deal with cup measurements in recipes is to take the amount by volume rather than by weight. Thus the equation reads:

1 cup = 240 ml = 8 fl. oz.   ½ cup = 120 ml = 4 fl. oz.

It is possible to buy a set of American cup measures in major stores around the world.

In the States, butter is often measured in sticks. One stick is the equivalent of 8 tablespoons. One tablespoon of butter is therefore the equivalent to ½ ounce/15 grams.

Liquid Measures

Fluid Ounces	U.S.	Imperial	Milliliters
	1 teaspoon	1 teaspoon	5
¼	2 teaspoons	1 dessertspoon	10
½	1 tablespoon	1 tablespoon	14
1	2 tablespoons	2 tablespoons	28
2	¼ cup	4 tablespoons	56
4	½ cup		110
5		¼ pint or 1 gill	140
6	¾ cup		170
8	1 cup		225
9			250, ¼ liter
10	1¼ cups	½ pint	280
12	1½ cups		340
15		¾ pint	420
16	2 cups		450
18	2¼ cups		500, ½ liter
20	2½ cups	1 pint	560
24	3 cups		675
25		1¼ pints	700
27	3½ cups		750
30	3¾ cups	1½ pints	840
32	4 cups or 1 quart		900
35		1¾ pints	980
36	4½ cups		1000, 1 liter
40	5 cups	2 pints or 1 quart	1120

Solid Measures

U.S. and Imperial Measures		Metric Measures	
Ounces	Pounds	Grams	Kilos
1		28	
2		56	
3½		100	
4	¼	112	
5		140	
6		168	
8	½	225	
9		250	¼
12	¾	340	
16	1	450	
18		500	½
20	1¼	560	
24	1½	675	
27		750	¾
28	1¾	780	
32	2	900	
36	2¼	1000	1
40	2½	1100	
48	3	1350	
54		1500	1½

Oven Temperature Equivalents

Fahrenheit	Celsius	Gas Mark	Description
225	110	¼	Cool
250	130	½	
275	140	1	Very Slow
300	150	2	
325	170	3	Slow
350	180	4	Moderate
375	190	5	
400	200	6	Moderately Hot
425	220	7	Fairly Hot
450	230	8	Hot
475	240	9	Very Hot
500	250	10	Extremely Hot

Any broiling recipes can be used with the grill of the oven, but beware of high-temperature grills.

Equivalents for Ingredients

all-purpose flour—plain flour
coarse salt—kitchen salt
cornstarch—cornflour
eggplant—aubergine

half and half—12% fat milk
heavy cream—double cream
light cream—single cream
lima beans—broad beans

scallion—spring onion
unbleached flour—strong, white flour
zest—rind
zucchini—courgettes or marrow